IRON SKIN

Iron Skin

A memoir

Brendan John Lee

ISBN: 978-0-473-60625-1 (paper)
ISBN: 978-0-473-60680-0 (hard)

Edition 1.1

Every triumph of this story,
and of my life,
I owe to my darling mother.

Preface

Initially, this book was to document a two-year period of my life.

However, as I started putting words on the page I noticed myself prefacing many chapters with stories of my childhood. Events and conversations I hadn't thought about in over thirty years suddenly became as clear and vivid as the events of yesterday. I realised in many ways, I have been writing this story since the day I was born.

I suspect many of you will find this book while fighting the same battle as I was. Perhaps you'll learn you've been writing this story since the day you were born, too. Writing is a battle in itself, but from the first chapter I knew this book had to be written, for you, for those who were fighting alongside me, and those who would inevitably come after me. I knew this because there were days I was inches from giving up, and the only place I found hope was in knowing someone had walked before me, and I was not alone.

I share this story not as medical advice, or life advice, or any advice at all. It is simply my story, the kind of story I wanted to find so desperately in the depths of my struggle. I never found it then. I also didn't realise I didn't need to find it – in the midst of my battle, by some miracle, I had been writing it myself.

Thank you for being here. Within our unique stories, we all experience pain, and all find different paths to healing. My only hope is that within these pages, you find something that takes you a few steps further along yours.

With love,
B.

IRON SKIN

A healthy man has a thousand different wishes.
A sick man has only one.

-CONFUCIUS

The Reason

There are many reasons people start running.

Some to lose weight.

Others to train for the upcoming basketball season.

Some out of habit, because they've been doing it since high school and the day just doesn't feel right without it.

Me?

I did it to heal.

But it doesn't feel like it's healing me. Right now, it feels like it's going to kill me.

This heat is thick. *Heavy.* In heat like this, just wandering down the sidewalk would be tiring. And I'm running. I've been running for four hours. My foot's been busted for at least three.

It buckles one more time.

I curse.

I take another step.

Curse again.

That's it.

I don't feel like this run is going to kill me.

I know it's going to kill me.

I pass another person sitting on the roadside, defeated. Add her to the collection. Already five, six, maybe seven athletes have collapsed around me. Heatstroke, probably. I'm next. I know I am.

Notice how I used the word *athletes*? Yeah, because that's what they call us. Athletes. Or sometimes, they call us runners.

I've got a better word for us.

Idiots.

We know it too. Spending our weekend out here, running this stupid race in the thirty-five-degree heat. All idiots.

I see the banner by the roadside.

Singapore Marathon: It's Ours To Run.

Yeah, exactly. Ours. Just for us. The idiots.

Nobody forced us to do this. Actually, get this – we paid to do this. And not just five or ten dollars. Hundreds of dollars. We could have gotten a foot massage followed by a steak dinner followed by a night of cocktails, and probably still had enough for an ice cream and a taxi home. One of those nice taxis too, like the Mercedes ones at the airport. But instead, we're out here. Running this stupid race, all of us damn near dead.

Of all the things I imagined I'd be in my life, marathoner is last on the list. Down the bottom, beside opera singer, and Prime Minister of New Zealand. In fact, if I were in Vegas and had to bet a million on which of those three I'd never be? I'd take marathoner.

If video games were my first love, running was my first hate, ever since the school cross country in Year 4. That week, my best friend Nilesh and I kept laughing about how not a single girl would be in front of us. Yet the race had barely started and girls were passing me left and right, the stitch in my chest already so painful I knew I'd never catch them. I haven't missed running since. Because why run? Why leave the comfort of your house to run to nowhere, around in circles, hurting and huffing and heaving, just to come right back to where you started?

Sounded like the dumbest thing in the world to me.

And then almost overnight, I had a reason.

2

Dr Sato was the reason.

I've never met Dr Sato, never talked to Dr Sato, never even heard Dr Sato speak. But he is the hero of this story. Of my story. He is the hero of thousands of stories, and will be the hero of thousands more. Remember the name – Dr Sato. I will tell you more about him soon.

That is, if I make it out of this race alive.

My foot buckles again, and limping under the Singapore moonlight, drowning in my own sweat, I make a promise to myself. This is the last one. No more races.

Then I laugh. Because I don't know why I even need to promise. *Of course* this is the last one.

Why would you even think about doing this again?

What are you, an idiot?

1

It is 1991.

I am five years old. There is a scab on my earlobe that I pick at constantly. It forms. I scratch it off. It bleeds and dries up. I pick it off again.

Sometimes, it leaves a spot of blood on my shirt.

Hey, there's blood on your shirt, my classmates say, pointing at my shoulder.

Yeah, I know. There always is.

At school, teachers and parents describe me as "the one with the skin". It has always been this way, since I can remember.

My ear is just the beginning. The back of my neck, the folds of my elbows and knees – these are the places people stare at. They are constantly red, constantly angry. I scratch them all the time.

Does it hurt? My friends ask.

No, not really.

Sometimes a friend's Mum or a teacher will take my arm and graze their finger over it softly. They'll look at me sympathetically.

You poor thing.

But I don't really understand why. To me, this is normal. I've never known skin to be any other way.

It's my first year of school. I love spelling. It's my favourite subject, and the teacher has already crowned me the best speller in class. In a few years, in the school spelling quiz, I'll spell at a level six years above my age. Maybe it's because my vocabulary is already filled with long and fancy words, words I hear in doctors' offices and pharmacies, and from my Mum every night before bed.

A is for apple, B is for ball. H is for hydrocortisone. S is for Sorbolene.

Sorbolene is my doctor's favourite moisturiser, and each night my Mum slathers me in it, while I stare at the bottle and sound out the syllables – *Sor-bo-lene* – in my head, over and over.

But even glistening in Sorbolene, my skin doesn't look like that of the other kids. It's still red, still broken. The only difference is now the rashes shine for everybody to see.

It is 1993.

I am seven years old. I've been to so many doctors I've lost count, and today I'm seeing another. He is going to do an allergy test.

Normally, they conduct allergy tests on your forearm, but because I'm so tiny – my arms are barely the size of twigs – he has to do it on my back instead.

I lie on my stomach and the doctor makes two long lines of pinpricks, around twenty of them, and drops a solution on top of each one.

Afterwards, I sit in the doctor's office while he explains the test to my Mum.

Each solution contains a different allergen, he tells her, and any spot that swells more than a millimetre indicates an allergy. Your son is clearly allergic to cats. But look at his result for dust mites. Your son's measurement is twelve! It's one of the highest I've ever seen.

This marks the beginning of my Mum's war on dust. When we get home she rips out the carpet. My bedroom now has concrete floors. Dust mite-proof. We go to K-Mart and purchase an extra expensive dust mite-shielding bedsheet. Apparently the thread count is so fine, dust mites from the mattress can't fit through.

I study the diagram on the packaging, of the mites getting trapped by the sheet.

Cool, I think. Maybe I'll finally have normal skin. Like the other kids.

I sleep with these new sheets for months, wondering how long it will be until my skin changes. But it never does.

It is 1995.

I am nine years old. We are going to a Chinese medicine doctor today. I don't know where Mum heard about him, but she tells me he's managed to cure lots of kids. Kids with skin like mine.

When we arrive, I'm instantly drawn to the photos on the wall. Dozens of them, all showing before and after pictures of kids. Some begin with skin worse than mine, and a few months later, they are milky and smooth like a baby on a nappy advertisement.

I stare at them, filled with hope. Does this mean I'm going to have normal skin like them too?

I won't remember much about this Chinese doctor. In ten years, I won't remember his face, his name, or what his voice sounds like. But I will always remember what his medicine tastes like.

It's a herbal tea, and after dinner that night Mum brews it up. It's black, bitter, sour, and smells like rotten grass. I don't care. I can hardly wait to drink it. It's not like any medicine I've been given before. It's a secret potion, like those wizards have in the movies, and it's going to heal me. I know it is.

Mum pours it into a mug.

The doctor had told us, if the taste is too strong, you can add some honey.

As soon as I take the first sip, Mum doesn't even have to ask. She gets the honey from the pantry and I load it into my cup one spoonful at a time.

By the time I've finished, I've drunk twice as much honey as tea. It's the most horrid thing I've drunk in my life.

Still, if it means I can have normal skin, I'll drink it every day. I'll pour it on my cereal if I have to. But I don't. After several months, we give up on the tea as well. My skin hasn't changed at all.

It is 1996.

I am ten years old. We are seeing a new dermatologist today. He's a Kiwi guy with perfect hair and a jaw like an astronaut. I take off my shirt and he looks at my skin the same way every other doctor has looked at my skin.

Then he tells us about something called evening primrose oil. The brand name is EPOGAM.

A wonder treatment, he tells us. You have to try it.

We arrive home with three containers of EPOGAM. They are soft gel capsules and oddly shaped – like peanut M&M's, but with a little point sticking out. Since I'm so tiny, they are too big for me to swallow, so the doctor says we can cut the little ends off with scissors and squeeze the oil into a spoon.

That night, I wish I were older, that my throat was bigger. Then I could swallow the pills whole and wouldn't have to taste them. Instead, I'm forced to drink the oil from a spoon and can taste every drop. It tastes like almond essence mixed with cooking oil mixed with old soybeans.

It's almost as bad as the Chinese medicine.

Almost.

Thankfully, I don't need to deal with that for long either. After a few bottles, we give up. My skin still hasn't changed at all.

It is 1997.

I am eleven years old.

Today, we are going to see my GP again.

My family's GP is a Jewish man by the name of Dr Stone. He has thick, dark hair with soft waves, a prominent nose and kind eyes. He not only sounds like a doctor, he looks like a doctor. If he were an actor, he'd be cast as a doctor every time. Either that, or a science teacher, or possibly the owner of an antique store. Somebody harmless, and intelligent. One of the good guys.

Dr Stone is from the same high school as my Dad, and my Dad often tells me what a smart guy Dr Stone is. Dr Stone returns the favour often, and tells me what a smart guy my Dad is. Of course, I have no reason to doubt them. I grow up thinking Dr Stone and my Dad are the two smartest people in the world.

Dr Stone runs a busy private clinic in our area, and knows everything about my brothers and me. But he knows me the best, because I see him the most. It's almost like he is part of our family. There was even a time, back when I was seven or eight, my skin was flaring across my face so badly I could barely get out of bed. It was a weekend. Mum was so worried, she got Dr Stone on the phone and he said we could come to see him at his house. Even my Mum was surprised.

This is so kind of him, she kept saying in the car. He really doesn't have to do this.

Maybe that's why Dr Stone has always felt more like an uncle than a doctor. He always asks about school and sports. As I get older, he'll ask me about exams, what I'm studying at university, what my dream job would be. His face saddens when he sees me in pain, and with my gut instinct – the flawless gut instinct you have as a child – I know he is a good man.

Dr Stone's house was big, in a nice area. Maybe the nicest area in town. At the time, E was for Elocon – a strong steroid cream I often used on my body. Dr Stone always told me not to use it on my face, but when I saw him that day he said, just today, just this once, you can use a little on your face. But only today.

Almost twenty-five years will pass before I'll learn how good that advice was.

We arrive at Dr Stone's clinic and I run up the stairs to the reception area like I always do. My Mum follows behind me and greets his receptionist,

Margaret, as we walk in. She's a small elderly woman with spectacles, close-cropped brown hair, and the demeanour of a school librarian. Dr Stone calls us in soon after. I stroll into his office like it's a friend's house, like I come here all the time. Because I do come here all the time.

Merry Christmas, he says. Enjoying the holidays?

We've been to Australia, I tell him.

He frowns. I don't need to say any more.

Let's take a look.

I stand up and take off my shirt. He examines my torso like he always does – like I'm an artifact, and he's an archaeologist. I have the same rash I always have when I come back from Australia after visiting my cousins for Christmas. Whether it's the heat, the humidity, or something in my auntie's house, I always come back with the skin of a lychee.

As I guessed, it's the same treatment as last time, and every time before that. Dermovate twice a day for a week. Then Elocon twice a day until it's better. And moisturise. Morning, afternoon and night.

He dashes off a prescription and hands it to Mum. Usually, that's it. We'll take it and say thanks, I'll ask for a jellybean and we'll go. But this time Mum has something on her mind.

We've been dealing with this for so long, she says. Why is nothing working? We've tried everything. We've done the allergy test, we've seen this dermatologist, that dermatologist. I've pulled the carpet out of the house. He stays away from cats. He moisturises every night, puts his creams on. It just feels like we've done so much, and his skin is still the same. What's wrong with him?

Yeah. Good question. What is wrong with me?

Dr Stone purses his lips. Thinks carefully about what to say.

Without doing those things, he says, like taking out the carpet, and making sure his creams are on, things could be a lot worse.

He speaks confidently and reassuringly, like a politician.

Maybe we haven't cured it, but we're treating it. We're stopping it from becoming much worse than it could be.

I look at my Mum. She nods, accepts this answer, but I can't tell if she's happy with it. This is the day I realise maybe my skin is even more exhausting for my Mum than it is for me.

As we do after every trip to Dr Stone, we go next door to fill his prescription. We spend so much money at this pharmacy we hit the threshold for the VIP discount every year. Over the years, Dr Stone has prescribed me an endless rotation of creams – Sorbolene, emulsifying ointment, cetomacrogol, hydrocortisone, Elocon, Eumovate, Dermovate. We started with the mildest steroid and now we're on the strongest ones he can give me. Over the years, there will be many more. But none of them will heal me. For the entirety of my childhood, I'll still be the one with the skin.

It is 2003.

I am seventeen years old. Things have improved. After puberty, the rashes slowly started to fade. Instead of having them constantly, they only flared once a week. Then only in the summer. Now only some weeks in summer. I play sport competitively now, and the daily training helps. That's Mum's guess anyway. A good sweat followed by a hot shower.

Now, the rashes only show up in one area of my body at a time. Maybe this week it's my forehead. At first sight, I nuke it with a steroid cream from my vast collection. They go away. A month later they come back somewhere else, maybe my neck, and I nuke them again. I visit Dr Stone every few months to restock my prescriptions.

Your skin looks great, he says every time.

Living on a constant supply of steroids isn't ideal, but it means I can live a relatively normal life. For now, eczema has become an afterthought, causing problems just a few weeks at a time. I'm no longer the one with the skin. I'm just a normal guy. And for someone who grew up like me, being a normal guy is everything.

2

It is 2019.

I am thirty-three years old.

Standing in front of the mirror, I run my hands over my forehead, again.

Hot.

Scorching.

I look like a burn victim.

My chest too. And my arms. Each red splotch connects to the next red splotch, until it wraps around my whole body.

Two days ago it was getting bad. Now it is bad.

This mirror I'm staring at, fearfully running my fingers over these rashes, is a long way from home. I'm in a little apartment, in the little city of Windhoek, in the little country of Namibia. Just a week earlier, I was in Cape Town, South Africa to attend a festival. It was one of the best weeks of my life. Prior to that, I had spent two months writing and eating my way through Malaysia.

For the previous nine years, this has been my life. Travelling and writing full time. My dream.

I sit down on the bed, but slowly, because even sudden movements hurt. I'm scared. Or maybe a better word is – confused. Confused as to why my skin is suddenly bubbling up like the plague. The rashes on my arms look different, almost like blisters. I thought I had seen every rash imaginable on this body, but I haven't seen ones like this.

Even worse is the itch.

I whimper. Then I scratch. I can't not scratch, even though it hurts. I scratch until it bleeds and then scratch even more. This definitely isn't normal eczema.

Normal eczema.

How's that for an oxymoron.

There's a saying we have in the travel community – always trust your gut. Since we're so often in foreign places, we can't know what is normal and what is not, but we always have our gut. Your gut has a lifetime of experience. When it tries to talk, it's best to listen.

I book the next flight home. For three days I've been holding out, hoping it will get better, knowing it will get better. One morning, I'm going to wake up and it will be gone. But now I listen to my gut.

It's telling me, this is not getting better.

It's telling me, this is bad, and you're going to need some help for this one.

Here's the catch: It's nothing compared to what's about to come.

My flight departs the following morning. I wake up and look in the mirror, hoping to see something good.

I see the opposite.

My arms are now covered in broken sores, like chickenpox. My forehead is crusting over bit by bit, a dark yellow, like a wave creeping down my forehead towards my eyes.

What if it goes into my eyes?

No. Don't even think about it going into your eyes.

I look at my back. Welts. Top to bottom. I pick at some loose ends on my forehead, and they peel off, like pastry. It's raw and pink underneath. Wet, and smells like metal.

My face is literally falling off.

What's happening to me?

In a few days, I'm going to find out. I'm going to find out I'm a drug addict. I'm going to find out I've been a drug addict my entire life, and I didn't even know it.

I sit on the bed and pep talk myself. I still need to dress, pack, call a taxi. Most of all, I dread the ordeal of surviving twenty-five hours on a plane. Like I said, home is pretty far away.

C'mon Brendan.

Just get home.

You can panic when you're home.

But *in my gut*, I'm not even sure I can do that. Packing a bag, twenty-five hours on a plane. I've done this hundreds of times. Hundreds. But not like this.

I look out the window. It's a warm day, but I dress as if it's winter, doing my best to cover every inch of myself. Jeans, sweatshirt with the hood up, baseball cap underneath. That hides my forehead, arms, and legs. I ghost through the airport with my head down, avoiding eye contact with everyone, and make it onto the plane.

Miraculously, I'm not itching much. Yet. Even so, I do touch my forehead every few minutes, feeling the scabs to see if they are getting worse.

They are. And they hurt.

I wonder if I'm just imagining it.

Surely, it can't be getting worse so quickly.

How is it getting worse so quickly?

Meal service arrives.

Would you like the lamb or the fish today, sir?

Lamb please.

But my hood is up and my face is turned. She can't hear me.

Sir? Lamb or fish for you?

I want to turn to face her, but I can't. My face won't let me. My pride won't let me. So I peer up at her, through the corner of my eye, and say it again.

Lamb please.

This moment splashes over me, like a bucket of ice water. For the first time in a very long time, I'm ashamed of my face. I'm ashamed to look someone in the eye. I'm afraid to be seen. In three short days, I've become a different person. This look I've given the stewardess – this side-eyed, shying my face away from every person look – I know it well. It used to be me, when I was eight years old with rashes flaring across my top lip. I'd forgotten what that felt like, but not anymore. Now, after all these years, I suddenly remember what it feels like to not want to be me.

Mum is waiting for me as I come out of arrivals. I am all covered up, so she can't see anything yet. I put on a brave face. I don't want her to know I've just spent over twenty hours in pain. But when we finally get home and she sees my body, she knows.

As she's examining me, my Dad walks in.

Wow, he says, gobsmacked.

I haven't seen him look at me like that before, ever.

But Mum is a little more pragmatic. She looks me over, studies me, like all the doctors have done over the years.

See these?

She runs her fingers over my back.

These look more like welts, or bites. But this ...

She grabs my arm, runs her eyes along it.

This looks more like eczema. Like you had when you were little.

As she taps her fingers along my skin, I'm reminded, this isn't new to her either. She fought this battle with me for years when I was a kid. Now, we'll do it again as adults.

That night, I spend hours with the greatest doctor of all time: Dr Google. During the last three days, and throughout that horribly long plane ride, I've had a lot of time to think, and I've been doing the same thing you do when you lose your wallet: Retracing my steps.

Malaysia. I'd been living there earlier in the year, when the first sign of trouble started. I'd used my regular steroid creams, and they hadn't done much, so I'd gone down to the pharmacy and bought a tube of Dermovate – the strong stuff I'd used often as a kid. I didn't need a prescription. Just some Malaysian ringgits and a smile. I thought that was fantastic. And the Dermovate was equally fantastic. Nuked those rashes in a day.

I'd moved to South Africa two months later, still having problems. Nothing I hadn't seen before, though it did seem odd that my skin was playing up for so long. It hadn't been like that since I was a child. I'd already used the entire tube of Dermovate from Malaysia, but that was the great thing about South Africa. You didn't need prescriptions there either. Just some South African rand and a smile. Their Dermovate was equally fantastic. Nuked those rashes just as quick.

A couple of months on, I'd made it to Namibia. The rashes still weren't gone, but I knew, in my gut, I had to stop using the Dermovate. Of course, Dermovate was nothing new to me, I'd been through countless tubes during childhood and my teens. But, even as a kid, I knew you couldn't use it forever.

Every time you use it, Dr Stone would always tell me, it makes your skin a little bit thinner.

I'd even asked my Mum that day – does that mean if I use it forever, all my skin will be gone?

She said yes.

I'm about to learn just how right she was.

It's the middle of the night. I'm jet-lagged, and can't lie in bed without scratching my life away, so I pepper Dr Google with questions. It's endless. That's the problem with Dr Google. She knows everything, but you need to ask the right questions. And it's only with a tiny stroke of luck that I find the right question.

In every story, there's a character who's in it for just a second, but he's pivotal. For example, the Russian guy in *Armageddon*. You probably don't even remember his name, but if he hadn't smashed the engine with his spanner in that one scene, they would never have restarted the ship, and the Earth would have blown up, and that would have been the end of mankind.

My story has that character too.

His name is Jon.

Jon and I are cousins, about five years apart, but one thing binds us. We both had shit skin growing up. I see Jon every Christmas when my family visits his in Australia. We've done that every year since I can remember, and even as a kid, I remember seeing his little tubes of steroid creams around the house. I knew exactly what they were, because they looked exactly like mine.

Then, after a lifetime of using them, he stopped. I'm not sure why. Probably the same reason I did. Not long after, his skin went bananas. Bananas isn't even the right word, unless there's a species of banana that's made of napalm and destroys everything it touches. Soon, he's bed-bound. His face ravaged so badly he's drinking meals through a straw. While on his search for answers he discovers a little-known condition: TSW.

Topical Steroid Withdrawal.

Only from Jon putting these words into my vocabulary do I know to punch them into the computer, and the second I hit search, I know.

The pictures come up.

It's like I'm looking at myself.

I read the people's stories.

They might as well be mine.

As I read more, the dots connect like a jigsaw.

Heavy use of steroids. Often for life. Rashes go away, come back worse. Prolonged. Common in eczema sufferers. Common in adults. Stop cold turkey. Severe withdrawal.

I'm not only seeing it, I'm feeling it. That's one thing about having shit skin your whole life. You become eerily in tune with it, always examining it, feeling it, understanding it. Almost like it's talking to you. Even though my skin looks like it's dying, I can feel it trying to heal. It's screaming and angry, pushing some kind of evil to the surface. I feel it as deep as the marrow in my bones. It's saying, if you just let me shed all this poison, all this rottenness, I will become normal again.

I believe it.

Soon, Dr Google leads me to the third character in this story. She's a Japanese woman in her fifties. Her name is Tokuko.

If Dr Sato is the unsung hero of this story, and my cousin Jon is the random but pivotal character who smashes the engine with his spanner, Tokuko is more important than both of them.

She's the star.

The character who saves the day, and maybe my life.

Jon is an X-Wing pilot. Dr Sato is Yoda.

Tokuko is the Jedi.

Fitting, because I'm about to find out, Tokuko is famous. Not *famous* famous like Beyoncé, but underground famous, like Brian Scalabrine. Tens of thousands of people, maybe even hundreds of thousands, are going through TSW right now, and nearly all of them know who Tokuko is. And they all found her the same way I did – through her blog.

I'm completely unsuspecting when this blog pops up on my screen for the first time. It's a no-frills blog, resembling an old Myspace page or a kid's blog from the nineties. But it doesn't need to be any more glam than that. When I first read her blog post, *"How To Cure TSW!"* it gives me the most important thing anyone can ask for in this journey: Hope. Because this blog post is going to allow me to be treated by the best TSW doctor in the world. The hero of the story I've been telling you about.

Dr Sato.

Here's how I know Dr Sato is the best TSW doctor in the world. On Tokuko's blog, she has photos. These are photos of her worst days. There's a photo of her leg, and it takes me a while to confirm it's actually a leg. It looks more like a pipe rotten with rust, pulled out of the ocean from a hundred years ago.

Studying this photo, I cannot find an inch of normal skin. I look for pink, but only see yellow, black and red. Crusts and scabs and blood. It's so bad that fifty years ago, the doctors would've assumed it was gangrenous and amputated it on the spot.

Then, after three months, it looks like a leg.

After a year, she could almost be a damn leg model.

I think to myself, if Dr Sato can cure that, he can cure me. He can cure anyone.

I barely sleep. I'm up before the sun, and this time, I'm not even hoping to look better. I already know I'm going to look worse. I go straight to the mirror.

Much worse.

My forehead isn't part yellow. It's all yellow. I haven't seen scabs like this before, but now they're everywhere. My forehead, my arms, my back. It hurts to the touch. And the itch.

Oh my gosh, the itch.

I go straight back to my laptop and pull up Tokuko's blog. Last night, I only got halfway. Today, I'm going to study everything about her.

Soon I see, Tokuko's story is my story. The one who has always been "the one with the skin". Now in her fifties, she's been dealing with this a lot longer than I have, but it's been exactly the same – new doctor, new steroid cream. Each steroid damages her skin even more, so she's given a stronger one, living in a never-ending cycle of steroid addiction. In Japan, it sounds even worse than New Zealand. They're giving steroid creams out like jellybeans. It's only after half a lifetime, when there's no stronger steroid to give, when her body has started imploding, Tokuko is referred to Dr Sato.

On her blog, Tokuko shares everything inpatients do while living in Dr Sato's hospital clinic. It's his entire treatment plan, translated into English. Whether she realises it or not, this one blog post will change more lives than she knows. TSW is not widely researched, but with this information, the whole world can be treated as if they're in Dr Sato's clinic. I devour every detail, and that's when I learn what the real miracle is.

It's not that Dr Sato healed her. It's how he did it.

In Dr Sato's clinic there are no creams. No drugs. No grafts or surgery. No injections. No therapy. No soaps. Not even showers.

His magic treatment is: Doing nothing.

For ninety days, just leave the skin alone and let it heal.

And it will.

Here's the interesting thing I will soon learn about doing nothing: It's the hardest thing I've ever done. It's the reason Dr Sato only does inpatient care – because he's learned that, when left alone at home, almost every patient will fail at doing nothing.

The rules are simple:

1. Go to bed before ten o'clock.
2. No showers or bathing.
3. No soaps.
4. No shampoos.
5. No moisturisers.
6. No creams.
7. Limited water intake.
8. High protein meals.
9. One hour exercise daily.
10. **No steroids.**

You'll go through withdrawal. It will be bad. Then you'll come out the other side.

I start immediately.

The following day I visit my dermatologist. My usual dermatologist, Dr Oliver, is away on vacation, so I'm seeing his colleague, Dr Lin.

Every kind of scab and wound rages across my back and chest. My arms are bright red, my forehead even yellower than before. The only part of my body that looks normal is my feet. Is that because I've never used steroid creams on my feet?

I'm hopeful as I walk into Dr Lin's office. I hope he is going to listen, and have an open mind. I've never seen him before, so I look up his profile on the website beforehand.

Dux of his school, winner of dermatology awards, reasonably young. It's promising.

But Tokuko saw many doctors, and they all sent her away with more steroids. My cousin Jon said his dermatologist told him it was just more eczema, and sent him away with more steroids.

Nonetheless, I'm hopeful.

I don't stay hopeful for long. I take off the long-sleeved, high-necked shirt and baseball cap I've been hiding under. He takes a close look at my body through his special glasses. Just for a minute. Hums a few times.

When did this start?

Few weeks ago.

I tell him about the no-prescription tubes of Dermovate.

So you've been travelling?

Yes.

Whereabouts?

I tell him.

He types a few things on his computer.

Scabies, he says finally.

Huh?

I sigh. Silently, on the inside. I've had scabies before. I know exactly what it looks and feels like, because I'm obsessive sometimes, and I read about fifteen research papers on scabies while I was going through it. I'm sure this isn't it. Ninety-nine percent sure. Point nine, nine, nine.

My cousin went through something last year, I tell him. A bad withdrawal, from his steroid creams. There's a diagnosis for it – Topical Steroid Withdrawal. I stopped all my steroid creams a few weeks ago, and now I look extremely similar to him. What do you think?

He glances at his notes quickly.

Not possible, he says, shaking his head. Something like that might only happen after years and years of steroid use.

Well, I've had years and years of steroid use.

He frowns.

You won't look like that after some Dermovate.

I've had scabies before, I tell him. I even saw Dr Oliver about it, if you look at my history. It didn't look like this. Didn't feel like this.

He studies me. My face. I hear him sighing, feel his impatience.

This is way too serious to be from some steroid creams. If this is how your body reacts to steroids, we'd be putting you on the strongest immuno-suppressants we have. There's just no way. The prednisone I'm giving you, we don't give that out lightly. You have eczema. It looks infected. I'll give you something for that. And scabies is the likeliest answer, based on your travel history. It's the surest diagnosis I can give you, without doing a bunch of other complicated stuff, like skin scrapes and so on.

I want to say, why don't we do that then? Isn't that what I'm paying you for?

But I don't. I've already given up. I just want to get out of his office and start treating. Tokuko's way. Dr Sato's way.

He starts typing a prescription.

Everybody in the house needs to do a full body treatment, he says. Use this scabies cream. Leave it on for eight hours. Wash your sheets in hot water. Put them out in the sun.

Then he explains the rest of the list. Two new steroid creams. Prednisone. Antibiotics.

His printer rattles it off. He hands it to me.

I thank him and leave. Get in the car. Throw the prescription aside. Drive straight home.

He's not my doctor anymore. Dr Sato is my doctor now.

Later that evening, I discover Tokuko's next gift to the world. Her Facebook group.

It is filled with people all over the world who are following Dr Sato's treatment. They post photos – photos that look just like me – asking for advice, sharing their routines, describing what has worked and what hasn't. Even the patients in his clinic are in there. I look at everyone's healed photos. Incredible.

Then I see Tokuko herself. Posting comments and answering questions. And, to my surprise, Dr Sato too. This is how they spend their free time.

Like I said, the hero of the story, and the star.

Sitting in front of my laptop, scrolling through these stories, my forehead literally falling off into a pile of crusts on my desk, I learn what to expect over the next few months.

Your skin will dry, they say. Break open. Ooze. Bleed. Scab up. Shed, layer by layer. Don't moisturise it. Don't put anything on it. One day, all the bad skin will fall off and you'll be pink underneath. You'll never need to touch a steroid cream again. You'll be healed.

I get it now. It's the scene in *Trainspotting*, where he's going insane, locked in a room and shitting in a bucket. That's going to be my skin. My drug addiction isn't quite as colourful, definitely not box office movie material, but the journey is going to be the same. Whatever addiction you have – drugs or sex or alcohol or crack – or steroids – the withdrawal is going to be hell.

Of course, I don't see myself actually going to hell. I'm different.

I text Jon.

I've only been upping my dosage for a few months, I tell him. I don't think mine is going to be that bad.

I hope so, he replies.

No, none of us believe we're going to hell. Until we get there.

My hairdresser's name is Kaori. She's a Japanese lady, tall and thick, with a round face, and small, warm eyes that she smothers with eye shadow. She's been cutting my hair for fifteen years. When I'm travelling, if I can stand it, I leave my hair to grow wild. I do everything I can to avoid cutting my hair until I return home for Christmas, because I only want Kaori to cut it. I love my hair too much. It's been this way since high school.

In fact, it's been this way since forever.

When I was thirteen, Mum and I went to Hong Kong for the school holidays to visit my Auntie Wai Hing, and my cousin Mark.

Mark is the same age as me and has a shaved head. A buzz cut, like he's in the army. One day, after finding out how much I love my hair, Auntie Wai Hing makes me an offer: A hundred dollars to shave my head like Mark's.

Auntie Wai Hing is rich. For her, it's all a big joke. A hundred dollars might as well be toilet paper. For me, it's the opposite. At thirteen years old, a hundred dollars is a fortune.

Still, my silky black hair is sacred. I can't decide. Every day she asks me again.

It's just hair! A hundred dollars! It will grow back!

On the verge of giving in, my Mum takes me aside one afternoon.

Don't do it, she says. You love your hair too much. If you go home with a shaved head, you'll be miserable.

Still, I agonise over all the basketball cards I could buy with a hundred dollars. All the bags of sour gummy bears. It's the biggest decision of my life.

A few weeks later, we get on the plane to return home.

I still have my hair.

Now, twenty years later, I wish I could go back and take the money. I'm about to lose my hair for nothing.

That's what I want though. I don't love my hair anymore. I want it gone. When I wake up, it's matted to my head. It's wet with ooze, and it smells. Scabs and flares cover my scalp, especially at the back above my nape and on my forehead along my hairline. And it itches. Oh my god. Like it's crawling with fucking fire ants sprinkling itching powder across my scalp.

My Mum fires up my brother's old head shaver. In other countries, when I need to get a haircut, the very sound of the *nrrrr* gives me a mild panic attack. I'm terrified of anyone bringing a shaver that close to my head, unless Kaori is doing it. But these lifelong fears have magically evaporated. I cannot give half a shit about my hair today. I look in the mirror and don't see how I could possibly look any worse, even without hair. I just want it gone, so I'm bare and bald, and can enjoy the pleasure of my nails running cleanly across my scalp with pure delight.

Around my neck, I have the haircut bib Mum used on us when we were toddlers. She runs the shaver up the back of my head. I feel my hair fall against my neck. I imagine what I'm going to look like. I haven't changed my hairstyle since I was thirteen.

When she's done, I hurry to the mirror. It's the first time I've seen myself with a buzz cut. I lean in and study my scalp. Red. Flaky. Hurting. I pick up my face shaver – the one that gives a clean shave, right down to the skin – and run it over my scalp, like the scene in *G.I. Jane* where she buzz cuts herself in front of the mirror.

It works. The one millimetre of hair left on my head comes clean off.

When I'm done, I run my palms over it, like a crystal ball. It's not the smooth polish I'd always imagined; it's rough and crusted with scabs and damp patches of ooze and blood. Still, I manage a smile.

I've always wondered how I'd look like this.

I look the same, but also different.

Older and younger at the same time.

One thing's for sure – I definitely look like shit.

I don't care. It's soothing. Freeing. There is no hair left to cover my crusted forehead, I see myself now exactly as I am. Ironically, my head has stopped itching at this moment, but I still run my nails over it and smile. The old me is well and truly gone. After this is all over, if it is ever over, I won't have just cured my skin. I'll have cured my vanity too.

3

It is Day 14.

As I do every week – and will do every week for the next three months – I set up my tripod and take some photos. Close-ups of my forehead, my back, my torso, my arms and legs.

As I load the images onto my computer, I am amazed. I don't feel any better. In fact, I feel worse. Each morning, I look in the mirror and struggle to believe this is my life now. But the photos tell a different story. One week ago, my forehead was covered with wet, yellow scabs. Now, they're dry and brown. My torso was bright red with raised rashes, as if I were covered in hives. Today, the rashes are smoother, gentler.

I upload my photos to the Facebook group.

This is my first week, I tell them.

Congratulations, come the replies. You look much better already.

Still, going through withdrawal this way is harder than I imagined. Most of us have never gone a day without putting something on our skin. Now we're supposed to do it for ninety. The no moisturiser, no soaps, I can handle. But not showering is bizarre. Covered in goo, waking up all clammy in the night, my skin is dead. I even smell dead. The first thing I want to do is jump into a hot shower and wash all the rot away. But that's the opposite of what your body needs, Dr Sato says. Don't shower, let your skin stay dry.

Leave the scabs there. Good things are happening underneath. When you're dry, you're healing.

It is Day 22.

June. The start of winter.

As if this season of my life wasn't looking miserable enough – Auckland winters are renowned for their misery.

I dig through my garage and pull out an old pair of Adidas sneakers. They are seven years old and barely worn. I lace them up.

This is the last thing I want to do right now, but if Dr Sato says I have to exercise every day, I'll do it. Still, I can't go to the gym looking like a leper, so even though I hate it – have hated it my entire life – I'm going to do it the old-fashioned way.

I'm going to run.

The sun is out. It comes and goes in winter, whenever it feels like it. Not that it will be touching my skin. I'm wrapped from head to toe, like Rocky during his snowy morning runs – hooded sweatshirt, hood tied tight, long sweatpants – all grey, just like the movie. When I step out my front door, the only things visible are my nose and my hands. I'm not ready to let anyone see my face. Or my body. Not like this.

Thankfully, my neighbourhood is quiet. My parents' home is nestled in a sleepy suburb, hidden away in a corner where, even with the address written down, some people struggle to find it. It's the type of neighbourhood where the street names don't even use the word *street*, instead, they use boutique names, like *drive* or *crescent* or *place* or *rise*. At a guess, I'll pass two or three people out there, if any. But even that's too many. This hoodie, these sweatpants, they're my new skin now. My shield between me and the world.

I head down my driveway, onto the roads. It feels new. Even though I know these streets inside out, every shortcut, every alleyway, it's been years, decades, since I've run here. Since I've run at all.

I head past the bus stop where I used to wait in the mornings as a teenager. Then past Laura's old house. Laura was a friend of my childhood neighbour, Kirsten. Kirsten and I used to ride our bikes down here and visit Laura sometimes, back in the nineties, when we were kids. I've actually seen her standing outside once or twice in recent years. Her parents still live there, after all this time.

I veer around the bend, up the hill that follows. This hill is where James, a childhood friend of my brother, used to live. He's the one who always came to our house and played Jewel on my guitar.

But as I start the climb, suddenly I don't have the oxygen to think about James or Kirsten or Laura. I can only think about my ribs, already scorching from this hill. How long has it been? Five minutes? Are my legs really dying after five minutes? Dr Sato said we need to exercise for an hour, but me surviving an hour on this run is going to be a bigger miracle than Tokuko's leg.

I reach the top. With my legs sad and screaming, but rebellious, I run past the park my brothers and I used to ride our bikes to as children. I haven't been there in years. It looks different now. A new playground, new signage. But I only glance at it for a split second. Then it's back to the road, my chest heaving, my lungs gulping oxygen in super-sized bites.

A downhill starts, finally. A gentle one, until I hit the next corner. This corner marks the halfway point of the loop. Now, it's back towards home.

The downhill steepens. I let my legs go. They thump the ground while I gasp, whimpering, my lungs bouncing up and down inside my chest as they burn. My legs are on autopilot now, rolling, I don't have the energy or strength to stop them. If I try to think, try to slow down, I'll tumble. So I let them churn over and over, and we make it to the bottom.

All that remains is the final hill back up to my house.

After two steps, my thighs feel that horrible ache, heavy like timber. I've never known this hill to be steep. All those times we rode our bikes down it as ten-year-olds, zoomed down it on rollerblades, it was just "that little hill down the road". But now, looking towards the top, home is an eternity away. That's when I know this hill is going to end me. I'm already half dead. Already look full dead. This hill just needs to finish the job.

But it doesn't. It spares me. After three gruelling minutes, I make it to the top. It's barely been twenty minutes, I should be going for another lap, but it's unthinkable. I head home, stumble past my letterbox, rest on my knees for I don't know how long. Until life starts seeping back into my head.

Dr Sato says no showers, but with sweat seeping into my wounds, my entire body on fire, there's no way I can't shower.

I get to the bathroom and gently peel my clothes off. They're stuck to my skin in many places. Once naked, I stare into the mirror. I always do that now. It's funny; when you look good, you stare in the mirror for a whole minute. When you look terrible, you stare in the mirror for a whole hour.

I examine my scalp. It's patched from back to front with small sores and crusts. I know I shouldn't pick them off, but I can't resist. I regret it immediately. Raw. And burning. The rest of my body stinking with sweat and goo.

I get in the shower. Dr Sato says if you really need to shower, you're allowed one minute.

I take three.

It is the best three minutes of my day.

Once I'm dressed, the first thing I do is go to my computer and pull up *mapmyrun.com,* a site my old colleague used to use. I type in my address, then map out the route I've just run, sure to do it as accurately as possible – every corner mapped tight, every last step up to my front door. When I finish mapping, the thin blue line zigged and zagged all over my screen, I see the total in the corner, and laugh.

2.21 kilometres.

Three days pass. I'm ready for my next run. I follow the exact same route. Same sweatshirt. Same pants. Same shoes. Even the flares taking over the back of my head. Still the same. The only difference is my ears, plugged with a brand new pair of wireless headphones. If I'm running, I'm going to need a few new toys to get me through.

I step out my front door, flick through the new playlist I've made on my phone. It's called *Run*. The first song is *Take A Picture* by Filter. Next is *3AM* by Matchbox Twenty. Then, *Torn* by Natalie Imbruglia. I have no idea why I've chosen this music. It's all music I listened to when I was a kid. Maybe it gives me comfort. Reminds me of a happier time.

Down the driveway. Turn right. Past Laura's house. Up the hill. Towards James' house. The music carries me.

I start to sweat. Two places on my body are flaring badly right now – the back of my head, and my groin. The sweat seeps in and stings, like pouring alcohol on a fresh wound. Every step I take, I wince. My forehead stings now too. I slap it. I don't know why I think that will help, but it's all I can do. Slap it once, twice, a few times. Then I give in. I slide my hand inside my hood and scratch. Hard.

There are two kinds of scratches – one that feels amazing, and one that just hurts because the skin is too raw.

This one is the second type.

Just finish this run, I tell myself. Then you can take a shower, and it will feel better. Which is only half true, but it's enough.

The first hill starts to kill me, again. But it's killing me less than last time. My legs remember it. They know they conquered it just a few days ago, so they can conquer it again today. Besides, I want my legs to hurt. I want them to hurt so much it makes me forget how much my skin hurts.

I make it to the top. Joyous, but half the joy is spent recovering while I heave oxygen. It's always a mental victory though, to scale a hill. Then the downhill starts. Down to the corner that turns back towards home.

Last time, sprinting down this hill winded me. This time, I run it slowly. Shuffling almost. Small steps. Slow steps. Downhill feels easier on the mind, but now I'm realising, it doesn't really feel easier on the legs. It's still hard, makes your knees cry. But I finally hit the bottom. Now we're back here, at the final hill. Home is at the top. I start climbing it slowly and *Take A Picture* by Filter comes back on. The drums in the intro are glorious, and they lift me.

C'mon Brendan. This is your hill. You own this hill. *This is Brendan's hill.*

I run harder. I haven't heard this song in years. My older brother used to love it. Sang it all the time. *Could you take my picture? 'Cause I won't remember.* As the guitar riffs in the background, I imagine myself in a movie, a classic nineties popcorn movie where everyone in the theatre is smiling and feeling good inside. And I make it to my letterbox.

Again, I'm dead. But less dead than last time.

It is Day 26.

I'm awake, but have not left my room. These past few days, I've deteriorated rapidly. It hurts too much to get off my bed. My skin is broken everywhere now, top to bottom. My arms, legs, neck, my lips, my groin. Even my balls. It's especially bad on my balls. I don't want to stand up. I don't want to look in the mirror. I don't even want to think. They all said it's going to get worse before it gets better. But I never thought it could get like this.

I sit up on my bed, stare at the painted blue walls of my childhood bedroom. This room, this entire second storey – sometimes I think it was built especially for me. Back when I was ten, maybe eleven, when my parents decided to renovate the house.

You're all getting older, they said. We need more space.

But only my room got moved upstairs, into the new storey, built only with wooden floors, no curtains, no upholstery. Only leather furniture. Safe from the carpets downstairs. A whole floor turned into a dust mite-proof chamber, just for Brendan.

Mum comes in. Mum never knocks. Ever. She catches me in my stare of hopelessness.

Oh, son.

She walks over, brushes my face.

I so hate to see you like this, son.

I feel myself start to cry, but I hold it down.

Don't worry, I say. This will be a fight ...

31

I clench my jaw so the tears can't come out, hold on until they subside, so I can talk again.

... but I'm going to win.

I know, son.

She kisses me on the forehead and leaves.

I hear the door close.

Now I can cry.

Getting ready for bed that night, I take a closer look at my groin. It's not just my balls. It's everywhere. Diseased. That's the word that comes to my head. It's the worst place in the world you want to look diseased, except for maybe your face. But that's no comfort, since I look diseased on my face too. I run my hand across my thighs. Raw flesh. And it's three colours. Red, brown and yellow. When it gets sweaty – which it always does at night – it itches, badly. And it smells even worse.

I get into bed, tuck a towel between my legs. It keeps me dry enough that I don't get woken up by the clamminess, and somehow, I make it through the night. But in the morning, it's back to square one. All the areas that had scabbed over, that were trying to heal, I've scratched them open. And my body is raw again.

It is Day 27.

The sun is out today. I open the curtains and stand by my window, naked. The sun's rays are only thick enough to hit the upper half of my body, or the lower half, but not both at the same time. I choose the lower. It's warm. And feels so good. Again, I stare at my groin. I can't believe this is my body. Didn't I suffer enough as a kid? I never had a normal childhood because of you. I was the one with the skin. I thought I'd served my time. Surely I earned myself some normal adult years. Why have you come back? Why me? Why now?

Lavishing the sun's warmth on my groin, I survey the rest of my body. My arms, legs, belly, still the same. Still bright red. The backs of my thighs too. There are patches everywhere, where skin has just kept falling off, until there's none left, leaving scatters of open wounds. I run my fingers across my forehead. Rough, and tender. Feels like frog skin. I've never actually felt a frog before, but I imagine this is what they feel like. Rough, scaly, scabbed over. Diseased.

And that's when I also get a big whiff of … me. I'd noticed the odour before, but now I'm finally realising – wow, that's me. It's a cross between metal and rotten meat, and a little sour too. And it lingers. In our Facebook group, everyone talks about the ooze smell.

I dab my skin with my finger, the places where it feels damp. Smell it.

No wonder everyone hates the ooze smell.

That afternoon I'm back on Tokuko's blog. Every time I read it, I find something I missed the previous time. This time, I'm trying to learn about the water limit. Because I hate the water limit. I thought counting calories was hard, but counting mils of water is pure misery. Tokuko described it as craving water like a dying person in the desert. She wasn't exaggerating. But if dying of thirst in a desert made her go from rusted-pipe leg to leg model, I'm listening.

Dr Sato says, limiting water stops the oozing. Your skin cells are damaged. The ooze is your body leaking plasma. When this happens, you're leaking protein. And that can cause something serious – a big medical word starting with H. But if you drink just enough water so that you're hydrated, and nothing more, the body won't be able to ooze. And the wounds will heal faster. Dr Sato says the skin heals when it's dry, not when it's moist. When the skin is very dry, it goes into survival mode. It sheds and regenerates. It's forced to create its own steroid. When it's very moist, it only gets more inflamed. Eventually, your skin will work properly again. You won't need moisturiser. It will create its own oils and moisturise itself. Like it was designed to. But only if you let it.

I'm not sure it makes sense. But it definitely makes more sense than a doctor telling me I have scabies.

Okay, Dr Sato. I'll do your water limit.

I start with Tokuko's limit – a thousand mils per day, including food. I only need a day to find out it's impossible. I drink one small bottle of water. Eat a couple of dates. Four mandarins. A slice of pineapple. Two kiwifruits. Knock it into my spreadsheet.

Way over.

I feel like I've barely had breakfast, but challenge myself to avoid eating or drinking for the rest of the day. Tokuko might think this is like dying of thirst in the desert. To me it's more like dying of hunger in the jungle.

I message Tokuko on Facebook, ask if it's really supposed to be this hard. To my surprise, she replies. When I get to know Tokuko better, I will learn she always replies. This is how she spends her days now, replying to people's messages about TSW. I also learn that, since my leg doesn't look like her leg – at least not yet – I don't need to be so strict. Maybe I'm allowed two thousand mils. Maybe even a tiny bit more. A monumental relief. Still, I fail to hit the target daily. In the nights, I wake up parched and slug water, as if I really am dying in the desert. Blowing through the limit every time.

The next day, I run again. It's my third run in a week – the most I've run in my life. I still hate running. But I hate TSW more.

I have a routine now. Sweats on, hoodie on. Pull the hood up, tie it tight. Headphones on. Wait for the *doo-dee-doo* so I know it's connected. Open my playlist on Spotify. *Take A Picture* by Filter comes on. I hear the guitar, the drums. And I know it's time to run.

Down the driveway. Turn right. Past Laura's house. Past James' house. Up the hill. Down to the corner. Back towards home. All the way to the final hill.

Only this time, when I get to the final hill, I feel good. Strong. Halfway through the hill, there's a side street. My classmate from primary school lived on this street. Jonathan something. Baker, I think. His street leads to my house too, but it's a longer hill. A harder one. But that's what I want. I don't know why, I just see it and think, that's going to be pretty hard. And I'm up for it.

I'm right, it's hard. I'm sucking air, climbing as hard as I can. I get to halfway in one piece. I run past Jonathan Baker's house. I can see the top. I get to the last twenty metres, just before I can see my driveway, and my lungs feel like they're going to pop. But I don't stop. I get to my driveway and I run up, all the way to my letterbox, my lungs don't pop, and I make it to my front door.

When I get out of the shower, I go straight to my computer and again, I map my run meticulously, remembering every point where I crossed the road, if I crossed it straight or on an angle, if I was running on the road or the footpath. Has to be perfect. Can't miss a single metre.

2.74 kilometres.

It is Day 29.

I already notice some improvements from the running. I don't know why I doubted Dr Sato. He's been doing this a long time. After I run, even though it's not close to an hour, not even close to half an hour, I feel better. The sweating itches at first, then it hurts, then stings, but by the end of the run, it feels good. Like I've purged something. Toxins? Steroids? I don't know. Something worth purging.

There's something even better about running. It makes me sweat, and sweating increases my water limit. Dr Sato says everything you sweat out, you're allowed to replace. As soon as I get out of the shower, I weigh myself. If I've lost two hundred grams, I'm allowed to eat an extra two hundred grams that day. That's an extra kiwifruit and an extra apple. It might not sound like a lot, but when every millilitre counts, a kiwifruit and an apple is like a three-course meal.

I eat a steak, some fish, some pineapple, an apple, a kiwifruit. Slug some coconut water.

Then for the rest of the evening, I snack on dates. Dates are my hack – they're sweet and filling, but have hardly any water. About five mils each.

I still fail to stay under the limit. But I'm getting closer.

The following day, I notice something strange. I'm shivering. It's early winter and it's cold but even while sitting indoors in front of the window with the sun shining on my face, I'm shivering.

I go to the Facebook group, search for "cold".

Dozens of posts come up about people feeling cold. There's an explanation: When we go into withdrawal from steroids, it not only weakens our skin, all its other functions stop working too. Our skin does many things, like sweating, creating oils, and retaining heat. Some people say they haven't sweated in months. Almost all of us are no longer creating oils. And most of us can't hold in heat. Our skin is like a screen door. The warmth just drifts out. Everyone reports feeling cold.

I am already sensitive to cold when I'm healthy. Now, I am ultra-sensitive. I didn't know feeling cold could hurt, but hunched in my chair, in the corner of my room, I'm shaking. I have never shivered like this before. Even walking through the snow in rural Switzerland, I never shivered like this. Living through winter in China, where your fingertips freeze as soon as you pull your gloves off, I never shivered like this. I want to get up and go downstairs, stand on the deck in the sun and get something to drink. But I can't move. It hurts too much. It's like I'm stuck to the chair, paralysed. Shivering violently. Mumbling to myself.

What is happening to my body?

I'm not sure how long I sit there. Maybe twenty minutes, maybe an hour. But eventually, I need to get up. I need to use the toilet. I groan deeply as I push myself to my feet. I can see the sun out the window, but it feels like there's a blizzard inside this house. I make it to the toilet. My urine is darker than usual and my flow is weak. On any regular day, I would be alarmed. But I remind myself this is okay. That's what it's supposed to look like.

Follow the protocol. Ninety days. Dr Sato always says: The treatment sounds unbelievable, but it works.

I believe him.

Then I go do that other thing Dr Sato said to do.

Sweatpants. Hoodie. Out the front door. Down the driveway, turn right, past Laura's house, up the hill, past James' house. But when I get to the corner towards home, I don't take it. I keep going. Straight ahead, towards the shopping centre. The same one I used to buy lollies at sometimes, on the way home from school. I don't know how far away it is in kilometres but in my mind, it's not that far. Even if it is, I don't care. It's either run or sit in my house freezing to death. So I run.

I get to the shopping centre. I don't turn around. I keep going. Another kilometre. Maybe two. Until I get to the park by the main road. The one with the skateboarding ramp. Here, I finally turn the corner, heading back towards home.

It's far, but I know if I just follow this road, it will eventually lead back to Laura's house. Which then leads back to my house.

I can do it, I tell myself. Keep running.

But halfway along this main road, my gas tank runs out. I don't want to stop, because cars are driving past and they'll laugh at me. But I'm barely moving. I'm plodding. Breathing noisily. Desperately. I need oxygen. I know I'm surrounded by oxygen, but it's not enough. My lungs are beating against my rib cage screaming, "Hey, we need oxygen!" but my chest is drowning, I can't breathe it in fast enough. Cars are passing me every five seconds. The people inside probably looking at me, laughing. Saying, look at this guy, about to die out here.

They have no idea.

I don't know what happens next. My mind blanks. Cars whiz past, and eventually, I'm turning up the street towards Laura's house. In five more minutes I'll be home.

How did I make it?

I have no idea.

But I will one day. One day I'll learn, this is a superpower I have. One we all have. During those runs where you know you can't take another step, your mind turns off. It's a trick, a survival instinct maybe, to save you from yourself. To stop you from thinking about how much you hate this run, how good it would feel to quit and never do this again. Everything blurs. You feel nothing. Then, suddenly, ten or twenty or thirty minutes later, you snap back to reality, and you're near the end.

I get to my letterbox. This time, I sit down on the driveway. How far was that? Ten kilometres? Twenty kilometres? Whatever it was, it was far. Further than I've ever run in my life.

I get out of the shower and don't bother getting dressed. I sit at my computer in my towel and trace my route – past the shopping centre, past the skateboarding ramp. Where did I cross the road? Here? There? Has to be perfect. Can't miss a single metre. I continue along the main road, back around to the little street up to Laura's house and to home.

6.67 kilometres.

Journal entry

21 June, 2019.

When I'm lying in bed in the morning, my thighs are all oozy, behind my knees and elbows all sweaty, my forehead stings because I've been scratching it all night. I know I need to get up and start the day, I need to exercise because that is what will heal me. I need to set out a meal plan for the day because that is what will heal me. I need to go stand in the sun because that is what will heal me. But I feel crappy because I didn't get enough sleep, and my body is broken, and I don't feel like getting up.

So I say out loud to myself, "Brendan, how strong are you?"

And then I reply to myself, "I'M TOO STRONG."

And I throw the sheets off, sometimes so viciously they fly across the room. And I get up and start the day.

When I'm running, and my legs are starting to hurt, my skin is stinging like fire because it's broken and the sweat is starting to seep in. I hate running. But I know I need to sweat because that is what will heal me. So when I look up at the final hill to my house, and I think about how much it's going to hurt, I say out loud, "Brendan, how strong are you?"

And then I reply right back, "I'M TOO STRONG."

And I keep going, and I finish my run.

When it's time to get in the shower, I strip off my clothes, sweat dripping off my body. I know I'm only allowed one minute, and it should be ice cold, because that's what's best for the skin, and the inflammation, and the immune system. And it's winter, so I'm dreading getting into this ice-cold shower. But I turn the water on, and I see it running, looking freezing cold and terrifying. And before I have time to talk myself out of it, I say out loud, "Brendan, how strong are you?"

And I reply right back, "I'M TOO STRONG."

Then, with my adrenaline pumping, I jump into the ice-cold shower and it's the worst thing ever for three seconds, and then it's the best thing ever. After thirty seconds I get out, and I look at myself in the mirror dripping with cold water, feeling invincible. And I say to myself, "Damn, you really are too strong."

When I wake up in the middle of the night, I'm scratching like crazy, lying in a pile of my own dead skin. I get out of bed because lying down only seems to make me itchier. I go downstairs and stand in the kitchen, pour myself 100ml of water to drink, since I'm not allowed any more than that. In fact, this 100ml is already cheating. But I don't mind, I need it. I sip on it until it's gone, and then I tell myself I need to go back to bed, and meditate myself to sleep, because that is what will heal me. And I whisper to myself, "How strong are you, Brendan?"

And I reply right back, "I'M TOO STRONG."

And I walk upstairs and get back into bed, and I force myself to sleep.

And then it's morning again. And I don't want to get up. But I know I need to get up and exercise, and make my meal plan, and get some fresh air and some sun, because that is what will heal me.

I ask myself, "How strong are you, Brendan?"

I answer, "I'm too strong."

And it starts all over again.

4

It is Day 38.

I look in the mirror, surprised at how fast I've improved. I'm happy – maybe even excited – to take my weekly photos. I set up my tripod, *snap snap snap*, then hurriedly load them onto the computer.

My back and torso have cleared. Patches remain, some scarring, but no red. My arms and legs are so dry and powdery, they look like they're covered in flour. But no red. My forehead has remnants of scabs and flakes, but nothing compared to the carnage that was there before, and barely any red. Of course I still don't look like the old me. I'm still discoloured and my skin is tight and thin, like cellophane. In place of the rashes are now wrinkles, like elephant skin. I look ten years older. But the cracks are gone, and the ooze, and the blood. And I'm not hurting anymore. That already feels like a victory.

I upload the photos to the Facebook group. I follow with an update of my thoughts, my emotions. It's only been four weeks, but it feels like a year. I don't usually write posts like this – soppy ones – but in this group it's like we're all therapists and patients at the same time. We're pouring our hearts out or we're listening. Usually both. I tell them about my runs. About my spirit, constantly breaking and growing. About how hard this has been. I write and write, because I can't stop.

There is a flood of comments. Ten times more than usual.

This is amazing, they say. Your sharing is a gift. Please keep posting. You're strong. You're inspirational.

Now that I no longer look like a burn victim – or at least a recovered one – I'm no longer terrified of being in public. I pack a gym bag and head down to the YMCA, just a few minutes from my home. Doing my daily exercise here will surely be less painful than on the wintery road.

The guy at reception signs me up for a trial week, then runs me through the complex.

Two pools, spa pool, two-storey gym, sauna.

Sauna? That sounds interesting. Maybe I'll try that.

But I head for the treadmills first. Even though I still hate running – hating it more every time I lace my shoes up – I keep going. The more I run, the more my skin improves. As long as that's happening, I won't dare stop. I can't run for an hour yet, but if Dr Sato says you need to run for an hour, I'll do it. I'll run every day until I can.

My last memory of running on a treadmill is training on a clunky machine in my garage, back when I was fifteen. Times have changed. The treadmills here are covered in graphs and buttons and flashing lights. As soon as I get moving, I notice how much of a reprieve the treadmill is, from running in the winter outside. No cold. No wind. There's a TV in front of me. Now the sweatpants and hoodie keep me too warm. I start to sweat, and it's like a steam oven inside my hood. Still, I keep my hood up and tied tight, to cover my bald and splotched head. My forehead starts to sting. The back of my head stings. It's awful, but I know it will only last ten minutes. It will go away if I just keep running.

I hit four kilometres. It feels good. Then I hit the weight room. For that hour or two of working out, all I think about is putting one foot in front of the other, lifting the bar as cleanly as I can for every rep. By the end of each workout, I'm not thinking about my skin at all.

Soon, the gym becomes my new safe space. My happy place. I go every day. When I'm at home staring in the mirror at the cellophane skin on my hairless scalp, when I'm in bed scratching, struggling to sleep, when I'm weighing out pieces of fruit on my kitchen scale, everything depresses me. I don't want to accept this is my new life. But when I'm in the gym, panting, working, my skin becomes soaked in sweat, and from a distance, in the mirrors on the gym walls, I almost look normal. For that small part of the day, I feel free.

It is Day 42.

I arrive at the gym slightly earlier than usual, around midday. The faint smell of chlorine hits me as soon as I walk through the front doors. Already it's become calming and familiar.

The guy at reception smiles at me, like he always does.

No rest days for you, huh?

Mate, I would spend the entire day here if I could.

Straight to the treadmills. Four kilometres, nice and easy. Then I lay out on the floor and stretch.

The trainer in the gym is a guy named Greg. He sees me on my lonesome, wanders over from across the room. Big smile on his face.

He points at the stereo in the corner.

You can put your own music on if you want! Just plug the cord into your phone.

Oh, yeah?

Yeah! Just no swear words.

Oh …

I'm just kidding!

He laughs confidently, like he's used that joke a hundred times, and it's worked every time.

One thing I've noticed about Greg – he's the gym trainer, but he never seems to be training anyone. Just waltzing around, chatting, putting back everyone's weights. He's short and stocky, about as old as my Dad, maybe a little younger. The way he grins and talks at the same time, the way he shuffles around the gym like he's wearing flip flops, he's the quintessential Kiwi bloke. But as he stands there chatting away to me, I start feeling uneasy, conscious of him being too close. I look normal from afar, but when you're near, you can see the flakes running across my forehead, the cracks in my lips.

Still, I take him up on his offer. It's the middle of the day, the gym is empty. I ditch my headphones, blast my own music from the speakers. *Could you take my picture? 'Cause I won't remember.* It feels like the gym is all my own.

As I finish my last set of stretches, I think about what I'm going to eat when I get home. I guess I've sweated around half a litre, and I've barely drunk anything, meaning I'll be able to add most of that to the day's water limit.

Then I have an epiphany.

Why don't I go sit in this sauna for an hour and sweat a bucket? Then I'll be able to eat as much as I want!

Genius.

I hurriedly pack my stuff and rush downstairs. I don't even know where the sauna is. I head to the pools, see the lifeguard as soon as I walk in.

Excuse me, ma'am, is the sauna in here?

She points to a tiny wooden door on the far side. You can barely see it.

Thanks.

Still, I'm not sure if I can actually go in there. For every second of every day I've been in this gym, my hoodie has stayed on with the hood tied tight, hiding my scabbing scalp, the crocodile skin that runs down my neck. Getting in the sauna will mean getting undressed. Exposed. Sitting in a tiny crowded room. In my underwear.

Really Brendan?

But if it's empty ... maybe.

I walk past, peer in the window. It's a small wooden room, the size of a rich person's Jacuzzi. It takes me a moment to see through the hazy glass and make out who's in there.

Just one person. A Chinese grandma.

I can handle looking like shit in front of a Chinese grandma.

I strip down to my underwear and hurry inside. The second the heat hits my face, I smile with bliss. My body hasn't been able to hold heat for weeks, now I'm bathing in it. It wraps my skin, the warmth filling my veins like a shot of heroin mixed with warm tomato soup on a rainy Sunday morning.

I take a seat opposite the Chinese grandma. She barely acknowledges me, a weak smile. I smile back. Then I close my eyes and enjoy the warmth and silence. The sweat comes quickly. It's liberating. Detoxifying. Feeling the droplets run down my back, I think about how many extra mils of water I'm losing, how much more I'll be able to eat when I get home.

Then after ten minutes, like a switch, comfort turns to effort. It's hard to breathe now. I open my eyes. Chinese grandma is sitting cross-legged, chest puffed out, breathing deeply.

In, out. In, out.

I try it. It makes it even harder.

Maybe that's the point.

Instead, I hunch over, hang my head. As I do, sweat runs off my forehead, not in drips, but in a steady stream. And then it drips off me from everywhere – my fingers, my chin, my chest, my nose. I watch it splatter the ground, like bullets. At this rate I'll be able to eat an eight-course meal and still won't break my water limit. If I don't pass out first.

I hear huffing across the room. I look up. Chinese grandma is waving her arms, doing tai chi, complete with sound effects. She's probably seventy, but has the body of a thirty-year-old. Maybe because other Chinese grandmas are at home watching kung fu movies, snacking on dried mangoes, and she's here alone at midday, doing kung fu in the sauna. I look back at the ground. Every part of my body is drenched. From my ears to my toes. That's when I notice – soaked in sweat like this, in the dim sauna lighting, you can't see the ugliness on me. The flakes, the red splotches, they're invisible.

I like the sauna. I think I'll come here every day.

It is Day 60.

Shaving my head each morning has become religion. Like morning prayer, I can't miss it. I stand in front of the mirror and zip the half millimetre of growth from the day before. Off with it comes a layer of dead skin. It floats through the air, a cloud of tiny flakes that look like sawdust. Watching them sail into the sink feels cleansing, satisfying. If my body is shedding this much skin, it must mean new skin is coming underneath. If only it would come faster.

It's perplexing, looking in the mirror now. I've gotten more muscular. I can run five kilometres any day of the week without a hiccup. Since all I do is go to the gym, sit in the sauna, and sleep, I might be the healthiest I've ever been – on the inside. On the outside, it's the opposite. My skin looks like I've aged eighteen years in eight weeks. The wrinkles on my forehead run deep. I've got no fat on my belly, but the skin there rolls up like elephant skin. My eyebrows are eighty percent gone from all the scratching. I'm Benjamin Button. Young and old at the same time.

Off to the gym.

I knock out my usual four kilometres on the treadmill, and it feels good. It feels so good I don't want to stop, so I don't.

Go for six, I tell myself.

I go for six. I get there. I'm still not tired.

One more kilometre to hit seven? That'll be a new record.

You're on.

The screen hits seven.

Can I keep going?

I check in with my legs, my lungs. They feel fine.

Let's go for eight.

I'm really working now. Sweat drips off my forehead like rain. Watching the treadmill screen move from seven to eight seems to take forever, feels like I may not make it, but when it finally hits, I feel good again. Energised.

Nine?

Why not.

I get to nine.

Well now. Can't come all this way and not go for ten.

It sounds unreal, to be on the brink of ten kilometres, but I'm here. Minutes away.

The screen hits ten.

People who run ten kilometres are crazy. I've known that my whole life. Now I'm one of them, and I did it almost by accident. And my legs still haven't stopped.

I watch the numbers still ticking up.

Another half a kilometre, and it's a quarter marathon. *Quarter marathon.*

That's the one, I tell myself. That's where we're going.

The screen slowly runs to 10.3, 10.4. Then it finally hits 10.5. I let it run to 10.8, just to be sure. Then I slam the Stop button.

The treadmill slows to a standstill. My legs wobble slightly as I step off and go to my bag. I sit down. Slug some water. Goofy smile plastered across my face.

Quarter marathon. How about that.

When I get home that night, I don't bother measuring my water limit. I eat until I'm full, and enjoy it. I don't look in the mirror for the rest of the night. It doesn't matter what I look like today. Today, I did something special. Nobody can take anything away from me today.

The next day, I take a break from running.

You deserve it, I tell myself.

Instead I head straight to the weight room, playfully throw some dumbbells around, then head to the sauna.

Chinese grandma is there. The big fat guy who always puts eucalyptus oil on himself is there. And there's a new guy. Huge, like Rambo. Muscles so chiselled, body fat so non-existent, he looks like an action figure. He walks in moments after me, sits down beside me. A cute blonde follows behind. I can't tell if they're together or just friends.

Should've brought some headphones, he says to her.

She shrugs.

Do you think they'll work though? They might get fried, eh?

She shrugs again.

I look up at him, and he looks right back at me.

What you think? If you bring a phone in here, will it fry?

I nod.

Probably. Yeah.

Mmm, he hums. Sucks.

He's friendlier than I expected.

You South African?

Yeah! He grins. The accent, eh? Still strong.

Kinda. I was in Cape Town actually, earlier this year.

No way! The hell you doing out there, bra?

I want to say, living my awesome life, with a full head of hair, before all this bullshit happened to me.

But I don't.

Festival, I say. Afrikaburn. Heard of it?

Nah, what's it, like a music festival?

More like ... an arts festival. In the Tankwa.

Ooh, says the blonde. I've heard of that. It looks awesome.

Yeah, I smile. It really is.

You're brave, he says. Going out there.

I shrug.

Cape Town? It's alright. Where you from?

Johannesburg.

And how you liking Auckland?

Oh, bra. Couldn't pay me to go back.

Over the next few minutes, I get the Cliffs Notes to his life. He's a personal trainer, and a fitness model, and just ate a chicken burger that his coach is going to be mad at him about. For some reason, it's really weighing on his mind, that chicken burger. He mentions it a few times.

Then we go silent.

This is what happens after fifteen minutes in the sauna. At first, everyone is chatty. Then the heat gets on top of you and there's no energy left to talk. All you can think about is trying to breathe.

We both hunch over, arms rested on our knees.

See who can make the biggest swimming pool, he says, as we watch the puddles of sweat growing at our feet.

I don't say anything. Just grunt.

He lasts another five minutes, then gets up to leave.

You win. I'm Shay, by the way.

He holds out his fist. I bump it.

Brendan.

Nice to meet you, bra.

Shay can afford to get out early, but I can't. Every drop of sweat adds to my water limit. Another five minutes might mean I can eat two more kiwifruits when I get out of here. I stay in there until Chinese grandma gets out, eucalyptus guy gets out, until it's just me moaning and sputtering, trying to squeeze out every last bit of sweat.

Then after ten minutes, eucalyptus guy gets back in. I peer up at him. He has a beer belly the size of a beach ball that hangs over his thighs. And then I notice, he has perfect skin.

It's not fair. I run every single day. Eat the healthiest foods. My calorie count is angelic. Yet this guy looks like he hasn't run more than forty seconds in forty years, and he has better skin than me. Guys eating McDonald's every day have better skin than me. Even damn homeless people have better skin than me.

I shake my head. So I'll work harder. Starting right now. I'm not getting out until this guy gets out.

It's not a good idea. I'm getting close to forty minutes, and I don't know if I have any sweat left. I look up at the eucalyptus guy. He's lounging against the wall, his face suffer-free, his tiny bottle of annoying scented oil sits by his side. Sweat runs off his perfectly round and oversized belly covered in spotless skin. I curse. Not at him. At me. At my pounding head and shortening breaths.

C'mon, fat guy. Get out.

I figure he can't last more than five more minutes. I look up at the clock, mark the time.

Another minute passes. His eyes are closed, making his face hard to read. I'm not sure if he's just enjoying himself, or trying to zen out the pain. I hope it's the latter.

I lean on my knees again, stare back at the ground. It's easier, looking down for some reason. Each breath feels cooler.

Someone opens the door and walks in. I'm sitting right at the entrance, and the five-second rush of cool air is a life saver. I look up at eucalyptus guy. He looks less at ease now, like he's starting to struggle.

Yes, c'mon. Please.

It's been four minutes. He must be getting close. I'm not close. I'm already long gone. I should have gotten out ten minutes ago. But he's got better skin than me, and I want what he's got.

It's almost six minutes. I've stopped sweating. If he doesn't move now, I'm going to die in here.

I watch him with one eye. Ten seconds. Twenty.

I guess this is the hill I'm going to die on.

No. You idiot. Get out.

Thirty more seconds, I tell myself. Until the clock hits twelve.

Deal.

It hits twelve.

He's not moving.

I wait ten seconds more.

Another five.

Another three.

Okay, fat man. You win. Keep your perfect skin.

Then, just as I'm about to stand up, I see him lean forward. He grabs his little bottle of oil. Slips his feet into his slippers. Gets to his feet and walks out.

I grind my teeth and follow right behind him, getting a whiff of big-man sweat and eucalyptus all in one.

The smell of victory.

The only thing better than the cool splash of air that hits my face after I walk out the sauna door is my after-sauna tradition. It starts with the car ride home. By the time I get to the gym carpark, my skin has already dried out to a crisp. My forehead feels like a piece of Weet Bix, bits of dead skin hanging off like wafer crumbs. The entire drive home, I run my fingers back and forth over my face, and flakes whirl around the car and blow out the window.

Once I get in the front door, I go straight to the kitchen. The fridge is loaded with fruits. Mangoes are usually a luxury here, but there's a mango surplus in Mexico right now, and they're being sold in the supermarket for less than a dollar. I take a few out, along with some kiwifruits and a chunk of watermelon. I peel them perfectly and chop them until I have a heaping bowl of rainbow-coloured love.

Then, still half naked, standing in my kitchen, I savour each piece one by one. Every bit of sweat gets replaced by a piece of tropical fruit. It is the favourite part of my day.

It is Day 86.

I haven't slept in three days.

I've been denying it, but I can't anymore. The second flare has arrived. With a vengeance.

It's talked about often in our Facebook group – the dreaded second flare – but it's taken so long to eventuate I thought I might have escaped it.

I guess dreams are free for a reason. Reality is sold separately.

My neck is the victim this time. Puffy, like marshmallow, and bright tomato red. It hurts to look left, to look right, or to move at all. I can't stand to look at it. Just so ugly.

Even worse than the neck, is the cold. It sails right through me, like a blizzard through an open window. If the shivers during my first flare were bad, these ones are apocalyptic.

Worst of all – I know, I can feel it – this flare is just getting started.

On days like these, when it's really bad, I know there's only one thing I can do that will take my mind off it. That thing. That thing that is going to hurt so much, and I hate so much, but always seems to work.

But I already know, I'm not running today. Today I get a pass. Even the strongest man in the world wouldn't be able to run today.

I hurry back to my room, where the heater is still on, and the sun is coming in through the window. I pull the heater close and huddle beside it. I can't cover myself, because my skin lets out so much heat that it gets trapped inside my clothes, and it becomes like a mini oven, my skin sweats and gets clammy. Then I'll scratch. And then things will get really bad. So I just sit there, half naked, shivering by the heater. I sit there the whole day. Looking through my phone. Wishing for sleep. Wishing for my life back.

I need to eat. It takes me a few hours to muster the strength to put on clothes and get to the car. But, as the day goes on and the house warms a little, I get there. I have my cap and my hoodie and my sunglasses, to cover my face, so I don't scare any children. That's what I tell myself, anyway. But it's really all for me. I don't have the strength to let the world see me like this.

I get in the car. The sun's been beaming down on it all morning, and it's cooking inside. Normally, this would suffocate me. I'd open the doors and let it breathe for a minute, wind down all the windows and blast the air conditioner. But now it's the opposite. The heat is precious, I quickly shut the door and trap it all in.

Bliss.

I pull into the supermarket five minutes later. Sitting in the parking lot, I pep talk myself to go inside.

Just go in, get your food and get out. Five minutes max.

But I can't move. It's too warm inside the car. It reminds me of when I was backpacking in Norway, snow on the ground, and we were all hiding in the wood-fired sauna, not wanting to make the long walk back to the cabin.

Five minutes, I tell myself. I'll go into the supermarket in five minutes. Just give me five minutes of this warmth, and then I'll go face the world.

Five minutes ...

I'm not sure what I see first.

Trees, I think.

Then my dashboard.

Or maybe it's the other way around.

It feels like one eye is opening before the other. I see my steering wheel next. And then in front of me, I can see the sun still shining, but on its way down.

I look at the clock. I've been asleep for four hours. I never suspected sleeping in a supermarket carpark could be so rejuvenating. It's the most sleep I've had in weeks.

I put my cap on, pull my hood up, get out of the car. I feel semi-alive now. Amazing what a few hours of shut-eye can do. I buy my dinner. Get home. Sit in my driveway for another half hour. Just to enjoy not shivering, feeling normal, for a little longer. Then I head inside for the favourite part of my day. Feeding time.

Once night falls, I am back at my chair, in my room, by the heater, staring at my bed. I really, really don't want to get into bed. If feeding time is the best part of my day, bedtime is the worst. I already know what's going to happen. I'll get into bed, and I'll put the covers on because I'm freezing. My body will try to make heat, but it just escapes through my skin like an air vent, and fills the sheets like a steam room. Then I'll be sweating and itchy. I'll throw the sheets off, scratching, tearing my skin apart, ripping all the scabs off, undoing all the healing my skin has done that day. Until I'm freezing again. Then I'll pull the sheets back on. And scratch, and throw them off again. I won't sleep a wink. And when I've scratched and sweated and my sheets are covered in bloodstains and dead skin, it will be morning.

No thanks. I've tried everything already — thinner sheets, thicker sheets, sleeping on the floor, sleeping on the yoga mat, thinner clothes, thicker clothes, more clothes, less clothes, no clothes. It's the same every night.

So I sit in my chair and stare at my bed, and it terrifies me. But I know I don't have a choice. I need to sleep, I need to at least try.

Besides, maybe this night it will be different?

So I get in.

And sweat, and scratch.

I don't sleep a wink.

My sheets are soon covered in bloodstains and dead skin.

And then it's morning.

It is Day 89.

I get out of bed. No sleep, again. There is blood all over my pillow. There's always blood, but never this much.

I run my hands across the bedsheet. Dead skin jumps off it. Piles of it. There's always dead skin. But never this much.

I go to the heater. I stand over it, like I'm bending over to touch my toes, but with the heater underneath me. It's the only way I can get my body close enough to feel anything. I'm still shivering, even though I'm less than an inch from the heater panels on full blast. Every few seconds I get too close and touch it, and flinch from the burn. But the heat is life. I'm there for a really long time. Hours.

As I stand hunched over the heater, I run my hand over the back of my head. It's lumpy, scaly, like concrete. And it hurts. It hurts to turn my head left or right. But I keep doing it, somehow hoping it won't hurt if I do it one more time.

Finally I go to the bathroom. As soon as I step out my bedroom door, I feel the cold hit me like a punch to the gut. I don't know how, but it gets inside me instantly, like someone pouring ice water right into my bones. It's confusing, because out the window I can see a few rays of sun. But I walk like a hunchback, shivering. On the way, I manage to laugh sadly at myself, bent at the waist, hobbling along. How ridiculous I must look.

I get to the mirror. At four weeks things were looking so good. At eight weeks even better. Now, this flare has brought me all the way back to zero. Sores bubble on my chest. My neck has broken apart like a volcano erupting. Why is it so evil, this thing? Gives me so much hope, a glimmer of my old self, then snatches it away. My face has never looked this bad. Never felt this bad. I stare at myself for a long time. My eyes are lifeless, black, like marbles. Not a flicker of happiness. I don't recognise this face anymore. I have no idea who it is, but it's not me.

And then an overwhelming sadness when I realise, yes, it is.

I want to cry. But I don't. I look into the lifeless eyes in the mirror and tell myself I'm too strong to cry, that I've cried enough already, that crying won't solve anything. I need to do something better than crying, like running.

I put on two layers of sweats. Covering every inch of my body. Lace up. Drive to the gym.

As soon as my feet hit the treadmill, I know I won't be lasting long today. My skin has been lit on fire. It's never been this sore. Not even close. From my neck to my waist, it's like my sweater is packed with hot coals. But, oddly, it seems the worse the skin feels, the more I can run. The suffering is no longer new, the run just lets me suffer on my terms. Nothing can hurt me more than me.

How strong are you Brendan?

Too strong.

I get to four kilometres. What got me out of the house was repeating "just four kilometres" inside my head, but now that I'm here, I'll give more.

Soaked in sweat, salts soaked deep into every wound, I can't feel myself anymore. I just stare ahead and go.

I get to five.

Push to six.

Make it to seven.

I already know I'm doing ten.

I get to ten.

No euphoria this time. Just a gross smelling body and a craving for a shower and fruits. I skip the sauna and head straight home.

When I'm finally showered and dressed, it's back to reality. My neck crinkles like tinfoil every time I move. All I want to do is sit in my chair and rest, to avoid moving for the rest of the night, but I need to eat.

I labour down the stairs to the kitchen. Shivering in the evening cold, getting down the stairs is a mission on its own, but I talk to myself as I move, tell myself how well I ran today, how I'm getting better every day.

How strong are you Brendan?

Too strong.

Yes you are.

I take a mango from the fridge. A knife from the drawer. I move in slow motion. It hurts less that way.

Then, just as I start to peel it, my hand quivers from the cold.

The knife falls and clangs to the floor.

This sound is like a bullet. The ringing of this dropped utensil is the final straw.

My legs go limp.

I collapse to my knees.

I've never cried this way before, this hard, this sudden, but now these tears are here, and they don't stop.

I'm not strong, I cry.

Tears free fall from my face and splatter onto the kitchen floor.

I know I said I'm strong, but I'm not!

I can't do it anymore!

It's too hard! It's too hard.

It's too hard.

I don't want to do it anymore.

The words come out between sobs, so mangled even God wouldn't understand them.

I call for my Mum.

Nobody answers. Nobody is home.

Tell them, I plead. Can you tell them, Mum? Tell them I'm not strong. Tell them I can't do this. Tell them I don't want to do it anymore. Tell them I can't do it anymore.

Journal entry

August 13, 2019.

On the darkest day, I didn't even recognise myself.
So I closed my eyes, and I saw the devil.
I asked him "What should I do, when I'm going through hell?"
He said, "Keep going."

5

It is Day 98.

I have a new running watch. It's a Fitbit. The fanciest one. I'm the guy who normally buys last year's model, the demo model, anything to avoid spending more than I need to. But they say you can't take your money to your grave, and it's true. The old me died months ago – the old me who smiled and told people to chase their dreams and lived free and never complained. Dead now, and none of his money went with him. So we might as well spend it.

I've never spent more than thirty dollars on a watch. Now, I don't even think about it. I order the most expensive one they have. It's three hundred dollars. If my entire body wants to look diseased and broken, at least my watch will be sparkling brand new.

When evening falls, I lace up my shoes and take my new watch for a ride. I can't lie, it's really cool. Touch screen and everything.

I don't know how far I'm going tonight. Maybe five kilometres. Maybe six. All I know is kilometres have stopped mattering to me. Every time I run, I just want to run until my legs hurt so much I don't feel my skin anymore.

I start the same way I always do. Headphones in. Down the driveway, turn right, past Laura's house. Up the hill, past James' house. Then once again, at the top, I don't turn back towards home. I keep going, towards the shopping centre. All the way to the park with the skateboarding ramp. And then I go somewhere new. Instead of turning left towards home, I turn right towards the city.

I take the first side street. New territory. I've never run here before. Never even driven here. It's flat for a while, then a massive hill. Huge. I don't care. I run it. My heart burns almost as hard as my legs. I wonder how far this run will be. Might be a new record. But I don't have to guess anymore, no more waiting to get home and check *mapmyrun.com*. Now I can just look at my new expensive watch.

I peek at the screen.

Four kilometres.

That's it? Four kilometres?

I liked it better when I had to guess.

Sweat starts to collect behind my knees. It starts to itch. It starts as just a tickle. I ignore it, sure it will go away. But it grows and grows.

Don't give in, I say. Don't let yourself stop your first run with your brand new watch to give in to some itch.

I continue up the never-ending hill, push the itch to the back of my mind, and focus on my steps.

Up, up, up.

The itch doesn't care. It's relentless, it grows even more. Soon it's at the point where it's tingling up and down my spine, making my leg twitch with every step.

I can't take it. I fall to the pavement. Drop my pants and go to work. *Oh my god.* I have never scratched like this in my life, but here I am – outside someone's house, writhing on the footpath, in the dark with my pants down, scratching like an animal. I don't care who sees me, who drives past, if people are watching me from the window. It is heavenly. It is crack cocaine, caramel ice cream and a full body orgasm mixed into a syringe and injected straight into the bloodstream. I can't stop. Each time I drag my nails behind my knees, I groan with pleasure. If you could buy this kind of pleasure, I'd be bankrupt tomorrow. I'm addicted. I sit on the footpath and ravage myself until my arms hurt, until my skin hurts, until blood and sweat and dead skin are caked under my fingernails, and then I scratch even more, even harder, hoping to feel it one more time.

When I'm finally done, when blood is smeared up and down the back of my legs, I start to feel the droplets. I don't know how long it's been raining, but I feel it now. Only barely.

When I was a kid, we called this type of rain spit. Is it raining? Nah, just spitting.

I get to my feet and run. This hill still isn't finished. But it feels easier, now that the skin behind my knees isn't showered with itching powder.

I'm smiling.

My gosh.

I still can't believe how good that felt.

As I reach the top of the hill, I recognise where I am – on the main road, near Meadowbake, the bakery my brother always raved about when we were young. *Chicken and veggie pies!* Every time we drove past. Further down is the dairy a friend of my parents used to own and the video shop, where we used to go for movie night. I used to choose Power Rangers, every single time. If you watched Power Rangers on TV, you only got one episode, but if you hired the tape, you got four episodes in a row. It was the greatest thing in the world.

I run past it all – Meadowbake, the dairy, the video shop. All staples of my childhood. I drive this street all the time, but it's my first time running it. It feels a lot longer when you run it.

The rain goes up three gears. Not spit anymore. Real rain. The kind of rain you see out the window and instantly know the lunch plans you made that morning are cancelled. The kind that makes you run for cover and wait in a shop doorway until it stops.

But I don't stop. Because I can't. There are no shop doorways for me to hide under, no car to rush to. If I stop, I'll just get wetter. The only thing I can do is run faster, so I do.

I look at my watch.

Five and a half kilometres.

I hate this watch. I paid three hundred dollars so every time I feel amazing, like I'm a movie star, like I'm running across the planet, this stupid gadget can punch me in the face and say nah, only five kilometres bro, LOL.

Forget the watch. Rain is pouring on my face. The pavement splatting with every footstep. Nobody else is out here. The harder I work out here, the faster my skin heals, and I'm working harder than everybody. That's the thing my watch can't see.

In the distance, I see a guy. Maybe only a block away, but in the darkness, in the wall of rain, I can't tell if he's just a guy walking home from work, or someone pumping out kilometres. But he gets closer, and I'm able to make out his stubby shorts, his running shoes. He's pounding pavement like me. It's bucketing down. Rain thumping so loud even if you screamed nobody would hear you. As we pass each other, we manoeuvre around a little hump in the footpath and catch each other's eye. He gives me a sly grin, a little jerk of the eyebrow. Half a second maybe, but it doesn't need to be any longer than that. His glance says it all.

Yep, you're just as crazy as I am.

I lift my knees even higher, pump my arms even harder. Feeling proud. This rain doesn't scare me anymore. I'll run in the rain all night.

Then, just as I make peace with the rain, it goes away. Back to spitting for a moment, then gone. As if it was only there to piss me off. Once it could see I didn't care, it decided to go somewhere else. I wish TSW would do the same.

I finally get to the turn-off that leads back towards my house. Head home or keep going?

I look at my stupid expensive watch.

Six kilometres.

Not enough.

I surge on ahead. This road I'm on now, I know it well. I drive it almost every time I leave my house. The gym is this way. The supermarket is this way. I used to drive to work this way. But I've never run it. Every road is different when you run it. When you drive a road, you know it only with your eyes, but when you run it, you feel it, you breathe it. You smell the dog shit someone didn't pick up. The curry being cooked in the kitchen you just ran past. The freshly cut grass. You even smell the rain. You hear the road. The muted sound of televisions from people's living rooms. The echo of the pavement. Your own footsteps, scratching like velcro on the wet concrete. And the air. Especially the air. You might smell it, you might hear it, but more than anything you feel it, especially in the cold. It hits your skin like a gush from a refrigerator door. Hurts at first. But after a few kilometres, as sweat runs down your face and your body heats up and your head pounds, you need it, you crave it. Anything to cool you down. Anything to keep you going.

I run for one more kilometre before I turn around and head for home. It is well into the night now. The hour when kids have been put to bed, when people are putting the kettle on to wind down with a book and a hot mug of tea.

I look at the stupid expensive watch.

Seven kilometres. One more kilometre to home will make it eight.

I'll be happy with eight.

The run back towards home goes faster than the run away from it. It's always like that. On the way out, forever. On the way home, quick. I get to the turn-off towards my house. Run past Laura's house. Up my driveway. Past my letterbox. The letterbox I've huffed and puffed in front of so many times.

I drop my arms to my knees, watch the fog blow from my mouth as I huff and puff in front of it again one more time.

If this letterbox could talk, it would probably ask, why do you do this to yourself each day? What are you running from?

And I would point to my face and answer – this.

It is Day 102.

I get out of bed, go straight to the window. A little sunshine is beaming in, not much, but enough to warm me. I brush my naked body down lightly with my fingers, as I do every morning, and watch the cloud of dead skin flakes snow to the floor.

Then as my fingers brush my lower abdomen, I pause.

Run my finger over it again and again.

What is *that*?

I open Dr Google.

lump near the groin between thigh and torso

Of course, the way my luck's been going lately, I fear the worst. Lumps are usually what? Cancer? Is there such thing as groin cancer? But after an hour of browsing medical sites, I think I have the answer.

I call Dr Stone's surgery. Tell the nurse it's urgent.

Well, semi-urgent.

Arriving at his clinic later that day, I grow anxious. It's been a while since I visited Dr Stone. I hadn't planned to see him during TSW, not wanting him to see me like this.

He comes to the waiting room, smiles, gently calls my name. Same as always.

Good to see you!

Yeah, I smile back. Long time.

I get into his office and sit. He has a fantastic poker face, Dr Stone. I know he's noticed my face, the skin under my eyes, red and peeling, my cracked lips, but he's given away nothing. I don't let the elephant sit any longer.

Been having skin problems, I tell him. As you could probably tell.

I wave my hands around my face.

Yes, yes, he nods, sympathetically.

I give him the three words. Topical Steroid Withdrawal. Ask him what he thinks.

He sucks the inside of his lip, thinking.

Well, he says finally, for that to happen you'd need to have been using very strong steroids, for a reasonably long time.

I recap the full story for him – from the tubes of Dermovate on my travels, which he frowns at, to the dermatologist and his scabies, which he laughs at. Then I show him the photos, of my first flare.

Oh my GOD!

He takes my phone, examines them more closely.

Why didn't you come and see me then?!

I shrug.

I knew you'd send me to the dermatologist. So I went straight there.

Right, right.

So, there's this doctor in Japan, I tell him. His specialty is TSW. I've been following his advice, which is to put nothing at all on the skin. Just let it … do its thing. And if we call this flare a nine out of ten, I say, pointing at my phone, I'd say now I'm probably down to a … six?

Definitely, he says. I agree.

Any objections?

He wobbles his head.

I guess if it's working, keep going. Doing nothing is always a good option. If it's working.

Exactly the answer I'd hoped for.

Anyway, believe it or not, my skin isn't why I'm here to see you.

Oh?

I stand up and lower the edge of my pants.

Notice anything strange?

Ahh, he says, squinting. He runs his finger over it. Presses it a few times, gently.

That is what we call an inguinal hernia.

Dr Google was right.

I sigh.

Was hoping you wouldn't say that.

Why's that? He sounds surprised.

Well, don't you need surgery to fix those?

Mmm ... yes. But. Well. Let's just take it step by step. First we need an ultrasound, just to be sure. Let's book you in for tomorrow.

He hands me the appointment slip, and I get up to leave.

And just so you know, he says, as I'm walking out the door. You're doing a really good thing getting off the steroids.

I nod with relief.

I hope so.

As soon as I get home, I pull up Dr Google again.

hernia surgery

Some YouTube videos come up. I watch the most detailed ones, from medical schools, where surgical interns are watching from the gallery, like in *Grey's Anatomy*. I squirm at the hot scalpel not just cutting, but burning, right through the patient's skin.

The next clip is a vlog of someone who's recovering from the operation.

Been about two weeks, he says, smiling. Can finally walk properly again!

Life has been punching me in the face lately, but this is the sucker punch. I can't sleep, can't move, can't smile. Now they don't want me to walk either?

I close my laptop. Walk away. While I still can.

The next day, I head to the radiology clinic across town. The nurse is a homely woman with a kind voice who looks like a young Bette Midler. I lie in the examination chair, surrounded by screens and trays full of machines.

Just lift your shirt for me, she says.

She gets her little gadget ready, and as she turns and sees the skin on my belly, she hesitates.

Don't worry, I say. I had ... an allergy. To some medication.

She nods understandingly, tries not to stare, then proceeds to rub ultrasound goo all over my pelvis.

As if my body hadn't been making enough goo already.

She circles the ultrasound stick around the lump in my groin. Points at the screen on the wall.

That's it right ... there.

I study the screen, but see nothing. Just a bunch of black and white splotches.

She prods at the lump with her stick a few more times.

Definitely a hernia, she mumbles to herself.

My heart sinks. Again.

Must say, it's been doing that a lot lately.

I'll just finish up these photos, she says, tapping away at her machine. And then we'll get the radiologist to take a look. He'll write a letter to your doctor in the next few days. But it looks like a definite hernia on the left. Possibly on the right as well. But you'll know for sure soon!

I know. I know life isn't fair. But how fucking unfair does it need to be?

It is Day 104.

Each day I think this flare might be getting a little better, I wake up, and it's decided to get worse.

My armpits are destroyed. No skin at all, which means I can't leave my arms down for too long, or the ooze sticks to my body. Groin is ravaged, from my belly button to my balls. And my neck, worse than both, which has made sleeping impossible. If it could be any more impossible.

The house is empty. My parents are overseas, thankfully. I don't want anyone seeing me like this, not even them.

I get out of bed, go to the window again. Run my hand over the flakes stuck to the back of my neck, then down my torso as I always do. Watch it all snow off me. Then I poke a few times at my new friend. My hernia.

Yep, still there.

It's constantly at the back of my mind now – the surgery. I've never had surgery before, and even though I'm too strong – I know I'm too strong because I tell myself I am every day – I don't know how I'm going to make it through an operation.

What if something goes wrong? What if I'm one of the ones with complications and I can't walk for weeks, or even months? Am I even allowed surgery with my skin like this?

I sit and spend the morning trying to move as little as possible. No running today, I say. Rest. Maybe you're going to need it.

The day ticks by, hour by hour. I don't want to stand up, I don't want to eat. I don't even want to think. I spend the day by the heater, dozing in and out of half-sleep.

Night falls. I've been dreading it and looking forward to it at the same time. With this ooze coming out of my neck, I know sleeping is going to be a miracle, again, but I also know that for all this to end, I need the days to pass.

How many days? I don't know.

That's what scares me the most.

I get myself into bed. Then I start preparing my four towels. I have four towels with me every night. One is wrapped across my chest and tucked under my armpits, to soak up the ooze. One is tucked between my legs, to stop my thighs from oozing and sticking together. One is wrapped around my neck, to hopefully keep it dry, soak up any gunk, although it rarely works. Which is why I have the fourth towel. During the night, if I manage to fall asleep for an hour, the ooze collects in the creases in my neck until it's soaking wet, like someone has poured it on me. So I take my extra towel and wipe it dry, I wipe my armpits, wipe between my legs. Because even with an army of towels, ooze still finds a way.

On top of me I have a bedsheet. Duvets are impossible now. They trap too much heat and I wake up steaming, dripping with sweat.

I don't know about tonight though. The cold is vicious tonight. I put the heater on full blast, tuck my towels in all the right places, pull the sheets on, but I'm still shivering. I pull the heater closer.

No change.

Finally, I pull a duvet on. Within minutes I sweat. I throw it off. This makes me shiver again, worse than before. So I pull it back on. Throw it off again. It exhausts me. This is nothing new, of course, but tonight, it's different. Maybe the lack of sleep has caught up to me, or maybe it's because tonight's cold is extra wicked, but tonight I have nothing left. The cold grabs me, and my body starts to convulse. I don't have the energy to fight it. I curl into the fetal position and my body jackhammers up and down. I don't know what's happening. This has never happened to me. I have never shivered this violently. I have never smelled this horrid. Has it been ten minutes or an hour? I have no idea. I just lie there, wrapped in towels, shivering so fiercely it looks like someone is shaking me. I feel the first tears run down my cheek and onto the pillowcase. I don't even complain. I just stare into the darkness, trembling, enduring it in silence. I've given up wishing for my old life back.

The tears start to run faster. I don't have the strength to lift my hand to my face and wipe them away. They collect in a small puddle on the pillow, and the pillow soaks into my face.

Okay, I whisper.

You win.

I quit.

I say it louder.

I quit!

I scream it.

I quit!!!

I tap the mattress with my fingers. Gently at first, then faster, and harder.

Nothing happens.

Tears free flow down my face. I keep tapping the mattress, waiting for something to happen.

Nothing is happening.

I'm not strong, I weep, hoping for someone to hear.

I know I said I was strong but I'm not strong! Please! I quit!

I scream it so loud even the neighbour's neighbours can hear me.

Still nothing happens. At my martial arts gym, in my old life, tapping is how we submitted. Your training partner got you in a choke, you couldn't breathe, you tapped and he let you go. We lived by that rule – you fight as hard as you can, but when you're being strangled and you know in a few seconds you'll be gone, you tap, and everything stops.

But nothing is stopping.

I can't understand why it's not stopping.

That's when it dawns on me. You can't tap out of this. This is your new life now, and you don't know when it stops. Maybe it's going to be years. Maybe forever.

My eyes flood. I scream it as loud as I can, I slam my hand on the mattress.

I QUIT!!!!

Hours pass. Nothing changes. The ooze is still there, dripping from my neck like it did last night, and the night before. My body still convulses violently in the cold. My skin still burns. Everything *hurts*. I lie dead-eyed, shaking, staring at the wall.

I know what I want now.

The bridge.

I want to go to the bridge. I want to jump.

I want someone to walk into this room right now with a needle and say, Brendan, I can end it for you right now. Just say the word.

I would say yes. I would say yes in a heartbeat.

But nobody comes. I start to wonder how I got here. What I did to deserve falling this far. How did this body become so impossibly broken?

What if tomorrow night is even more painful?

I can't.

Now I finally see the place I never thought I'd see.

I wish I was dead.

Journal entry

September 2, 2019.

These nights, when you don't sleep, you have a lot of time to think. And you think about life, and every night that I lie there dying, I just think, I don't deserve this.

I believe in karma. For this shit to happen to me, I must have caused this much suffering somewhere, for it to come back around this way. I just think about all the bad shit that I've done, and I think, do I deserve this? Maybe I deserve this?

*But even if I think of all the worst things I've done I still think, surely that's not enough. I deserve **this**? This is the kind of thing that makes you question if you even want to be here.*

I'll just say that I get it now. I fucking get it. Anyone that decides to jump, I fucking get it, bro. Because it's just all this pain, all this suffering, all this hopelessness, you just want it to be over so bad, and there's one really easy way for it to all be over. You can just climb up on the bridge. You fucking jump and it's done. I could finish this right now. This could all be over right now.

6

Morning.

I lie still, not wanting to move – not only because it will hurt, but because I can feel the semi-dried goo between my legs. I prefer to pretend it isn't there. I don't even need to peel the sheets off to release the odour. I know I smell like a corpse.

Rise and shine, I whisper.

I've cried so much during the night, there are no tears left to cry. All that's left is a grim smile.

This isn't so bad. And I laugh.

When the anger is gone, the self-pity, the pleading, and all you can do is laugh at how disgusting you are – that's when you know things must be really fucking bad.

Still, it feels like a storm has passed. All the things I said last night, I start to take them back. One by one. I don't quit. I don't want to die.

And then I say again: Rise and shine. Rise. And shine.

Seriously Brendan – can you rise? How high? How high can you rise from nothing?

I throw the sheets off. Immediately, the cold smashes into me like a freight train. Still, compared to last night's jackhammering in the midnight cold, this could almost be a Hawaiian summer.

I pull my knees up to my chest, roll onto my front on all fours. Then, one foot at a time, I get to my feet. My sheets are a disaster zone of stains and piles of dead skin. My body stinks of dirty metal. I hunch over and shuffle to the heater, wrap myself around it, trying to hide from the cold. But I know there's only one thing I can do, to feel alive again.

It is barely six a.m. I open my bedroom door and grimace at the sudden hit of the Auckland winter morning. The heater has been blasting all night inside my room, so it's bearable. The rest of the house: Antarctic. Hunched over, I waddle to the laundry basket and put on my sweatpants, my hoodie. I hobble down the stairs. Lace up my shoes.

How high can you rise from nothing?

I don't even know what it means. I just mumble it to myself. Again and again. Like the last line of a song you hear just before you leave the house, playing over in your mind.

I screw my headphones in, put on my usual track. Those drums. It's always those drums, that get me in the zone. I pull my hood up over my head. Open the front door and step outside. The morning frost punches me in the face like a straight right hand. It's been raining. There's dew in the air. I feel the wind not just on my skin, but in my bones.

How high?

Down the driveway. Turn right. Past Laura's house. The neighbourhood is still fast asleep. On summer mornings, it's normal to see some other walkers or joggers, but this deep into winter? Not a chance. I have all the roads to myself, silent, other than the wind and the pitter-patter of my shoes. I fasten the strings on my hoodie again, so tight only my eyes and nose are bared. That small bit of extra snugness makes all the difference. If the hood is just a tiny bit loose, a little whisper of wind gets in and it's enough to chill your whole body. But tight, like this, I feel safe. Ready. In minutes, I am steaming and warm. I think about how filthy this body is going to smell soon, once I sweat and everything just turns into a steaming pile of dead.

Wonderful.

I get to the first hill past James' house, and sprint it, like TSW is chasing me. Today I won't slow down, not for anything. If last night was the night I died, this is the morning I'm about to be reborn.

How high?

My whole body breaks into a sweat. The open skin on my groin stings mercilessly, my forehead stings, my neck stings, the back of my head stings. Everything stings. The backs of my legs itch so fiercely, no amount of grit or stubbornness can overcome it. I stop and scratch them wildly, like an animal. I can smell the blood, see the scabs and dead skin under my nails. But it feels so *good*. I can't believe this broken, rotten thing is my body. But I know if I just keep running, if I sweat even more, if I start to hurt even more, it will start to feel great. Soon the sun will come out and I'll still be here. I will sweat all this horridness away, and while I'm on these roads, everything will be okay for a while.

Then I feel it. First on my hands. Then my face. And then everywhere. Raindrops.

It comes down lightly at first. In this cold, it's the last thing I need. I tell myself it will stop. The world is not this evil. I know it will stop.

But it comes down harder.

I look at the sky. I can see the whole world up there – all the powers of the universe, conspiring against me. Like they had wanted me to die last night. Like they sent the rain because they were bitter. They wanted me to stay broken, and here I am the morning after, becoming indestructible.

I grind my teeth. Laughing. Growling at the sky.

I'm too strong!

I scream it.

There's nobody out here but me! Can't you see? I'M TOO STRONG!

Rain splats against my nose and eyelids but I fix my eyes ahead, and all I see is the road. I feel myself about to cry, but I don't. I refuse to. I cried enough last night. I've cried enough to last the rest of my life. All I want to do now is run.

Your rain can't stop me. Nothing can stop me.

I'll show you.

I'll show you how far I can fucking run.

I go for another lap. Then another. And another. Today, I am unbreakable. I can run forever. The rain clears. A guy in his driveway is getting ready for work, stares as I run past his house. I'm screaming something about how strong I am, how high I'm rising from nothing.

He thinks I'm mad.

I am mad.

On the next street, a guy peers up at me from his garden.

How high Brendan? How high can you rise from nothing!

He hears me, but he smiles as if he knows exactly what this moment is. As if, maybe he's had one of his own.

I run up the final hill of the lap, chanting over and over:

You weak, Brendan?

No! I'm strong!

How strong are you?

Too strong!

How high can you rise from nothing?

REALLY FUCKING HIGH.

More laps. Past Laura's house again. Past James' house. Past Jonathan Baker's house. Around and around. I don't stop chanting. I don't even know what I'm saying anymore. I hold my arms out, like I'm crossing a marathon finish line. It feels good. Feels really good.

I step inside my front door. I bounce upstairs, strip and get straight into the shower. I'm not allowed hot showers, but today I am. Today I'll have the hottest, steamiest shower, like old times when life was good and I didn't have nights where I wished I was dead. I moan as soon as the water hits my body, almost lose my breath at how alive I feel. As it blasts against my head, I watch the water disappear down the drain between my feet, washing away the layers of gunk. I don't care about TSW, I don't care about Dr Sato's time limit. I stand there and savour what it feels like to be human again.

They say we don't recognise the important moments of our lives while they are happening. It's true. This feels like just another run I had to survive, like the one before it, and the one before that. But when I look back on my life, I'll point to this day and I'll know. This run I've just done, this night I've just been through – it is a moment that has split me in two. There is the person I was before today, and the person I am now. They are nothing alike. Nothing about me will ever be the same again.

marathons in new zealand

A year ago, this is the last thing I would have typed into Google. Now, it's the first thing on my mind. Still butt naked, still steaming from my shower, or my run, or both, I watch the results flick across the screen.

The first one is Auckland Marathon.

I click it.

Seven weeks from today.

Perfect timing. Almost poetic.

I read through every page on the website. Every FAQ, every rule. I watch every video. The highlights from last year. And the year before. Before today, marathon and impossible might as well have been the same word, but not anymore. Because I saw it. I saw myself crossing that finish line.

I browse through the training plans. The photo galleries. What strikes me is the clothes, the special running singlets, everyone's colourful shoes. It's only now I realise – running is a real sport, with real competitions and real champions and special gear. Not just some crappy thing people do in the mornings to stay fit. It even has its own lingo – *taper weeks* and *aid stations* and *pacers*.

I fill out the registration form. I'm not convinced I'm going to actually send it. But I fill it out. Just to see.

Then I get to the payment page. I punch in my card number.

I lean back in my chair. Study the screen.

There's a photo of someone crossing the finish line. She is smiling. I think about what it will be like if I pull this off. If I not only survive this thing – this *evil* – but along the way, I manage to achieve something great, something impossible. How proud I will be.

I click Submit.

A big yellow page pops up on the screen.

Congratulations. You are registered for the ASB Auckland Marathon 2019.

7

There's this feeling you get when you hear a speech or go to a concert or watch a special interview. It lights something up inside of you, and suddenly you're super confident and inspired and motivated, so you commit to something big, something courageous – because for that moment the world is yours and anything is possible.

Then a few days later, it wears off and you wonder what the hell you were thinking.

That's how I feel right now.

Reading these marathon training plans – eight kilometres, ten kilometres, fifteen kilometres. And they're calling these the "short runs". Then on Saturdays, it's the "long runs".

One of them is thirty-three kilometres. *Thirty-three.*

It seems obvious now, but I hadn't realised when you sign up to run a marathon, you actually run more like twenty marathons. Your whole life is just running, every day until race day. Run, run, run.

I know nothing about this sport and decide I better learn, quick. I start devouring books about running. *Born To Run. Ready To Run. Running To The Edge. What I Talk About When I Talk About Running.* Anything that has the word Run in the title, I read. I learn little tips from all of them. Tips about shoes. Tips about stretching. Tips about gait and cadence and overcoming pain. Tips about races. Tips about running one more kilometre when the last thing you want to do is run one more kilometre.

When my brain has had enough of books, I watch videos. I spend my nights watching YouTube channels from running nerds. They pull up clips of amateur runners and tear them apart.

Look how badly his hips sway to one side!

Look how her body is leaning backwards while her legs are trying to move forward!

Look how his heel strikes the ground too early!

Geez. I wonder what I look like.

I go to the gym the next day, take a video of myself on the treadmill. Then watch it back, hoping to be impressed. I'm not. I'm horrified. My legs fan out like chicken wings with every step. My head is corked back like a slingshot. My top half leans back while my bottom half moves forward. The running nerds would have a field day with me.

I study more. I watch hundreds of videos, clips and breakdowns of the world's best runners.

One – just one – stands out, stays seared in my memory. It's some running coach, breaking down a video of a triathlete named Patrick Lange.

Look at how easy he moves, he says adoringly. Look at his arms ... how they rock back and forth, just to the centre line of his body, but no further. Look how he leans, always forward. Look at his chest, always forward. Look at his head, balanced. Look at his eyes, always forward. It's just so darn pretty!

I nod as he says it.

He's right. It is darn pretty.

Instantly, I know this is my guy. My running spirit animal. Every time I run, I want to look like Patrick Lange.

After seeing this, I'm not worried about the special runs on those training plans. There are tempo runs and repeats and Zone 2 runs and Zone 3 runs, but it's like trying to learn Portuguese. I just want to look darn pretty when I run, like Patrick Lange. Besides, race day is in seven weeks. I'm not going to learn fifteen types of runs in seven weeks.

I stick with the basics – short runs and long runs. I write up a training plan. Three short runs per week. One long run.

Seven weeks to learn to run like Lange.

It is Day 107.

I'm training every day. Running. Stretching. Getting stronger. Fitter. I still leave a trail of dead skin everywhere I go, I'm still constantly picking at bits of dried ooze on my neck, but the pain is gone. Days are no longer hours of constant suffering.

I think, maybe, I'm finally healing.

Maybe, I might actually pull this marathon thing off.

Then, as I'm getting ready for the day's run, I take a quick scroll through my phone and freeze.

There's an email. It's from the clinic.

My heart falls through my stomach. It takes my spleen and a kidney with it. I don't want to open it because I already know what it's going to say. I've got two hernias and they're scheduling me in for surgery. I know it.

Just like that, no more running. No more marathon. Just as I thought something good might be happening, they want to cut my leg open, send me back to days lying in bed.

Don't open it, I say. Ignore it. Go for this run, and fuck anyone trying to take anything else away from you.

But I can't resist.

I open the email. Click the attachment.

It's a letter from Dr Stone.

Hi Brendan,

Your scan report arrived. Good news. The lump is a swollen lymph node. **There is no definite hernia seen.** *No follow up tests are required.*

I read the email twenty times. And then I read it again.

I'm sure it's not real, it's a practical joke.

Good news?

Since when did my life start to include good news?

I will later learn that swollen lymph nodes occur in people experiencing extreme stress, which makes all the sense in the world. But I don't know that yet. To me, the letter makes no sense at all. It's a mistake. A miracle. Maybe both.

When I'm sure I've read the email correctly, I click the reply button.

Doc,

This is the best damn news I've heard all my life.

Thank you.

I click send, and manage a smile. Just a small one.

But there's good reason to smile, because this unlikely piece of good news indeed marks a turning point. A point where things will finally – *finally* – start changing for the better.

It is Day 124.

I'm at the lake. The lake I've never actually been to until a month ago, despite it being only ten minutes from my house. Despite having driven past it thousands of times over the years. Probably even more. Every day, to and from middle school. Every day, to and from my martial arts gym. Driven past it, never looked twice.

Now, I'm here almost every day.

This is where I run now.

It's a three-kilometre lap. It starts innocently. The path is wide, you run under some trees. It's nice. You run past the sailing club. On Sundays, like today, there are Dads taking their boats out onto the water, hosing them down on the ramp, standing around talking in the sunshine. Always in the sunshine. If it's not sunny, they're not here.

Minutes later, you get to the playground. There are usually a few kids. They stare sometimes. I used to smile back at them, but now I don't. Now I keep my eyes aimed straight ahead. My knees driving forward. My chest forward. Breathing. Just focusing on those four things leaves little room in your mind for anything else.

Two minutes on, you get to the grassy part, the track lined with people's houses on one side. Their backyards open out onto the running path.

I like this part, because it feels homely, and it's also where the first marker is. It's a steel plate, sealed into the pavement, with a big 1KM on it.

First kilometre down.

Then onto the first bridge. It's a tiny wooden bridge, about four metres long. You turn sharply to get on it, and within a second you're off it, but it's a landmark. And it feels cool, running over it. Like you're in the woods or something.

Next comes the nice long stretch, right beside the water. I call it The Straight. It's not actually straight, it winds like a snake, but it's perfectly flat, and somehow it feels straight when you run it. On the weekends, there are people sitting on the rock wall that runs alongside it, chatting or listening to music or eating sandwiches or just sitting. Thinking. They always stare at you. Every single time. I guess that's normal. I probably did that too in the past, whenever I saw someone running. Watched them run past and thought, why would anyone want to do something like that?

As The Straight comes to an end, you go past the second playground, past the drinking fountain, then into a much lonelier spot. Here, you run side by side with the water too, but there's never anyone here. At night when it's dark – like it is right now – it even feels a little spooky. But it's a good spot because it ends with the second marker, another steel plate in the pavement with a big 2KM on it.

You don't notice that one as much though. Because as soon as you run over it, you're at The Hill.

The Hill isn't big, to be honest. It's mildly steep. Maybe thirty seconds long. But after a couple of hours, after six or seven laps, it starts to look like damn Everest. Every time I waddle up there, I say to myself, don't walk, don't walk. I allow myself to run as slowly as I want, but I'm never allowed to walk.

Then it's downhill. I always thought running downhill was supposed to be great, and it is, compared to running uphill. But it's still twice as difficult as running on a flat. Running on a long straight flat is a dream, especially when you're fresh, and the sun is out. But running downhill? It's hard. An optical illusion. You see it and your mind thinks, yes! But your knees, they cry silently at the punishment.

Then comes the second bridge. The real bridge. As in, if this bridge collapsed while you were on it, you'd probably die. It's an old, rickety wooden thing running high over the water, about as long as a tennis court, and narrow as an aeroplane aisle. But it feels sturdy somehow. How can something be rickety and sturdy at the same time? I don't know. That's just what it feels like. I ask myself that every time I run across.

As you come off the bridge, and make the sharp turn back towards the carpark, you can see the end. Where you started. Especially in the night, you can see those carpark lights. This is when I move. I call it The Home Stretch.

In one of those books – *Running To The Edge* – you learn about legendary running coach Bob Larsen. "The edge" is his secret sauce, his formula to winning. It means if you think you can run faster, run faster. Keep running faster until you know you can't anymore. That point is called the edge. That's where you stay, for as long as possible. That's how you get fast. Countless marathons have been won by training at the edge. His protégé – Meb Keflezighi, Olympian, Boston Marathon champion – became Meb Keflezighi by running to the edge.

So that's what I do when I hit the Home Stretch.

Run to the edge, I say.

Over and over. I whisper it to myself. When you're breathing that hard, only whispers come out anyway. Everything comes out as a breathless whisper. But I just keep saying it. And I keep running to the edge. I don't know why. I'm not trying to win a marathon, I'm just trying to finish one without dying. But on The Home Stretch, I can't resist. All the way to the 3KM marker, that's all I do. I blurt out – run to the edge! And I run faster and faster until I get there.

But not today.

Today is the twenty-eight-kilometre run day. And I can't run to the edge today. I can barely walk to the edge today. I told myself when I started in the afternoon, when the sun was still out and my legs were fresh, to go slow. Nine laps. Just do them one at a time. Doesn't matter how slow you go, as long as you finish them. And I did start slow. It didn't matter. First lap was great. Second lap was great. Third lap was pretty good. All downhill from there.

It's my seventh lap now. It's around nine o'clock, but it might as well be midnight. It's pitch black. The sun has gone. The Mums and their prams are gone. The couples doing their evening walks are gone. That extremely pretty girl who looks like Pocahontas and runs like a pro athlete is gone. There's nobody left but me – and one other person.

That person is the reason I'm still out here.

She's tiny. A little Chinese girl. Probably five foot two, not particularly athletic looking. By the way she runs, I'm guessing not a particularly avid runner either. But she's doing better than me.

Correction: She's destroying me.

We're running around the lake in opposite directions, so we pass each other twice per lap. She has pink sneakers on. A face mask. Under her mask, I can see her face is tomato red.

I can also see she's suffering, like she's going to collapse at any moment. Every time I see her, I'm sure she's done. I know the next time I see her she'll be walking, finished, or I won't see her at all. She'll have gone home. But she's still here. She was here on lap three. She was here on lap six. She's still here on lap seven.

I'm on The Home Stretch of lap seven now, and I can see her in the distance. Still flailing those arms, still churning those awkwardly out-turned feet. I try to catch her eyes as we pass each other, to give her a nod, a smile – anything to keep her going. To keep me going. She's pushing me, inspiring me, I need her, but she doesn't even blink at me. Probably hasn't even noticed me. Just zooms on past. Like she won't stop for anything in the world.

I don't know what she's running from, but I can see in her eyes, it must be heavy. Diagnosed with some disease. Husband left her. Been given one year to live.

Maybe all three.

I imagine telling her my story. So ... I have sore skin. I'm not allowed to drink too much water. I wanted to kill myself because, well, I had a rash on my neck and couldn't sleep.

All seems so stupid now.

I start lap eight. I really doubt I'm going to survive lap eight, but if you can't survive lap eight, how do you survive a marathon? So I make a secret pact with the Chinese girl in the facemask. If the Chinese girl in the facemask is going to survive lap eight, I'm going to survive lap eight.

We both survive lap eight.

I look at my watch.

25.08 kilometres.

One more lap.

Since my watch is on the running screen, I can't see the time of day, and I dare not fiddle with the buttons. Not in the middle of this run. I guess it's about ten o'clock. It feels like it's two in the morning.

Halfway through the lap, I see her. Right on cue, near the beginning of The Straight. She looks the closest to dying that I've seen, on the verge of tears, but is running stronger than ever.

Man, whatever she's going through must be FUCKED UP.

Even Dr Sato can't cure those demons. Three bottles of tequila and some sleeping pills won't cure those demons. But a thirty-kilometre run in the middle of the night?

Maybe.

I get to The Hill. I give in and walk it. It's either that, or watch my feet fall off. Even walking it is hard.

I wonder if the Chinese girl in the facemask is walking her hills yet.

Doubt it.

At the top, I get back to running. Slowly and sadly. It's always worse when you stop to walk, and then start again. It's like you told your legs, we're done! And then sixty seconds later, just kidding! Your legs hate that. They make you pay for it. Make sure to hurt twice as much as before.

I get to the bridge. I cross. Make it onto The Home Stretch. It feels like forever. That's the big problem with The Home Stretch. It looks short, but it's deceptively long. You can run it for two or three minutes and the carpark doesn't even look any closer. Sometimes, it looks even further away.

Like clockwork, the Chinese girl is here. In the distance. Flailing. Hurting. Smashing me to pieces. She runs past me. Doesn't even look at me. Just huffs and puffs as she goes past, and zooms off into the darkness.

I cross the steel plate in the ground. My watch beeps to tell me another kilometre is done. I look at the screen.

28.01 kilometres.

I don't stretch. I don't sit down and rest. I don't do anything except get straight into my car and drive home. On the way, I feel like there's one thing I should have done. I should have waited for the Chinese girl in the facemask to finish. So I could say hi and thank you and bye and you're amazing.

Maybe if I come down and look for her in the morning, she'll still be running.

It is Day 131.

Sunday. A beautiful one. Sun higher and brighter than anyone could ask for. In the afternoon, I head down to the lake. It feels like half of Auckland city is here. Playing with their kids, taking an afternoon stroll. Of course they're here. For most people, Sunday is the best day of the week.

For me it's the worst. Sunday is long run day. I don't even think I've half recovered from the last one.

As I'm jogging The Straight, I see a familiar face. My friend Terry from high school. He and I have become closer recently. Each of us struggling with our own pile of life's bullshit. We don't see each other much, but talk more often now, check up on each other. With my face dripping sweat, my hood pulled up over my shaved and scabbed up head, I hope I look normal. Or at least, not diseased. But I know it's fine, because even if he notices, Terry's the last person who would say anything.

He sees me as I approach. A shade of surprise appears across his face. I stop, pull my headphones out. Put on a smile.

How's it going?

We bump fists.

He's walking around the lake, with his beautiful wife and daughter. Just like everyone else at the lake today. His wife, Helen, smiles warmly at me. She always looks like she takes two or three seconds to pre-plan her sentences before she says them. She's planning one right now.

Do you run here often? She finally asks.

Yeah, I'm here every Sunday. What about you guys?

We come here sometimes on the weekend, she smiles.

I turn to Terry.

How's everything man? Doing okay?

Yeah, he nods. You jog now?

Nearly every day. Join me sometime.

He shrugs.

I'm not a good jogger.

Neither am I.

He laughs, looks down at my pink shoes.

That's bull.

I want to say, no my friend, it's not bull. Let's ask my legs and feet and knees right now. Let's get them a microphone. I'm sure they'll tell you very quickly, it's the furthest thing from bull.

His daughter is timid, holding onto his leg.

What's your little girl's name again?

Adeline.

That's right, Adeline. Hi Adeline.

She looks straight through me, like she's studying the clouds behind my head. Probably wondering if I'll hurry up and leave so she can go to the playground. How much simpler life was back then.

Enjoy it, kid.

Anyway man, I'm cooling down.

We bump fists again, I wave goodbye to his wife and kid. As I take off, I look at my watch.

Four kilometres down. Eleven to go.

That night, I hit up Terry on Facebook.

Hey man, good to see you. You look well.

Thanks bro. Never seen you there before.

Just started running there, a few months ago. You?

Well, he starts, I've been avoiding that place for a long time actually. Only recently been able to go back. Had some tough times down there.

I don't say anything back. Just smile to myself.

So have I, brother. So have I.

It is Day 138.

I have a new song now.

Days In The Sun, Ziggy Alberts.

It's upbeat, but poignant, and soulful. It makes me miss my old life more than ever. But it also makes me smile. Most of all, it makes me grateful. I listen to it before I sleep. When I wake up. When I write. When I run. Strange how a tune that's not about you, sung by someone you've never met, seems as if it was written for you and only you.

It's morning. Seven a.m. I've never been a morning person. Always late for school, late for work. My entire life, waking up early was impossible. Now, sleeping in is impossible. My skin is no longer oozing with open wounds – it's now dry and flakes constantly like filo pastry – but still leaves me writhing and itchy, unable to sleep. So I don't lie in bed for a second longer than I need to. Thanks to TSW, I'm now a morning person.

As Ziggy Alberts blasts from my phone, I lie in the lounge and foam roll my thighs. Up and down, like pizza dough.

Up so early? My Dad asks as he comes down the stairs.

He's going to make his oats. My Dad always eats oats for breakfast.

Can't really sleep, I tell him.

Still?

Yeah.

Itchy?

Yeah.

Hmm, he grunts.

Maybe try one of those humidifier machines. Might make you feel less dry in the night.

Yeah, good idea.

My Dad is a fixer. Always has ideas on how to fix things. But only other people's things. Never his own. Not because he can't – the opposite, actually. My Dad is an engineer, and ferociously smart. At my high school, the walls of the school hall are engraved with the names of honour students, and if you look for the year 1974, you'll see his name staring right back at you. But if Mum asks him to fix the sink, even though he knows exactly how, he can't take the first step. The sink stays broken for months. Then someone else decides to try and fix it, and within minutes, my Dad will be taking over saying, no, no, do it like this. But that fits his personality, as a typical Chinese Dad. Chinese Dads are fixers. They always remember little details about your life. Get very concerned about your small problems. And then try to fix them all. That's how you know they love you. Because of course, a Chinese Dad never actually says it. I've never heard him say the words I love you in my entire life.

Who's singing? He asks, stirring his oatmeal.

An Australian guy.

I already know he won't recognise the name and his next question will be, where's he from? So I just skip straight to that answer.

Australia's made some good singers, he says.

It's true. John Farnham, Delta Goodrem. Natalie Imbruglia. Tell me you can put that Natalie Imbruglia song on and not be singing along within thirty seconds. You can't. But this Ziggy Alberts song is just as good. Maybe even better. I don't know it yet, but a year from now, I'll put this song on and tears will well in my eyes, every single time.

Not right now though. It's not a memory yet. Right now I'm living it. Dying on top of this foam roller, trying to turn these legs into marathon legs. You wouldn't think it from looking at one, but foam rollers are a special kind of torture. It's bizarre, how they can feel so soft, and look so innocent, yet have you whimpering within a minute. But I keep rolling. Up and down, up and down. Since that twenty-eight-kilometre run, with the superhuman Chinese girl in the facemask, this knee hasn't been the same. Now, any time I run longer than an hour, it feels like someone is taking all my nerve endings, scrunching them up and hammering them in the side of my leg. So along with the pitter-patter of my footsteps – left, right, left, right – there's also an ouch, ouch, ouch, ouch coming from my knee.

The plus side of all this running is, my skin is improving. It's improving to the point where I don't think about it twenty-four hours a day. In fact, when I'm not lying in bed scratching or staring in the mirror, I can almost feel like a normal person. I don't even look like an extra from *The Walking Dead* anymore. I'd say now I'm more like The Hound, from *Game Of Thrones*. Just the face. Not the muscles.

Foam rolling is done. Or it's not quite done, but I can't do it anymore. I fall off the roller and lie on the ground for a moment, let out a huff of relief. It's an annoying kind of pain – not so sore that you scream out in agony, but sore enough that you just think about how much it sucks the entire time you're doing it. A bit like TSW right now.

I have thirty-three kilometres on the training plan today. It's the longest training run I've had or will have. I've been resting for a couple of days, foam rolling my knee religiously. Preparing for today.

As I get in the car, I make a quick video journal.

Don't know if I'm going to be able to finish this run today, I say.

Then I quickly correct myself.

What am I talking about? Of course I'm going to finish. I have to finish.

I get to the lake. It's a perfect day. Rare for September, but not unheard of. It must be a sign. God gave me this sunny day so I could complete my thirty-three kilometres. I look at the cooler bag on the passenger seat. It's filled with three litres of electrolytes. Some energy bars. Everything I'll need. I screw my headphones into my ears. Ziggy Alberts. I squint out over the water, bathing in sunshine, and envision myself in a Michael Bay movie, like this is the final training scene where it's impossible to fail.

Eleven laps. Thirty-three kilometres. Let's go.

The first lap goes down a treat. Three kilometres done. I feel even better after the second lap. Just nine laps left. Only nine. I don't tell myself I have twenty-seven kilometres left, I don't tell myself I have three hours left. Sounds too hard. Hearing those numbers, I'd probably quit on the spot. But nine laps – nine laps sounds easy-ish. So I say to myself, nine laps.

I pass the 3KM plate in the ground again. My watch beeps.

Eight laps left.

I feel beautiful. My legs are churning, I'm breathing easy, my knee feels perfect. It feels so perfect I can't feel it at all. I'm going to do it. I'm going to do thirty-three.

Four laps down. Running has never been this easy. In just two more laps, I'll be past halfway. It's paying off, all this training. All this foam rolling with Ziggy Alberts in the background. Today, I will join the 30k club.

And then, like a light switch, the knee turns on. Every time my foot hits the ground, it sends a jolt of electricity into the side of my leg.

Zap, zap, zap, zap.

Ouch, ouch, ouch, ouch.

It's going to go away. After this lap, it will go away.

I get halfway through lap five. It hasn't gone away. It's worse. I run through it. I get to The Hill. I bounce up The Hill on tiptoes. My thighs feel strong. Feet feel strong. Knee feels like it's made of Lego. And not real Lego from Toyworld. Fake, knock-off Lego from that Chinese dollar store in Onehunga.

I get to the bridge. Hobbling now. Skipping. Leaping. Leaning. Trying to run in whatever way I can to make my knee not hurt. Nothing works. It just hurts and hurts and hurts.

Ouch, ouch, ouch, ouch.

I pass the 3KM plate in the ground, near the carpark, and go straight to my car. I look at my watch.

15.21 km. Almost halfway.

Rest, I say. Drink. Stretch. Maybe it'll cool down.

Ten minutes pass. I take another swig of water, give my knee a little rub.

You ready?

I throw the bottle aside and get out of the car, pumped.

Let's rock, B. Seventeen more kilometres.

I don't even make it seventeen centimetres. As soon as I get up, my knee stiffens like a board and squeals like nails have been hammered into it. I fall back down into my seat.

We're done.

Live to fight another day.

I spend the evening with an ice pack strapped to my knee, walking like a one-legged pirate.

Race day is in three weeks. What if this happens on race day?

It won't, I tell myself. You're going to be smart, and you're going to be ready.

I hobble up the stairs, deflated, frustrated. No studying tonight. No stretching. I'm going to put on a funny movie, rest my leg up on my desk. I'm going to give this knee all the love it needs, not walk on it for a second longer than I need to. I'll massage these ice packs against it harder and harder, until the pain freezes into ice cubes and melts away.

Limping past the lounge, I get a glimpse of my parents' computer screen, sitting on what my Dad has been looking at during the day. Humidifier reviews.

Figuring out how to fix me.

I open the door to my bedroom. Limp inside. Collapse into my chair. Then as I plonk my leg up on the desk, I can't help but let a little smile come to my face.

In the corner, beside my bed, is a brand new little humidifier machine, humming away.

It might be the closest thing he's ever done to saying I love you.

Journal entry

September 20, 2019.

Sometimes when the sun is out, I like to go out on the balcony, get some Vitamin D. And it's a good time for me to just think about stuff. When the sun is out, it obviously means it's a nice day, which is a reason to be grateful. So I like to come out here, and just think about all the stuff I'm grateful for.

That can help you through a really tough day. Just the other day I was running the lake and I was so tired. I was on about 13 km or 14 km at that point. And this girl went past me in a wheelchair. She looked so happy, she had her phone out, and she was taking selfies, and I thought to myself, man, I am such a dick. I'm here, with two perfectly healthy legs, maybe the skin on them isn't healthy, but they work. I'm running around this lake. And I thought that girl — probably every single day — dreams of doing what I'm doing right now. She would swap places with me in a second.

Little things like that help me put things in perspective. Definitely, I've suffered so much. But it could be so much worse. At least I've got hope my skin will get better. I remember watching Oprah once, this lady had her whole body burnt. She'd had 500 skin grafts or something. Not exaggerating, it was really like 500. And her skin was just smashed, non-existent, and she was so beautiful before it all happened. I just think, yeah I've lost stuff, I've suffered and I've lost, but nothing compared to her.

That's the kind of stuff I think about when I come out here. Just be grateful. Like, be grateful you can get some Vitamin D today and it's not pissing down with rain.

What a learning journey this has been. Learning to be grateful all over again.

8

It is Day 152.

Cold. That's what I feel. Like old school mornings, mornings before work, mornings before soccer on Saturday when I was eleven. Staying huddled under these covers because – cold.

It's three a.m. I can hear my parents outside my room, already up, in and out of the bathroom, going up and down the stairs. They slept earlier than me. They're up before me. They talk in whispers, maybe to keep from waking me up. As if I'm playing in Wimbledon.

Are you excited? Mum had asked the day before.

I shrugged.

Oh c'mon! If it were me, I'd be super excited!

I should've realised it then, but it won't be until many hours later – not until my Mum's eyes are red from crying just like mine – that I'll realise this isn't just my big day, but our big day.

This is her first marathon too.

Though it's cold, it's not hard for me to get up. Sometimes, you don't even have time to think about it – when you have an exam, a flight to catch – you just get up. Today is one of those days.

Race day.

Among all the firsts we have in life, we celebrate the easy ones. First words. First steps. First birthdays. The irony is, we don't even need to work for those. Everyone gets them. But first paychecks, first dates, first race days – those are the ones you have to work for, maybe even bleed for. Especially first race days. Of all the firsts I've had in my life, this will end up becoming the most special of them all.

I go downstairs and foam roll. Work on my knees. Do the ten or fifteen different exercises that are supposed to keep your knees in line, stretch them out, keep them loose. It reminds me of those mornings, cramming bullet points before an exam. It's so last-minute, you wonder if it's even worth the effort. Then you remember – even if it gets you just one more percent, it will be worth it.

The race starts across the harbour, a short ferry ride from the city centre. The drive to the ferry building is silent. Auckland is still asleep. We arrive in the city and make the walk downtown towards the wharf. That's when I start to see them. It's four in the morning, pitch black, but in all directions are crowds of people in running gear. Everywhere. Swarming the ferry building with their yellow Auckland Marathon bags, Nike jackets, special running leggings. Some are immune to the cold, wearing nothing but singlets, race numbers already pinned to their tops. They can't wait.

We board the ferry and take the first free row. I just want to sit. To rest these legs for every second I can. Mum is excited. Dad is curious. Staring around the cabin, whispering his thoughts to me.

Look at all these Chinese runners! He says.

Dad always seems to get excited seeing other Chinese people, like they might be related or something.

I have other things to worry about. I pull off my socks, run my fingers over the dried blisters on my toes. No matter how carefully I tape my feet, each blister comes back worse, every time. I tape them anyway. Then I massage my knee. The knee that has tried to run fifteen kilometres twice in the past four weeks, and failed both times. I dig my thumbs into the muscles around my kneecap, knowing it probably won't do anything, but hoping.

And then I say to it: Please behave. Just for today. And I promise, I'll never make you run again.

The ferry docks. We are among the earliest to arrive at the start line. It's five a.m. and the street is near empty. It's a residential street, lined with houses. Nice ones. A huge blow-up arch – like a bouncy castle – stands in the distance. START is written across the top.

We still have an hour until the gun. I sit on the sidewalk and massage my calves, my glutes, and my knee. I stretch. In front of me is a guy who's jogging on the spot, maybe in his forties, wearing a fancy looking race belt. It has two mini drink bottles, loaded with some kind of secret potion, one strapped to each hip, like a pair of revolvers. He's wearing compression leggings, and colourful Nikes. A few metres away, another guy is jogging up and down the street.

Forty-two kilometres not enough for you guys today? Need a couple to warm up as well?

On days I've had to wake up at ungodly hours for flights, I've seen these guys sometimes – out running in the five a.m. cold – and always wondered, who *are* you people? Now I know, this is where you find them. On a marathon start line. This is their drug, their happy place, what they live for. Probably been waiting for this day all year. I look at my pink running shoes with ultra-thin soles, which I only bought because I read about them in that stupid book. The singlet I'm wearing is from ten years ago. I don't even know whether these shorts are mine or my Dad's.

This is madness. I'm not even supposed to be here.

And then I look at his perfect skin, and I remember, that guy hasn't been where I've been. Were his sheets covered in bloodstains too? Where was he when I was going through *that night*? Maybe I'm not supposed to be here, maybe I don't have any secret potions to strap to my waist, but I'm going to run every single kilometre, just like him.

The sun starts to rise. Slowly. The crowd fills up. By the time the sun is peeking over the horizon and the sky is bluey orange instead of black, the street is full. Hundreds, thousands of us.

At fifteen minutes until gun time, I pull my race number out of my bag. It is my first ever race number.

Number 4552.

My name – BREN – is written in bold across the middle.

In small letters, it says MARATHON in the top right.

I pin it carefully to my chest, while my Dad snaps a photo. My university degree? I have no idea where it is. My Chartered Accountant's degree? Gathering dust somewhere in a cupboard, maybe. But this piece of paper – I've never looked at a piece of paper with so much pride. I already know I'll be keeping it forever.

They call all runners to the start line. I pull off my hoodie, my sweatpants. The cold bites, but I feel it only for a second. I give my Mum a hug. My Dad a hug.

Good luck sweetie.

Good luck boy.

The beginning of a new tradition.

The start line is arranged in groups to allow runners to seed themselves in their expected times. I see the four-hour group beside me – a group of pacers holding the big 4:00 balloon. Then the 4:15 group behind them, followed by 4:30, 4:45, and so on.

I drop in with the 4:45 group.

The start line is way in the distance, hundreds of keener and faster runners lined up in front of us.

I look behind and see the rest of the crowd, stretching into the distance – 5:00, 5:15, 5:30.

I start building a strategy. If I stay under five hours, I'll be happy. If I break four and a half, I'll be ecstatic. So let me at least stay between these two groups. Then I think, maybe just focus on finishing. How about that?

Yeah, good idea.

For another ten minutes, the announcer riles everybody up.

You've done the training! Now you're here! This is your day!

Everyone cheers. The gun goes. We start walking. We have timing chips under our race numbers, so our timer only starts once we cross the start line. It's still fifty metres away.

Slowly we begin to jog, until we run under the big blow-up arch. I see the start line pass beneath my feet. Like one of those plates at the lake.

Welcome to the marathon.

I have never run at six a.m. before. Not just during training, but ever, in my life. It feels good. Surprisingly good. We run through suburban streets, then turn onto a hill. It's a mild hill – kids probably ride it on their bikes and barely notice it's a hill – but it's long. So long you can't see the end of it. I don't care. All around me, I see nothing but hundreds of people running this hill and not complaining. I won't either. I don't check my pace. I just stay with the crowd, and we run.

Even at this hour, people are out on their porches, clapping us along. Some have signs. Some scream. All are smiling, like proud grandparents.

At four kilometres, the first aid station arrives. Auckland Marathon is one of the few marathons where you can deposit your own drinks. You drop your bottles at athlete registration before the race, then on race day, they're waiting for you on the special drinks tables.

From a distance, I see it. A bunch of bottles, lined up on a special table, ten metres before the water station. I see my bottle waiting for me. I know it's mine, because I wrapped it in yellow ribbons, I can see it from miles away. It's glistening. Glowing. I don't even slow down. I run past and snatch it, suck down as much as I can. It sings on my tongue. Glorious.

As the aid station ends, I take one last gulp and toss the bottle onto the pavement, into the huge pile of paper cups on the curb. It feels cool when I do it, like I'm an Olympic runner, like I should be on ESPN and I'm running for a gold medal.

Over the next kilometres the crowd changes. It thins, and the roads widen. They're quieter now. Even though Auckland is my home, I rarely come to this side of town. We wind through the suburbs, up and down hills, roads and streets with names I've never seen or heard of.

There's a tall, muscular guy in front of me. Polynesian. Samoan probably. Looks like a rugby player. He runs with a sharp lean to his left, on tiptoes, his calf muscles pulse through his skin every time he takes a step. He's wearing headphones. A lot of people are. One girl not far from me has full-sized Beats headphones on, like she's in the recording studio. One guy has a speaker hanging from his backpack, blaring out rock music.

I don't know what's weirder, that he's running with a speaker, or running with a backpack.

I have earphones too, but they're not on my head. They're in my pocket. Earphones take you out of the moment, and during training, that's exactly what you want. Anything to take your mind off the razor blades in your feet, the five or ten or twenty kilometres you have left to run. But just before the starting gun, as I reached for my earphones, I stopped. Standing in the buzz of the crowd, I realised I didn't want anything taking me out of the moment today. Today I want all of the moment. If this is going to be the race of my life, I want to see and hear and taste every single kilometre, every cheer. Every footstep.

I look at the rugby player as I pass him. He's hurting. I can tell from his face he's tough, he'll be okay, but we're not yet at the second aid station, and he's already hurting.

I'm not. I feel good. We approach the second aid station, and again I see my bottle waiting for me. It's like being a pro — no queue, maybe only five or six bottles on the table. I run past and grab mine like it's my personal refreshment centre.

Bottle in hand, I run past the queue of people at the regular aid tables. They run awkwardly trying to drink from cups, trying to weave through the crowd, while I run and gulp from my bottle with ease, barely breaking stride.

As I toss my bottle into the pile of paper cups, feeling like an Olympian again, I grin at my good fortune. I had thought special drinks would be the opposite — in some obscure place, hard to find, set up begrudgingly for the high-maintenance people like me. Maybe you'd need to wait in line and ask for your drink, while everyone else grabbed their cups of water and zoomed by you. But it's not. It's right there, the first station you see. You get your drink set out for you like a VIP.

All these months, I've been asking to be the lucky one. Just once, let me be lucky. Give me something good. And now God decides to give it to me. Of all the days, he chose today.

Good choice.

At ten kilometres, we hit the Auckland Harbour Bridge. I don't even realise we're near the bridge until we're on it. It's one of the big calling cards of the race. People are always saying, you get to run over the bridge! One of my Mum's friends signed up for the quarter marathon, to walk it. Just so she could walk over the bridge.

But you learn very quickly, there's nothing special about the bridge. It's a farce. As soon as you're on the bridge, nobody wants to be there anymore. The wind is twice as strong. It's long and steep. It doesn't look steep when you look at it from the harbour, doesn't feel steep when you drive over it, but when you run it after ten kilometres at seven o'clock in the morning, say hello to the world's steepest bridge.

Half the crowd starts walking. I've never liked walking hills. Bad for morale. Seems to hurt just as much. And worst of all, it's slower. Makes the hill even longer. The race even longer.

I labour up, like I've done so many times on The Hill at the lake. Slower than usual, but I move. Pass a few people. There's one weapon you have on race day that you never have during training: Adrenaline. It's a superpower. It makes your lungs less heavy, your legs bouncier than usual. Best of all, it puts you in denial. If your thighs start to hurt, your feet start aching, you just say, sorry, not today. Today is race day.

It's the biggest hill I've ever run, but race day energy doesn't let me stop. I grind and grind, wondering if I'll pay for it later, but also not caring if I do. All that matters right now is conquering this bridge.

I get three quarters of the way up. Most people are walking now. Some have stopped and are taking selfies. One girl even hands her phone to a race volunteer and poses for a few snaps. I can see the top, I'll be there in two minutes.

One minute.

Thirty seconds.

It levels off. I look out over the harbour. Smile. Water starts to splatter against my face. I'm not sure whether it's rain or ocean spray. We're a little high for ocean spray. There's too few clouds for rain.

Does it even matter? It's race day. Just keep running.

Then, the reverse. What goes up, must come down. It's the universal law. It applies in politics, in science, in the stock market. It applies in the playground when you're five years old. And it especially applies in running. The descent is just as steep as the way up. I take extra care to descend slowly, and my knees hate it.

Then I think, why waste all this energy trying to go slower?

So instead of leaning back, I lean forward. I run down, fast.

Immediately my knees feel better, freer. On the way down, I pass the 4:30 pacer group. There's about thirty of them, running with three ladies holding the 4:30 balloon. I go even faster. I can't stop now, even if I want to. I blast the second half of the bridge at full speed, all the way to the bottom.

We've been running for over an hour. As the bridge ends, we turn into an obscure grid of suburban roads I didn't know existed. All these years living in Auckland, I had no idea people lived this close to the bridge.

Then, as we start to wind through these streets, the half marathon pros emerge from behind and begin zooming past us.

They are like robots. Tall and wiry, arms and legs with zero fat on them, like they've never eaten a chocolate bar in their lives. They all wear the same uniform too – stubby shorts barely a few inches long and quick-dry singlets. Nothing else.

We 4:30 marathoners are the opposite. Some of us wear skins, some of us shorts, some of us yoga pants. Some have bandanas, some baseball caps. Others have headphones and drink bottles strapped to their waists. We're like the Little Giants. As we dawdle along the course, they run like cyborgs in perfect form, shooting by us like we're not even there.

I look at my watch.

Eighteen kilometres.

I may not be a cyborg, but I have never felt this strong after eighteen kilometres. I've never felt this strong after eight kilometres. As I approach the upcoming aid station, there's a trio of race photographers sitting under the trees. There's nobody around but me, so they all focus on me and *chish, chish, chish*. I flex for the cameras and roar. I feel so good, so strong. One of them reveals a huge grin as she turns her camera down.

You're awesome! She screams.

I can't talk, can't interrupt my breathing to say anything, but I raise my hand and fist pump the air, hear her laugh behind me.

She knows that means thank you.

Then I pump my fist again, to myself.

You're doing it, I say. You're really going to do it.

I get to the aid station. It's filled with school kids. They are boisterous and full of endless energy.

I go to grab two cups of water. Two young kids are manning the table, and they cheer as I take them.

You're the man, Bren! THE MAN!

I forget my name is written on my race bib. I don't smile, I barely look at them, but their words lift me. More than I could've expected.

We start approaching the city's outskirts. I see the skyscrapers in the background, not far from the waterfront. Finally, familiar territory. My old office is barely three blocks away.

We run by the cafes along the water, past the fish market that's been there forever. Years ago, I walked these roads during countless lunch hours, countless nights after Friday drinks with the boys, hungry and intoxicated. Never once did I imagine I'd run them. Certainly not like this.

As we approach Victoria Park – the big central city park where the finish line awaits – the road forks. Two big signs are erected:

HALF MARATHON RIGHT.
FULL MARATHON LEFT.

I veer left. I'm hungry to veer left. In an hour I won't be. In an hour I'll be cursing every footstep, dreaming of going back and turning right. But for now I veer left and feel proud.

This is what I came here for. The main event.

The home of the second half of the marathon is the Auckland waterfront. It stretches from the heart of the city centre all the way to the beachfront suburbs, many kilometres away.

On this end, where I am now, is the central station where I used to get off the bus for university. On the opposite end, where I hope to be in about an hour, is one of Auckland's favourite beaches – Mission Bay. During my office years, I drove this entire road end to end every day, bumper to bumper both ways – cold and grumpy in the mornings, cold and tired at night. Halfway along is the park where I used to play touch rugby every Tuesday. Not far from there is the watersports club, where my class had our sailing lessons in primary school. I used to come to the beaches along this waterfront as a five-year-old with my parents and brothers. As a twenty-five-year-old with my friends. I know this road better than almost any road in Auckland. In the world.

Today, I'll get to know it even better. I hit aid station number six, not far from the bus terminal. If I'm ever at this bus terminal at eight-thirty in the morning, it's because I'm tired and hungry, still half asleep, wishing I didn't have to get out of bed so early. Today, I'm tired and hungry, but there's nowhere else I'd rather be. I'm twenty-three kilometres down, nineteen kilometres to go, running the race of my life. All I'm wishing for is my knees not to break. Or my feet.

One of my wishes comes true. My knee behaves, like a child on a mission, hoping for the best video game console for Christmas. My feet don't. They start acting out like juvenile delinquents, stabbing me with pains as if I'm standing on a stapler with every step.

I check my time. My pace is normal. I tell myself I'm okay. The 4:30 pacer group is still behind me. I don't know how far, and I don't look back to check. I just know I'm in front, and I keep going.

Every kilometre on the waterfront is marked with huge signs on the lamp posts. It seems like an hour passes between kilometres twenty-four and twenty-five. A decade goes by between aid stations six and seven. I look to those running near me for company. Or comfort. It's the same thing. If they haven't collapsed yet, then neither will I.

An Asian guy is running in front of me. He's wearing the freshest looking Nikes, has the freshest Korean style haircut. I've been tailing him a while. Suddenly he starts to run differently, awkwardly, with straight legs. He's swinging his legs forward, like balls on a chain.

I know why he's doing it. His knees hurt. Even then, I'm not moving any faster than he is. We both plod along, for a twenty-sixth kilometre that never ends.

Crowds are approaching now, on the opposite side of the road. Coming towards us. Not spectators. Runners. They've already reached the turnaround point, and are on their way back. Until now it's only been elite runners coming towards us, you can tell from the numbers on their bibs – #2 or #5, one of the numbers reserved for pros – instead of #4552 like me. And you can tell by the way they run. Like machines. But now those running towards us are different. A ragtag group of weekend warriors.

The 3:30 pacer group goes past.

That is so fast, I think to myself.

Not long after, I see a grandma running up behind them. And not one of those special forty-year-old grandmas. A real grandma. Seventy years old, maybe older. She runs with a hunched back and a pronounced lean to her right side. The kind of person I'd offer to help carry groceries to her car, if I saw her walking through the supermarket carpark with more than one bag. But she has the eyes of a prizefighter. About to fight for the heavyweight title of the world. I try to make out the name on her race bib, but I can't.

She runs with straight arms, and looks like she's power walking more than running. But she's almost an hour ahead of me, and she's not slowing down.

Two words come to mind.

Holy shit.

Before we reach twenty-six kilometres, the 4:30 pacer group catches me. As they run by me I sift in amongst them.

I'll stay with them, I pledge to myself. They'll keep me going.

One of the pacers ends up by my side. She's a Kiwi lady, maybe in her forties. If you saw her walking down the street, you'd never guess she can eat a marathon for breakfast. But clearly she can. We're twenty-six kilometres in and she looks brand new.

She turns to me.

How you feeling?

It takes me a few seconds to process the question.

Fantastic, I reply.

That's the spirit!

Aid station number seven arrives at twenty-seven kilometres. In the distance, I see my bottle waiting for me. I think, this is what walking into heaven must feel like. Kilometres one to twenty went by in a flash. Kilometres twenty-six and twenty-seven took half a century.

As we enter the aid station, I hear the pacer ladies talk amongst themselves. One of them sprints – *sprints* – to the toilets. These ladies are androids. They're not real.

We can slow down a bit, another says. Let's walk the aid station then, says the third.

Great. I can't let them pass me. Not after this long. I grab my bottle and suck it down, then bolt out ahead. Stay ahead of them, and you'll run this thing in 4:30. How incredible that will be. You're going to do something incredible today.

As I take off, I imagine the gap between us growing with every step. I tell myself they're still walking through the aid station. They've slowed down. I tell myself how well I'm doing. I tell myself I'm going to do this well all the way to thirty kilometres.

I don't do well until thirty kilometres. I do well for about thirty seconds. Then I hear those ladies behind me. Two minutes later they're next to me. I slot back into the group. Two minutes after that, my knees are twinging. My feet are crying. It's too fast. They're too fast. I let them go, watch them drift off ahead.

Say goodbye to 4:30.

The Asian guy with swinging legs is back. I thought I'd left him in the dust a few kilometres ago. Now, I don't know if he was just a few steps behind all along, or if I've slowed down so much he's caught me. He's running normally now. Sometimes a burst of energy finds me and I pass him before slowing down moments later. Then it's his turn. He runs ahead, just for a moment. Then slows down. And we're side by side again. It's a silly game, this entire race is a silly game. But it keeps us going.

I pass the twenty-eight-kilometre marker. A new record. The furthest I've ever run. Miraculously, the knee is in one piece. But I think about the fourteen kilometres I have left before I get to taste that finish line, and my spirit takes a punch in the face.

That is *so many* kilometres.

I think back to the Chinese girl with the facemask, the night I ran twenty-eight kilometres for the first time. How much steel she had in her eyes. That's the kind of steel I need right now.

I'm given a second boost moments later. As I run past Mission Bay, I see my Dad on the sidewalk. Most of the spectators have congregated here, where the sidewalks are wide and the coffee shops are open. He's got a proud smile on his face and his phone pointed right at me, snapping photo after photo. I don't have the energy to lift an arm and wave, but I smile. Then I look for Mum. She's on the opposite side of the road, waving and shouting at me.

Now I know – after seeing them both – there's no way I'm not crossing the finish line today.

The turnaround marker arrives like an oasis in the desert. There's no aid station here, no shower of cold water, no cup of hot soup. Just a medical station and an orange cone. But it feels special, like conquering the bridge. At the barrier, a small crowd waits to cheer on their loved ones as they arrive.

I slow down to make the U-turn, and my knees buckle. My feet feel like jelly. I never imagined turning around could be so difficult, but after running in one direction for three hours, it's almost like I've forgotten how to run the other way. I walk the turn, carefully, a few people cheer my name as I do it. And then slowly, I get back to running. The final leg.

I see my parents again a kilometre later. I smile at my Mum. I have them there for twenty seconds, if that, but it's vital. To know I'm not running just for me. To remind me this day is going to be good for all of us. But only if I finish.

I make it to thirty-two kilometres.

Ten kilometres left.

They say, this is where a marathon really starts. Where things really start to hurt.

Can that be real? Can my feet really hurt more than they do now?

I'm going to find out.

Things start to become eerily lonely on the course. We're rarely in groups of more than three or four. Half of us are walking. The other half, barely running. Some have stopped completely. There are no spectator zones here. It's just us.

But I refuse to walk. I won't let myself. I know if I stop running, it will feel too good, I won't be able to start again. I'm barely moving. These are the slowest kilometres I've run in my life. But I'm running.

There are three aid stations left. Just three. I get to the first one at thirty-three kilometres. It's a big one, and once again, I see my bottle waiting for me.

Finally, for the first time, I stop to walk as I drink it. I tell myself it's okay to walk right now. Take a beat to drink slowly, and a lot. And once you pass that drinks table up ahead, start running.

So I drink slowly. And a lot. I walk past the final drinks table. I start running.

There's a cute Chinese girl ahead of me. She's in a bright purple shirt, on the back it says, "I'm running for mental health." She stops to walk and, gradually, I pass her. She turns and smiles at me. I smile back. But it's not a regular "Hey how's it going" smile. It's a "Yeah, this shit is crazy, right?" smile.

Half a kilometre on, I start gaining on another guy. He's doing the classic run-walk strategy – run for a minute, walk for a minute. On the back of his shirt it says SUDDEN CARDIAC ARREST – then a date, and underneath – BUT I'M STILL HERE!

Warrior. I'll be proud to run behind you for a while. So I do. He run-walks, I just run super slowly, and while staring at the back of his shirt, I realise what should have been clear all along. These people aren't crazy. We're all the same out here. All regular people, just fighting our demons. Something tries to break us, tries to kill us, and this is our way of saying, fuck you.

I run with the cardiac arrest guy all the way to aid station number ten. It's the second to last aid station, right at the thirty-six-kilometre marker. The guy at the special drinks table grins at me. I roll my eyes.

Fucking glad to see you.

He laughs.

Not long to go, mate.

I suck my bottle down and then catch sight of the toilets.

Yeah, maybe I should.

I hop into the cubicle and my urine is hot like coffee, and orange. My legs shake. It feels weird standing still for this long. It's only half a minute, but feels like five.

When I get out, it's nearly impossible to get the legs moving again. I try, but dawdle like a penguin. Six kilometres left. That's two laps around the lake. Just two. But my legs aren't hearing it. For them, it might as well be a hundred.

Somehow, I move. My mind blanks the entire way. I don't know who's around me. I don't know how long it takes. All I know is running has never been this lonely. Nights at the lake were never this lonely. Early morning runs in the rain were never this lonely. This is the loneliest place in the world right now. Misery loves company, but I don't see any. All I hear is my legs begging, quit, quit, quit, quit. For a moment I relent and walk a few steps. Then I realise something. Nobody's coming to save you out here. If you quit, you still need to walk to the end of this thing to get home. If you cry, it won't make the course any shorter. You can't buy these final kilometres. You can't pray for them. The only way out of here is to run them on your own two legs.

They are the most lifeless and lonely kilometres of the race, of my life, but soon we emerge into the city. It brings my eyes to life, if not my legs. We're in the city centre now. Victoria Park is just there. I know it is. I've walked this road a thousand times. It's so close, but also an eternity away at the same time.

Aid station eleven arrives. The final one. I throw down two cups of Powerade. Forty kilometres done. Two to go.

A surge suddenly fires through my feet. I don't know where it comes from, maybe my body was storing it in a secret compartment just for this moment, but it's here. Like a shark that smells blood, my legs can feel the finish line is *right there*. I lift my feet, lift my knees. For the first time in hours, I'm running normally. I run past the bus station, past the Carpark nightclub we used to go to on Fridays, into the office backstreets, where we used to go to yum cha for lunch.

The crowd of spectators is growing. They're all strangers, but they clap and cheer, scream my name.

C'mon Bren, you're looking strong!

So close now!

And remember to smile!

Remember to smile. *Remember to smile.*

They are the three most perfect words anyone could have said to me.

Look at where you are, I remind myself. Look at what you're doing. Look at where you came from. This race isn't lonely. Your legs don't hurt. There is nothing here to cry about, because you were right. You were never supposed to be here, and here you are. You made it here from the gutter. You made it here from *that night.* One kilometre left in the most impossible moment of your life. God isn't just smiling down on you today, he's been smiling down on you since this started. He brought you all the way here, because he wanted you to know, this is what you can do. This is what you've been capable of all your life. He just needed a way to show you how.

There's a crowd of other runners beside me now. I don't know where they came from, but we all run strong, like we're just starting the race.

In the distance, I see the fork that split us twenty kilometres ago. Back then it was full marathoners left, half marathoners right. Now, I only see one road, just for us. I run through it, into the chute towards Victoria Park. The barriers are packed with crowds, screaming and waving us on.

We speed up, and as the cheers grow, I feel my spirit grow, as if there are hands on my back, pushing me. In this moment, the last six months flash through my mind. I think of the photos and stories in our Facebook group, the messages we write to each other on our darkest days. The warriors who've been on this journey with me. How much we had to *suffer* together. I feel them now, they are right here, all running beside me. Tears roll down my face. Now I realise, this moment is not just for me, but for all of us. To show the world who we really are.

As I turn the final corner, I see the huge arch, the word FINISH in big bold letters across the top.

It is ten seconds away.

I saw this moment, on that run. That morning I was reborn. I never forgot it. I visualised it over and over, during every training run. Every single time, it caused tears to well in my eyes. But the finish line isn't imaginary this time, it's real, right in front of me, booming with noise and screams and colour. The tears don't just well, they pour. The crowd is huge, I can't make out the faces through the flood in my eyes, but above all of them, I can hear my Mum screaming *Yesss Brendan*!

I cross. I fall to my knees. I can still hear my Mum screaming my name. I'm not sure how long I stay down. Long enough for me to stop crying. Then I stand and a young boy puts a medal around my neck. I don't look at it, just hold it against my chest with my palm. A girl hands me a Powerade. Another hands me a banana. As I exit the finisher zone, I see my parents waiting. My Dad is grinning ear to ear. My Mum's eyes are red and puffing.

She hugs me and holds my face and looks me in the eye.

I am so proud of you, son.

9

I can't walk down the stairs. I can go up, but coming down takes me forever. Each step makes my knees squeal with agony. I don't care. I asked my knees to behave today, and they did. Now they can do whatever they like.

I reach the bottom of the stairs and my Dad sees me from the kitchen and smiles.

Here comes the champion!

He is so impressed. So is Mum. So am I. It is not even two p.m. Usually I'm still in my underwear at two p.m. Today, I've run a marathon.

That night, I post about the race in the Facebook group. It takes me an hour to write it. I never thought writing a Facebook post could be so emotional. I thank them all for being there beside me, running to the finish line. I thank them for suffering with me. For answering all my questions. For giving me hope. For reminding me that healing happens. I tell them I wouldn't be here without them, and I don't mean here with a marathon medal, or here with healing skin. I mean here, on Earth. This group has literally saved my life.

The next day, I drive down to the lake. I park in my usual spot, take my medal from the glove compartment. I go stand by the water. I'm not here to run. I'm not quite sure why I'm here, to be honest. I just feel like the lake was there for me, every time I needed it. Like a coach, like a training partner, a best friend.

I hold up my medal, show it to the water.

Look, I say. I did it.

And thank you.

It is Day 155.

My hands have healed.

Oddly, I already take it for granted, that they look like normal hands. Only a few months ago they looked diseased. My wrists and the roots of my fingers were particularly bad. I couldn't get my hands wet or all the scabs would open up. Of course they got wet with sweat when I ran, but I wore gloves when I washed vegetables and dishes, just dipped my fingertips under the tap after using the toilet. Slowly, they would scab up and crust over with dried ooze that was the worst shade of yellow. Then at night, I'd scratch it all off in my sleep – if I managed to sleep – and we'd start all over again. But each time they healed a little stronger, a little faster. And now they look normal.

In our group, the advice is always the same. Time. Healing will happen if you just give it time. Skin regenerates cell by cell. Scars heal. Life comes back to normal. You just need time.

But in the hellish periods, time is the last thing you want to give. During those times I would think, I would give anything else – all the money in my bank account, everything I own and will ever own – if you could just end this suffering and heal me now. Please. I can't do this for another minute, another second. I'll give anything but time.

Yet time is the only remedy. The ironies of life.

Now I realise, almost by accident, time is exactly what this marathon has given me. The weeks of training, worrying about stretching, my bung knee, my diet, running hundreds of kilometres – it was all the perfect distraction.

I look in the mirror now and I see myself. I don't see a monster anymore. I don't see a face that needs to be covered so I don't scare kids at the supermarket. Of course it's still not my face, not the old Brendan who smiled at everyone and never thought twice about leaving the house. My eyelids still flake and flake, every morning when I rub my eyes, the flakes are so large I can feel them fall across my fingers. The patches under my eyes remain, but the skin has changed from bright red and hot, to light brown and faded, and the skin is intact. No wounds. Just battle scars.

Maybe it's only half healed, but it was the half I needed. Now, I'm just ugly.

I can do ugly. After what I've been through, I'll take ugly any day of the week.

It's been three days since the marathon. Every day I wake up and it's the first thing I think about. Each night, I see my medal on my shelf – sitting on top of my race number like a paperweight – and something curdles in my stomach. It brings the tears back, the happiest kind of tears. Each time I walk past, I pick it up, run my fingers over the grooves and smile.

The official race photos are released a few days later. I sit and stare at them for hours. The one of me flexing at the camera, taken by the photographer who told me I was awesome – it's hard to believe it's really me.

Later that evening, while watching marathon videos on YouTube, I find a clip of Ashton Kutcher doing an interview. I love Ashton Kutcher. Been a fan since *The Butterfly Effect*. Sometimes, when I'm driving and my phone beeps, I grab it and look, even though I know I shouldn't, and that film still pops into my head after all these years. Because that's the butterfly effect – just one poor decision, one tiny ripple, can whirlwind your entire life. Even something as innocent as a glance at your phone while you drive. Or a tube of steroid cream.

The interview has Kutcher telling a story about himself and P. Diddy They're friends, and Kutcher loves to run. So Diddy joins him one day Paparazzi show up. Just as they do, Diddy starts to gas out. He tells Kutcher, slow down, don't make me look bad. He can hardly breathe

Kutcher uses the word *skunked*. It's a good word. I know exactly what it feels like to get skunked on a run.

But Diddy is a winner. He's so pissed about skunking on this run, he decides to run the New York Marathon right in that moment. Starts training for it the next day.

I want to hear Diddy's version of the story. I search for more interviews.

In a news article, I see his time.

4:16.

Twenty-one minutes faster than mine.

I don't know if I'm impressed or jealous. I guess both.

An *Oprah* segment pops up next. She's retelling the same story. She says, after Diddy signed up for the New York Marathon, he called her for advice.

He told her, he's going to beat her time.

Oprah ran a marathon?

Who knew?

I look up her time.

4:29.

Oprah beat me too?

I start to replay the race in my mind. I wonder if maybe I could have started a little faster, those early kilometres, where I still didn't know if I'd finish. Maybe I could have held with that 4:30 group a little longer. During those dire moments between kilometres thirty and thirty-six, maybe I could have given something.

Dug a little deeper. Just an inch.

If I'd had to run two more kilometres, could I have done it? Or did I really have nothing left?

I spend the evening browsing marathon stats. Global averages. Mean times per hemisphere, age, gender. I find the worldwide male average. It's 4:16.

4:16.

I already know what this means.

One day, I'm going to run again. And I'm going to beat 4:16.

It is Day 159.

It's been a week since the race. I still haven't been for a run. Just watching my blisters shrink, eating toasted sandwiches for every meal. I open my inbox, see an email from Auckland Marathon. I figure it's to say, congratulations, well done, thanks for coming. How nice of them. But it's something else. Something more interesting.

You could be part of history at the Singapore Marathon on Saturday, November 30 in its first year as a night run!

Imagine starting in the Formula One pit lane and running past some of Singapore's most iconic sights like the Super Tree Gardens and the Merlion under Singapore's beautiful sunset!

I look up the Singapore marathon on YouTube. There's a promo video. It starts with drums. Lots of drums. Huge crowd. Huge race. Smiling faces. Singapore's magnificent skyline. Gardens at the Bay. Marina Bay.

It's been years since I visited Singapore, but I remember it well and recognise each place. It closes with two people holding their medals.

Singapore Marathon: It's Ours To Run. November 30.

Six weeks away.

I mention it to Mum. She's intrigued. She mentions it to my Dad.

Huh, he says. Which means, that's interesting.

I spend the day imagining another six weeks of training. Dieting. A trip to Singapore. If it's really in my heart, to do it all again.

Sleep on it.

The next day, I'm in the kitchen, meticulously peeling an orange. I've inherited my Dad's method, after watching him peel a million oranges since I was a toddler. Sharp knife, and wheel it around once, taking off the rind. Then do it again, this time more carefully, taking off the white. My Dad is beside me, washing vegetables. He has no idea this is one of the hundred things I've learned from him, without him actually teaching me.

While we both stand at the sink, he brings up Singapore. Out of the blue.

Have you decided?

Not yet.

Better make up your mind.

And then he says, talking at his vegetables: If you do decide to go … we'd really like to come with you. To be there for you. To support you.

It's the second closest he's ever come to saying I love you.

Lying in bed that evening, I open the email again.

I think about beating Oprah.

I think about beating P. Diddy.

I think about beating the average.

Most of all, I think about beating TSW.

One week later, I'm registered for Singapore.

10

It's evening when I land. Singapore Airport was the transit point for many of my backpacking adventures through Asia, but it's been five years, at least.

Last time, I stayed in Little India, where the hostel beds were cheapest and the air smelled like naan bread and cumin. This time, I get the subway to Fort Canning Station, where the buildings are tall and fancy, and the air smells like car fumes and noodle soup.

First thing I see when I exit the station is the huge park across the road. It's a maze of greenery and stairs and bridges, with running paths that wind up an enormous hill in the centre. I already know I'll be getting to know those paths well. But first, to the apartment.

I follow the map on my phone, lugging my old backpack behind me. Hearing the wheels rattle on the pavement, watching the blue line trace the map on my screen, it triggers vivid flashbacks of my previous life. In all my years of travel, my first hour in a new country always started this way – hunting down the address of my accommodation, already fantasising about the new adventures I'd have in this city before I'd even gotten in the front door. How much I missed this. How angry I was that for years I'd built this life, and overnight it was all taken away. All the hours I stared in the mirror, doubting I would ever get this back. Promising I'd never take warm summers and good skin and travelling for granted ever again. Now – already sweating in the humidity, with an almost-normal looking face, walking the streets in another country – I feel my heart smiling wider than my lips.

Everything taken from me. Time to take it all back.

My parents aren't due in Singapore for a few more days. I've come a week early to acclimatise and train. I check into the big family apartment Mum has booked – a high rise that looks over the Singapore River and Fort Canning Park. I collapse on the couch, admiring the luxury. On a backpacker's budget, you could never. But on a Mum budget, sit down and put your feet up.

It's eight p.m. Time for dinner. But from the window, I eye the park opposite the station. It's huge and well-lit and begging for it. Even though my body is gluggy from the twelve-hour flight, I know it needs to be done.

I lace up. Take the elevator down.

The humidity hits my skin like a steam sauna. Just the short walk to the park gets my sweat glands moving. After the most miserable Auckland winter of my life, I love it, I've craved it.

Once at the park, I set my watch and go. It's a recovery run, a reset run, whatever you want to call it. Slow and soothing – at least as soothing as a run in thirty-degree heat can be – just to lubricate the muscles, let the feet know that running in Singapore isn't too different from running in New Zealand. But it is. The air is different. The smell is different. Even the way people stare at you is different. And the heat – definitely different. Just like six degrees in Auckland winter feels like minus twenty, thirty degrees in Singapore feels like forty-five.

I start along the main road. Long and flat. My favourite kind of road. After a block, I see a small gate leading into the park. I take it. It's a winding path, through gardens, Pleasantville-esque. I run past a few guys in basketball gear, one or two couples taking their evening stroll, an old man who looks like he works there, but I'm not sure. Eventually, the path winds around like a snake, back to where I started.

I look at my watch.

Just short of a kilometre.

Perfect. Five laps of this and I'm done.

My left foot starts to pinch early, barely into the second lap. I ignore it, tell myself it's just a nervous foot. It hasn't felt these roads before. It will get to know this loop as well as it knows the lake back home, and then it'll be fine.

It works for a while, then it doesn't. My feet never hurt this early in a run. I try to guess why, maybe the flight, maybe the heat. I'm soaked in sweat, like someone has taken to me with a fire hose. Maybe I'm dehydrated.

Get through these five laps, I say. And we'll figure it out later.

When I get back to the apartment, my body has turned upside down. Earlier, my foot felt fine, but my head was gluggy. Now my head feels fine, but my foot is mashed. I peel off my socks – the fancy compression socks I read about in another stupid book – and give my toes a wiggle.

Well. It's not *that* bad. Then I look at my feet side by side, and raise an eyebrow. Maybe it is that bad. I hop around the living room, try to figure out if it's anything more than a bad swelling. I have no idea. But it looks like it needs a rest. Just like my knee needed last time.

Maybe I could use a rest too.

Good idea. No more runs. Not until race day.

Despite my balloon of a foot, I wake the next morning in the best of spirits. Since I can't train, I have the perfect excuse to spend the week doing something else, something I actually want to do. Exploring Singapore, like the old days.

I head downstairs in my slippers and bask in the tropical weather. Some ladies are doing Zumba in the courtyard. Rows of men are sitting on the benches, in business attire, eating cup noodles. I wander toward the station, enter one of the shopping malls. In the basement, there's a gourmet Japanese supermarket. It's enormous. My heaven. Not only because I have a love affair with Japanese food, but because this is the food I need. I didn't carbo-load for the Auckland race, but I'm going to try it for this one. And this supermarket is a carb fiesta.

I stack my shopping basket with calories, beautiful, beautiful calories – fruits, sweet potatoes, bread, and the best one of all – sushi. Then I hurry back to the apartment and feast. Eating hasn't been this much fun for a long time. Maybe ever.

That night, I head down to the apartment gym. It's small, but tidy, and there's an exercise bike in there. Not a regular one, but one with a large seat and a backrest, like it's been designed for old people. Or lazy people. Perfect for my marshmallow foot. I pedal for twenty minutes. The foot warms, feels okay. I decide I can give it fifteen minutes on the treadmill. There's a mirror in front of me. I watch my foot like a hawk as I run, make sure it's landing straight every time, on the ball, that my knees are in line. The foot jars at times, but I pretend it doesn't. Eventually my eyes drift from my foot to my face, and I stare myself down as I run.

Good foot or bad foot, you're gonna kill this race.

And then I can't help but look myself in the eye and say, I'm proud of you, man.

My parents arrive three days later. Even though I came early to get some running in, I've been doing nothing but eating Japanese food, bathing my feet in ice, and riding that elderly person cycle in the gym downstairs. I say nothing about my foot.

We go to the marathon check-in the next evening to pick up my race number. It's enormous. Ten thousand people are running. One of the biggest marathons in the world.

My Dad comes with me to the desk to pick up my race bag. There are arches for each event – full marathon, half, quarter, kids run. A crowd of volunteers is milling about.

Full marathon? The girl asks.

Yes.

She points me through the first arch. It's all so official, I feel like a pro athlete.

As we walk through the running expo that follows, a huge race map has been erected in the middle of the floor. I study it. There are aid stations every two kilometres. Sometimes even less. It's going to be twice as many aid stations as Auckland, and not only do they serve water and Singapore's favourite energy drink – 100 Plus – but some of them have gels, bananas, pretzels. Even ice.

Double the aid stations, three times the aids.

I wonder, why would a marathon need twenty-one aid stations?

But there's no need to wonder. Soon I'll learn why. We all will. The hard way.

That evening after we get home, I go to the 7-Eleven downstairs and buy five kilograms of ice. Take the biggest pot from the kitchen and fill it with ice cubes. Dunk both my feet inside.

It burns. Then numbs. Then feels mildly pleasurable, in a masochistic way. I make it through five minutes, then pull them out and look at them again side by side.

Better?

Maybe a little.

I pull my foot up and rest it on my knee. It's soft and fluffy, ready to be roasted on a campfire. I have no idea what's wrong with it, and there's no time left to find out. I prod at it, massage the sole with deep, gentle strokes.

And then I whisper: Please behave. Just this once. And I promise, I'll never make you run again.

124

11

It's been fifteen kilometres. Fifteen and I'm done.

I should've known. I think I did, actually. Right after I hugged my Mum, my Dad, went into the starting pens, I was already soaked in sweat. We all were. Like ten thousand animals just waiting for slaughter. That was a sign, we just weren't paying attention. Or maybe we were, but were in denial.

Like I said. Idiots.

Even though my rule is to never walk, I'm walking. At four kilometres I took off my singlet and tied it around my head. At ten kilometres I stopped at the aid station and took a time out to drink. Now, at fifteen kilometres, I'm walking. My foot is fucked. I don't know exactly what's wrong with it, but I know it hurts like fuck and moves like fuck.

Lots of runners write about stress fractures. Is this what a stress fracture feels like? I don't know. All I know is I'm not finishing this race.

Twenty-seven more kilometres, on this foot?

Dreaming.

I take comfort in knowing it's not just me. Everyone seems to be walking. It doesn't even feel like we're fighting against kilometres anymore. This heat will kill us before the distance does.

I look at the guy next to me. Bewildered. He's ready to call it. So am I. But I don't even know how to do that. How do you quit a marathon? Just put your hand up and a taxi comes to get you?

That's when he finds me. That guy. That voice that lives in the corner of your mind. Like he's been waiting for this moment.

Look around you. Look at where you are!

I look up. See the huge tree line running against the night sky. The sea of blue shirts around me.

Singapore! One of the greatest marathons in the world! Did you ever think you'd ever be here? After everything? You want to give up **here?**

He's right.

Sweat runs down my face and into my mouth, hits my tongue like seawater. I stare at the endless stream of heads up ahead of me. Thousands of us. We've taken over the city.

You're telling me all of them can keep running, and you can't? Have you fallen over yet? You've quit, and your legs haven't even quit!

He's right again. He's always right.

For that split second, everything that I need to flash through my mind flashes through my mind. Like a tape hidden in the back of your brain. An emergency reel. For when your mind is broken and your spirit is broken and your body is broken, maybe even your bloody earlobes are broken, and it plays. Every day you didn't want to train but you did. Every freezing morning you found the will to lace up and head out the front door. Every lap around the lake you never thought you'd survive. And then, it's *that night.* And I don't need to see anything else. Because I'm never going back to that night. I'll run a hundred marathons in Singapore before I go back to that night.

I look at my watch.

Twenty-seven kilometres left.

Maybe you won't make it. Maybe you will. But until they drag you out of here on a stretcher, we run.

Deal.

I start to move. I can't quite run, so I waddle. Like a seal pup. It's ridiculous, but it takes weight off my foot. With each step I push the air backwards with my arms. I have no idea why it works, and I don't care. Running with our arms, we must have learned this centuries ago – an evolutionary trait, a survival instinct, learned during our ancestors' long migrations, like the wildebeests. Whatever it is, and no matter how stupid it looks, I'm doing it.

It's working.

Not only is it working, I'm passing people. Lots of them.

The voice is back.

Look at all these walking motherfuckers! You deserve to be in front of them! Keep going!

I dig into my race belt, eat a date, and then another. Maybe these carbs will do it. I've got a whole race belt full of these things. Carbs were supposed to be the saviour for this race, but all those sweet potatoes I feasted on this week, all that sushi, it's feeling about as helpful as a pair of bricks tied to my shoes.

Chewing on dates, I tell myself, just get to halfway. Twenty-one kilometres. Maybe it will be a different race after that.

I don't know why I say that. It's a lie. It will be exactly the same race after that. But I believe it. Six more kilometres and it's a new race.

I survive six kilometres. Turns out, it's true. It is a new race. A worse one.

The half marathoners veer off to the left, the rest of us continue onto the winding paths of a city park. It's dark, the road overhung by trees that block out the moonlight. With half the runners gone, the road feels emptier, lonelier. In races, you can feel the energy of the pack. It rises and falls, like tides in the ocean. As the half marathon finish line approached, the energy lifted. Some people smiled and ran with bounce. But now they're all gone and it's just us. Heads down. Walkers. Exasperation. The faces of a crowd looking down the barrel of twenty-one more kilometres.

I grimace with every step. I don't know how much longer the foot will last. So I make myself another offer: Get to the aid station, and you can walk it.

Deal.

When I finally see the huge green aid station sign in the distance, I feel that tiny piece of bliss flutter in my lungs. It's the secret to the marathon, that tiny feeling of bliss when you hit a new kilometre or see an aid station. It only lasts ten seconds, but remembering it, anticipating it, can make miracles happen.

I slow to a walk and grab two cups of 100 Plus. With the half marathoners gone, the aid stations are uncrowded, barely a handful of runners. I grab a third cup for the road and walk, slowly, sipping it. If I'm allowed to walk through this aid station, I'm milking it, taking it for every last centimetre.

Then, when it's finally gone, when I can no longer see it behind me, no longer hear it, I toss the cup and run.

Same rules. Get to the next aid station and you can walk.

My foot doesn't jar anymore. Just dull pain. Numb. My mind is empty, switched off. My body has only enough energy to power my brain or my legs, but not both. So it powers my legs. The course blurs. Everything blurs. I don't know who's around me, where I am. All I know is one thing. Forward. To the aid station.

I get through two aid stations. Then three. Four. Five. The aid stations are only one and a half kilometres apart in this stretch, but I believe they're two kilometres. Though it's a blessing to not know this. To believe I'm running further than I am. Lie to me. Tell me I'm doing well. Let me think I'm doing better than I am. Anything to keep me going. Forward. To the aid station.

The twenty-eight-kilometre aid station arrives. I barely believe it. I wouldn't have bet fifty cents on me getting here an hour ago. But now, seeing the twenty-eight on the sign, something changes. I see a flicker. That thing I lost a long time ago. You were ready to quit at fifteen kilometres.

Didn't think you could make it to twenty-one. Now you're almost at thirty, and if you can get to thirty, you can get to thirty-five. And if you can get to thirty-five, maybe you can get to ... forty-two?

So I make myself another offer: Get to thirty kilometres, and you can walk one full kilometre to thirty-one.

Best offer I've had all day.

I make it to thirty. The walk to thirty-one is blissful, at least compared to the thirty kilometres before it. The last ten kilometres has been a blackout, like the scraggly grey and white static on a busted TV. I don't know where we've run, who's been beside me, how long it's taken. It's the most recent hour of my life, and I remember none of it. But now my eyes are working again, my ears. I'm in a park, walking beside grassy banks on a tree-lined street. Several runners are sitting on the park benches with their shoes off, maybe they've given up. Maybe just checking their blisters. Maybe a toenail has fallen off.

My foot doesn't feel any better. But it doesn't feel any worse. I look at my watch for the first time in a while. It's stopped, still stuck on twenty-five kilometres. I must have pushed a button by accident somewhere.

Of course I did. I've never done that before, ever, but of course the first time it would happen is today. At the one moment I really want to know my distance and my time, I don't know my distance, and I don't know my time.

Then I realise neither would help me anyway.

I make it to the thirty-one-kilometre marker. The strategy hasn't changed. Get to the aid station and walk. My foot isn't any less broken, I'm not moving any faster, but now there's one big difference from before: At fifteen kilometres, I was sure finishing was impossible. At thirty-one kilometres, I'm sure it only might be.

I make it to thirty-three kilometres. It's almost ten o'clock, the sky is pitch black. We continue to drown in the humidity, like wet smog. I never imagined kilometres could feel this long, running could be this miserable. It's so miserable, nobody is even running. People are sitting, walking, straggling, waddling like me. Anything but running. You can't even quit if you want to. How? Sit on the side of the road, wait to be picked up? There are already people sitting on the side of the road, and nobody's picked them up. Nobody even knows they're there. The only option is to move. Forward.

Thirty-five kilometres.

Every medical tent is full. They come every two kilometres, like the aid stations, and they're overflowing. Not just five or ten people. Thirty or forty. It's a warzone. It's us against the pavement, and the pavement's winning. A massacre. As we approach the next tent, I see the row of people lying on stretchers while being nursed. Many sit outside on the curb, drinking water, pouring it on their heads. A crowd of runners are standing around, spraying something on their legs that smells like menthol.

As we hobble past, this spray drifts onto the course. The girl beside me coughs. Then I cough. The guy next to me coughs. Then our eyes start to hurt. We turn away, waving our hands in front of our faces, wondering why they're covering their legs in pepper spray.

As we cross the small bridge that follows, I notice a guy sitting against the railing. He's on the verge of passing out. A volunteer crouches beside him, holding him upright, shouting on the radio to someone.

A kilometre later, a girl collapses ten metres in front of me. The guy behind her flinches and manages to catch her before she hits the pavement. He pulls her to the curb, while another guy stops to help.

Minutes later, weaving through the crowd, I see the medic running towards me with a wheelchair and a bag of ice.

Down there, I tell him, pointing.

He nods and sprints past.

As we come to exit the park a few streets later, a guy suddenly peels off the course, into the bushes. I think he's going to pee, until I hear it. He pukes once, twice. We all turn and look. Vicious. A few of us manage a wry smile. None of us are surprised.

Gardens By The Bay now. I know this place. It's one of the first sights I came to see when I visited Singapore, many years ago. But we're not sightseeing now. We run past it, barely giving it a second look.

A bridge. Long and narrow, crossing the river. Halfway across, we shuffle into single file to dodge another girl lying against the railings. She's one of the pacers. Two medics crouch beside her, holding her up. One of them speaks calmly into his radio.

I need ice on the bridge please. Right now, ice on the bridge.

But as I run past them my first thought is, I know that won't be me. We're almost five hours in, but from here, we can finally see the bright lights of the finish line, way in the distance. Now that it's in sight, I can't fail. I'm going to make it.

We hit thirty-seven kilometres just around the corner. Seeing it is music to my eyes, and gives my legs a new life.

Five kilometres left.

I run that for breakfast. Blueberry pancakes. Ain't even two laps around the lake. Less than two laps around the lake, and I'm home.

And then I see it. The final hill. Huge. Gargantuan. I wonder what kind of evil weirdo would plan a course this way. Five hours of running in end-of-the-world heat, and they decide to put this monstrosity in front of you. A hill like this in the last five kilometres of a marathon – it's not a coincidence. It's a big unmistakable fuck you to ruin your day. Only one thing you can do – give a big fuck you right back.

So I don't walk it. I run it. I run it as hard as I can, my foot winces but I don't care anymore, I enjoy it, I crave it. I make sure it's my fastest kilometre of the night. And I sign it off with a big fuck you.

From the top, I can see the finish line. It's down below, on my right, glittering in all its glory. That's when I know, this course is more evil than I thought. This hill was bad enough, now they let us see the finish line, let us hear it, make us feel like we're almost there – but of course we're not going there. The finish line beckons on our right, the hill descends and veers left.

Still four kilometres to go.

After the hill, the course reverts back to glumness. It's almost midnight. The humidity suffocates. Almost everyone is walking. Beside me, I catch a glimpse of a girl's face, barely moving forward with each step. She's demolished. She doesn't want to be here. I don't want to be here. None of us want to be here.

Thirty-nine kilometres.

Now, the crowd thickens somehow. I don't know where everyone came from, but we're here – maybe fifty of us. And now that we can smell forty kilometres, we start to move.

Jogging slowly, but steadily, we run through a small gate and enter another park. As we turn the first corner, a guy running in front of me suddenly stops and drops his hands onto his knees. He stands out – he's not wearing the official blue singlet, he's dressed in black, all black. He's tired, but he's not done. I can tell.

I hit him on the shoulder as I run past.

No, c'mon! We're almost there!

As soon as I say it, his head shoots up like a whack-a-mole, and he's back to running. Flicked a switch. He runs beside me until we hit the final aid station at forty kilometres.

Enjoy this one, I tell myself.

So I don't just walk, I stop. Grab two cups of water. Gulp them both. Grab another two. Drink them slowly.

Then I turn to get moving again, and I see the guy in black, waiting for me. He doesn't say a word, just stares at me with glinting eyes. He nods his head towards the road.

Oh yeah? Okay. I'm in.

I toss the cups of water and run. He falls in beside me. Bursting out of the aid station, we pace each other. Fast. Faster than I've run the entire race. I don't feel my legs, I don't feel my bung foot. All I feel is forward. Like TSW is chasing me. His legs are suddenly strong, and he pushes the pace even more. Maybe something is chasing him, too. We pass ten people. Twenty. Fifty. All of them walking, limping. Nobody is running but us.

But something is wrong. We should be at forty-one kilometres by now, and we aren't. I keep my eyes peeled in the distance, searching, hoping for that green kilometre marker, but it never comes. It feels like we've run two kilometres since the last marker, maybe three.

I manage to blurt out: Where the fuck is forty-one kilometres?

Maybe the sign was smaller than usual, or hidden. We must have missed it. Some joker probably took it down. Maybe the wind blew it over. All I know is it's not here, because we should've passed it long ago.

But my new comrade says nothing. Just grunts. I can tell that means, just keep running.

Good plan.

Then I see it. Far away, but it's unmistakable. Green sign. A big 41 on it. I guess time is just deciding to move slowly for these final kilometres. Like it's been doing all night. Time flies when you're having fun, drags when you're in misery, but during a marathon? Time stops altogether. Goes for a coffee. Takes an afternoon nap. Bakes some cookies. Then, when you're hallucinating and starting to look like a raisin, it finally decides to get moving again.

But we're too close now. Nothing can stop us. Not even time on its afternoon tea break.

One kilometre left, I say.

My comrade grunts again. Nods.

My foot buckles.

C'mon, he says. C'mon!

It's the first time I've heard him speak. He couldn't have chosen a better time. Or a better word.

Finally, we see some spectators along the rails. They cheer and it lifts us, because we know we're minutes away. Towering on our left is the big Formula One building. The finish line is right there, on the other side.

The final green sign passes. Forty-two kilometres.

Two hundred metres, I gasp.

He nods.

Let's do it.

As we turn the final corner, we see the finish line laid out before us. A hundred metres away. How glorious it looks. It's big and blue and green with flashing lights and there's nobody in front of us. All the photographers from the course are now here – six, seven, eight of them – and all we can hear or see is *click-click-click* and *flash-flash-flash* as we run towards them, side by side.

He holds his fist out. I bump it with mine.

We cross.

I roar with joy. Pump my fists in the air.

A few people finish seconds later and roar with me.

I look around for my comrade, see him floating in the corner, taking it in. I give him a high five, a hug, a slap on the back. All those nights you never wanted to train. All those hours you spent suffering on the course. The entire race, we wonder why on earth we're doing it. And then these thirty seconds, sixty seconds – this little moment of magic after crossing a finish line – reminds us why. There is nothing in the world like it.

We collect our medals. My time is 5:37. I don't care. We survived. And if I've learned anything this year, it's that surviving, is everything.

12

It is Day 196.

My parents have flown home. It's just me.

Lounging alone in the apartment with no return flight scheduled, I try to figure out how to spend my remaining days in Singapore, and where to go next.

Home? Or …?

And it hits me. I'm back. Here. Travelling the world again – no race to train for, no plans on where to go – just a blog to write and open road ahead of me. Where I dreamed of being every minute of every day just six months ago, and it seemed a century away.

Staring in the mirror later that night, I run my hands across my forehead, around my mouth. Still flaking, red. Still healing. But no longer angry, no longer the first thing I think about when I wake up. No longer the only thing I think about every second I'm awake. My pillowcase is still covered in flakes of skin every morning and I don't know how many more flares are left, but the days of blood and ooze seem to be over. Other than looking like I've got a good sunburn, I feel normal.

I smile into the mirror, finally at peace with what I see. I guess this is who I'm going to be for a while. Sunburned Bren. Pleasure to meet you.

I'm checking out in three days. I spend the evening trying to browse flights, but my mind drifts. It's still replaying the marathon over and over. I find myself on YouTube, again, watching race highlights and interviews and recaps.

Then, among some highlights, a new video is suggested.

Ironman World Championship.

I click it.

It starts with a pan of the ocean. A paradise. Hawaii. A voice begins:

It began with some words, an idea on the back of a napkin. For thousands, it is now a calling.

I watch the crowd of athletes in the pre-dawn darkness, shining their bike helmets.

What are they doing?

He answers me:

They are here to truly discover what they are made of. What lies deep in their souls. Deeper than most of us ever go.

Chills run down the back of my neck.

I watch them slip into wetsuits, wade into the ocean.

Today, they will take on the most challenging day in sports that's ever been dreamed up.

I watch them floating in the water, waiting for the gun. Kayaks are paddling up and down the start line, keeping them honest. The narrator rattles off their names. He says them as if they're gladiators, as if everybody in the world should have heard of them, but I recognise none. And then – bang! The gun goes. Except it's not a gun, it's a cannon. *A cannon.*

For the rest of the night, I don't move. I don't blink. I forget I'm in Singapore, forget I need to book a flight. I am glued to my seat, my eyes are glued to the screen, I watch race after race after race.

It is Day 198.

My final night in Singapore. I'm invited to dinner with two friends I haven't seen in years. Old classmates from my time in Shanghai. There is

Tatsuya – Japanese, wickedly smart, about my age, also ran the marathon. Blitzed it in just over four hours. Then there's Yale – Korean, preppy, well-mannered, playboy.

Both their careers have brought them here to Singapore.

Yale chooses a Mexican joint for us to meet at. I get off the subway in a part of Singapore I've never been, walk in circles while I struggle to find it.

Since TSW started, I'd come to hate this. Hated being in public. Rushing in and out of the supermarket, not wanting anyone to see my face. Now, wandering the streets of Singapore in circles, I smile. Before TSW, this was a favourite pastime of mine – strolling through foreign cities on warm nights. Finally, I'm allowed to love it again.

I find the place. It's small and inconspicuous on the front, but opens out into a huge terrace in the back. I spot Yale sitting alone along the wall. He sees me as I walk in. His trademark wide smile spreads across his face.

He stands and we hug.

Yale is tall, with broad shoulders. Dark-rimmed glasses. A tidy comb-over to the right. He looks exactly the same as he did eight years ago.

I know I don't.

Fucking good to see you, man! Congrats on your race.

Was a killer.

I can imagine.

We sit and flick at the menu.

So, how'd you end up here?

Work, you know. And my fiancé also just moved over, so …

I raise an eyebrow, and he smiles.

Yeah. I'm engaged now.

He grins, knowing it sounds as ridiculous to me as it does to him.

I know. Everyone's surprised.

Nah, man. Congratulations.

We talk a while – about her, about work. About Tatsuya still being at work.

The waiter arrives. Filipino guy.

Sorry, man. We haven't even looked yet.

He smiles, says he'll come back.

I tell Yale about the race, my skin, what's been happening. I can see him surveying my face for the redness, the scars.

You're looking better now though.

Thanks.

The waiter comes back. Yale orders a cocktail and nachos for the table. I order a mocktail.

After a thousand drunken nights together in Shanghai, now he's the one looking surprised.

I smile.

Two years sober.

Good on you, man. I should do that too. Seriously though my boss is this German guy, and he's fucking insane. There's no quitting drinking while you're working for him.

As we're finishing the first round, Tatsuya arrives.

Tatsuya is also tall, with a boyish smile and big eyes. He also looks the same, except now he's grown a beard, so he looks older without having aged a day. All that running might have something to do with it.

As soon as we've all hugged and shaken hands and sat back down, I tell him:

I had no idea you were such a beast runner!

Yale agrees.

I was browsing your Instagram. You ran 3:30 at Hawaii!

Like most of us, he's not great at receiving compliments. He shrugs it off.

The waiter comes back.

We order a plate of every taco on the menu. More cocktails, more mocktails. Talk about grown-up life. Reminisce about Shanghai. But conversation always circles back to the race. How hot it was, how horrible it was.

Never again, Tatsuya says.

Then I tell them – I've been watching these races on YouTube. You ever heard of ... Ironman?

They shake their heads.

I shake mine even harder.

So there's a swimming club and a running club having an argument. Out in Hawaii, back in the day. Who's the better athlete? The swimmer or the runner? Then this other guy who's eavesdropping butts in and says, some scientists figured out it's actually cyclists who can go the hardest. So these crazy guys decide to settle it. They dream up this race. The Waikiki Swim – 3.8 kilometres – followed by the Oahu Bike race – 180 kilometres – and the Honolulu Marathon. The three hardest races in Hawaii combined into one. The winner gets crowned the *Iron Man*.

They stare at me, intrigued. Waiting.

So who won?

I have no idea.

We laugh, start to Google it. We spend the whole evening talking about it. Looking up all the records. All the races.

They do the swim in only forty-five minutes!

He did the bike in four hours!

Tatsuya and I bounce ideas off each other.

Maybe if you do the swim ... then rest for half an hour ... then do the bike ... eat some McDonald's. Take a nap. I mean, that only adds an hour to your time right? The time limit is seventeen hours. Think you'd still make it?

We both shrug, laugh about it. Days after suffering through the most miserable marathon, it's too ridiculous to think about.

So when's the next one? He asks.

There's one in New Zealand next year.

You gonna do it?

Hell no.

He laughs and nods with me.

Yeah, he says. I think it's impossible.

13

I spend the evening wandering Singapore's streets with Yale and Tatsuya. Window shopping, snacking, talking about nothing. Like old times.

It is almost midnight when I finally get back to the apartment. I need to decide where I'm going next. I'm checking out tomorrow, and still have nothing booked.

After an hour of browsing flights, I narrow it down to Bali or Thailand. I can't choose. I ponder it until two a.m., when I'm finally forced to decide.

Thailand.

Flight leaves in seven hours.

I spend an hour packing. Get three hours of sleep. Wake up. No breakfast. Cab to the airport. Make it onto the plane.

Two hours later, we're landing in Chiang Mai.

It's joyous, almost surreal, feeling the plane hit the tarmac. It's the last place I expected to be to end the year. I'd thought maybe I'd end it in bed, with blood-stained sheets, sleep-deprived, counting every last drop of water going into my body. Instead, I walk out of the airport and the Thai humidity wraps my skin like Egyptian cotton, I can hear the chatter of beautiful Thai accents, I can even smell the fish sauce and vinegar drifting from somewhere nearby.

To my right, a group of men ask if I need a taxi, taxi, taxi.

I have never been so happy to be harassed by airport taxis in my life.

I continue to the main street, to the bus stop. I know where I'm going – to the Maya Mall – supposedly the best mall in Chiang Mai. Though I don't know how to get there. The maps for the buses are modern and clear, just one problem. They're all in Thai.

I ask a kind-looking man sitting at the bus stop with a suitcase.

You take same bus like me, he says.

The bus arrives and I follow him on. We coast into the city, and out the window I enjoy my first look at Chiang Mai. It's a common city on the backpacking trail, but for some reason I never made it here during my nomadic years. Now, I finally see the charm in its rickety storefronts, interspersed with new-age coffee shops, dirty grey sidewalks, tropical juice stands and massage shops, all among a sea of docile Thai faces.

It is everything I have ever loved about Thailand.

Fifteen minutes on, the kind young man from the bus stop is waving at me.

You take Maya Mall here, he says urgently.

I can tell he's been waiting for us to get here, petrified, not wanting me to miss my stop. I thank him three or four times as I get off.

I only need to walk two blocks before I see Maya Mall in the distance. It's big and new and would be a fine mall in any city in the world. My apartment building is right next to it, but I don't check in yet. I have no training session to do, no schedule to keep, no skin flare to rush home and nurse. This new freedom, of travelling in a new city, wandering in the sunshine in the middle of the day – it's intoxicating.

Towing my backpack, I walk the little maze of boutique cafes and dessert shops beside the mall. I see why so many foreigners move here. With all the western comforts, affordable, trendy, it's like a special hub of Thailand, catered just for us.

Afterwards, I sit for an hour on a bench under some trees. It's hot, the kind of hot I like. I simmer there, watching the foot traffic go back and forth. Girls carrying iced teas from 7-Eleven, backpackers in their flip flops, grandmas with their shopping carts, young men and women zooming by on scooters. Sitting on a park bench with a smile – this used to be so ordinary, boring even. Now, I breathe it in, savour it, remembering how many kilometres I had to run to get here.

My apartment is cosy – a balcony, a small lounge, a tiny bedroom attached. A little cooktop in the corner that should sear a steak just fine. I dump my bags in the corner, then head back downstairs, ready for some exploring and grocery shopping.

Down on the driveway, I find the security guard for the building milling about aimlessly.

His name is Kiet.

Kiet is short and podgy, probably nearing fifty. He had a beaming smile when I arrived to check in, has an even more beaming smile now as he sees me again. For a guard, he's hardly imposing, without a gun or even a stick, and with the belly he's sporting, I doubt he can run half a mile. Should a robber run in and snatch a handbag, he'd probably just smile at them too.

One thing I've noticed – in Thai condos like this, the security guards always get treated like they're invisible. Residents walk right past them, so I make sure to smile at Kiet, and say hello, *sawatdee krap* – one of the twelve Thai words I know (the others are numbers one to ten, and thank you). He smiles, waves, nods, smiles again. Like I'm his boss or something.

It takes me three minutes to walk to the Maya Mall. In the basement is a supermarket, an obnoxious one, designed to bankrupt people. Ribeyes imported from Australia. Pumpernickel from Germany. I don't care. It is the last month of the year, and I just want to eat heartily, even if it costs a fortune. I roam the aisles and nothing is off-limits. Japanese salmon, tropical fruits, the fanciest loaves of bread. I have missed them all. I buy them all.

Later that night, while working on my blog, I'm distracted again by YouTube. I watch Ironman Kona 2018, again. I am losing count of the number of times I've watched it. Lucy Charles smashing everyone on the swim, winning the bike, only to get pasted halfway through the run. Patrick Lange – my running spirit animal – nowhere to be seen after the swim, then destroying everyone's faces with a course record. Daniela Ryf – stung by a jellyfish, then coming back to win it all.

Nobody thought Lucy Charles would come out this quick! Patrick Lange has taken the lead! It's a perfect day here in Kona today. Will he get a new course record?

I know the commentary almost by heart.

As I watch the final kilometres of the marathon, the competitors' grinding faces, their legs looking heavy like tree logs as they rain with sweat, my brain tells me what it's been telling me ever since I first watched it that night in Singapore. The same thing everyone's brain tells them. This is an impossible race, only for lunatics. But my heart tells me something different.

Lying in bed that night, I toss for an hour, unable to sleep. And this time, it's not due to my skin. It's because I'm imagining myself zooming down a bike course in my first triathlon, fantasising about an Ironman finish line. I pull out my phone. It's four o'clock in the morning. I start watching the Iron War, the famous Ironman World Championship from 1988. It's Dave Scott, five-time champion, and Mark Allen, the guy who had tried to beat him five times and failed. But Allen says the sixth time will be the lucky time. They are neck and neck all race. It takes them eight hours to finish, and it turns out he's right. His sixth time is very lucky. He wins by one minute.

I shut my phone off and roll over to sleep. But having this on my mind at four in the morning, I already know what it means.

We start tomorrow.

It is 1997.

I am eleven years old.

Not only was I born with bad skin, I have bad lungs, too. I have asthma. Have had it my whole life. I have a brown inhaler and a blue inhaler. I have to puff the brown one twice every morning, twice every night. The blue one is for emergencies. I keep it in my school bag, in my pocket, in the car. It goes everywhere with me.

Do you have your inhalers?

It's the first thing Mum says to me, every time we leave the house.

One day, while sitting in class, I feel my throat closing up. I reach into my bag for my blue inhaler, but it's not there. I panic. Maybe I left it in my soccer bag. Relax, I tell myself. Maybe some fresh air is all you need. I ask the teacher if I can go to the toilet. Mr Deegan, may I? He says sure, thinking nothing of it.

The toilets are in another building, so I walk down the hallway, down the stairs and make it halfway across the school courtyard before I collapse to my knees. I can't breathe. I think if I just breathe deeper, just rest here for a second, I will be able to breathe again. But I can't. They say having an asthma attack is like breathing through a straw for an hour. Now I know they weren't lying. That's exactly what it feels like.

Quickly, I start to realise — I need to tell someone I can't breathe. I need to tell them I don't have my inhaler, otherwise I'm going to die.

But I also know if my Mum finds out I forgot my inhaler, I'll get in trouble.

So I decide it will be better to just die.

I have no memory of what happens next. Does a teacher find me? Do I just manage to get a few deep breaths and recover? I'm not sure. But obviously, I don't die.

This asthma is the reason my Mum forces me to go to swimming lessons. I would guess most parents send their kids to swimming lessons so if a ferry capsizes, they'll know how to tread water, or if they go to the beach, they'll be able to enjoy the ocean without dorky floaters on their arms. But my Mum only ever gives me one reason.

You need to strengthen your lungs, she says. Swimmers have very strong lungs.

I hate swimming. Especially in winter, going to swimming is worse than going to Chinese school on Sundays. Before swim class, standing shirtless by the poolside, just looking at the water makes me tremble. After class, deep in the winter months, it feels as if my toenails will freeze off by the time I run from the pool to the changing room. There are only two showers in there, so we all huddle around – two or three of us at a time trying to get just one or two seconds of hot water before we get shoved out by someone else.

Two years pass. Two years of swimming every week, twice a week. Everyone in my class can swim handsomely now, so our coach – his name is Mike – makes up strange strokes for us to do. He is a Polynesian man with a crew cut and a big booming voice. Sometimes he makes us swim with only our left arm, or only our right arm, or only using our legs, or only breathing on one side, or keeping our heads cocked and breathing the whole time. All these stupid strokes, it drives me insane. Every week, I dream about quitting swimming and never coming back.

I can already swim! I don't need lessons!

Mum won't hear it.

You have asthma! You need to strengthen your lungs! Swimmers have very strong lungs.

So the next week, and every week after that, I show up to swim school, thinking what a waste of time it is to swim lap after lap after lap, week after week, complaining to my Mum on the car ride there, on the car ride home.

Now, twenty-five years later, I am about to find out what I should have known all along. Mum was right, again. She saw the future.

As soon as I wake, I open my balcony door to let the air in. The air in Chiang Mai has a unique aroma – like the countryside and the inner city blended into one. I love it. It is cool outside, but the sun is high and shining. Ironman videos still playing in the back of my head, only one thing comes to mind.

I want to train. And I want to swim.

I go to the bathroom, do the usual morning exam of my face. Red patches under my eyes, but faint. Peeling around my mouth. Nothing I haven't seen before. I think about taking a few more days off, of relaxing, maybe eating a little junk food. But if Dr Sato were here, he'd tell me to keep going. Keep doing your daily exercise, he'd say. Keep doing your short showers. You're healing. Don't stop now.

He probably wouldn't want me to swim, but I'm compromising.

I spend the morning Googling Ironman training plans until I find one I like.

To undertake this training plan, you should already be capable of running fifteen kilometres and should already know how to swim.

Thank you, Dr Sato. And thanks, Mum.

It's a short, intense plan. Twelve weeks, the exact number of weeks until Ironman New Zealand. Weeks one to four are torturous. Weeks four to eight sound impossible. Weeks nine and ten are definitely impossible. But the design is clean and pretty – and it's free. I feel good when I look at it. Not too many words. Simple. Fits my personality.

One week, I say. We'll try it for one week. Then we'll see if I'm crazy or not.

There's only one fifty-metre pool in Chiang Mai. It's at a stadium, fifteen minutes away. I start getting ready, then realise my obvious problem.

I have no goggles.

There is a sports store on the second floor of Maya Mall. I walk down there and ask the guy if he has swimming goggles. He speaks little English, so I make a swimming motion with my arms, then put my fingers around my eyes in circles, like you do when you say glasses in sign language.

This we don't have, he says, shaking his head.

I nod, but I know he's just misunderstood me. In a place as hot as Thailand, in a sports store as big as this, of course they have swimming goggles.

I walk every aisle, scan every shelf.

No goggles.

There is a Nike store next door. I take a look.

Still no goggles.

I go to the information desk, ask the pretty girl where I can find swimming goggles. She points to the sports store.

I shake my head.

Been there already.

Then we don't have. Try the Kad Suan Kaew Mall. Down the road.

I refuse to believe there is not a single pair of swimming goggles in this enormous mall. For the next hour, I walk through all six storeys, go into every home store, every clothing store. I end up at the movie theatre on the top floor. I go stand out on the balcony, take in some sunshine. It's too bizarre. Hundreds of shops in here, selling five hundred different pairs of useless sunglasses, Batman masks, they even sell octopus sushi imported daily from Japan, but no swimming goggles? Is that a sign, maybe?

Finally, I relent and listen to the girl at the desk. I walk to the mall down the road. It takes me fifteen minutes, and in the Thai humidity, my armpits are dripping by the time I arrive.

Consider it a warm-up.

The mall is old, and worn, and empty, but still large and full of shops. I wander through, see the sports store up on the second storey, and sigh. It's the same chain as the one at Maya, just a smaller, older, crappier store.

Exhausted, ready to give up on swim day, I decide to take a look anyway. I ride the escalator up, walk inside.

Right in front of me, the first thing I see – a big wall of swimming goggles.

The cab ride to the pools is smoother than expected. We hit the highway and the roads are free-flowing, especially compared to the gridlocks of Bangkok. We head out of the city and it feels like we're in the countryside by the time we finally arrive. I look up at the big archway as we drive under.

700 Year Stadium, it reads across the top.

Once we pass through, it feels as though we've entered an abandoned city. There's not a person in sight. It's walled by trees, and there's an enormous carpark that can fit hundreds, maybe thousands of cars, sitting empty from back to front. I do not know this yet, but this is the stadium built for the 1995 Southeast Asia Games. All these Olympic-standard facilities, built twenty-five years ago, now sitting here unused and forgotten. After today, it will become my favourite place in Chiang Mai, like a personal training facility, put here just for me.

The complex is so big, we can't find the pools. My cab driver speaks some English, enough to tell me she's lost.

Do you know where is pool?

I shake my head.

Truth is, I'm not even sure it exists. I only read about it this morning, on some blog.

She points at a pair of guys – security guards or cleaners, probably both – sitting on some benches by the main stadium.

I will ask them, she nods.

She drives up to them, says a few words in Thai. They point into the distance.

We drive for another few minutes, past more big buildings and empty carparks. Finally, she points with relief, as if to say, there it is.

As I'm grabbing my stuff to get out, she gets out before me.

I will just ask this man. To be sure for you.

She talks quickly with the security guard. Waves me out of the car.

Right place! She smiles.

Walking across the long courtyard towards the pools, it's a ghost town. There is nobody. Literally. Just me. Dead silent. There are multiple entrances, but all are closed except for one. I walk towards it, see a man sitting behind the counter, watching a television the size of a toaster. He looks as surprised to see me as I am to see him.

A big sign hangs on the wall.

FOREIGNERS – 50 BAHT.

LOCALS – 25 BAHT.

I happily hand him a fifty baht note. Then, as I head towards the pool, he stops me.

Take your shoe off, please.

Yes, of course.

I leave my shoes by the counter, and finally get up the stairs to the pool. It's grander than I expected. Much grander. An Olympic pool, crystal clear water, glistening in the Chiang Mai sun. Eight lanes with no ropes, stadium seating on either side. And one other person. A fat guy, swimming laps on his lonesome.

I've never been so excited to swim. Then I dip my toes in the water, and all that inspiration shrivels into a tiny raisin. Everything shrivels into a tiny raisin. I can't understand with the sun so bright, how the water can be colder than Frozen Coke. Then I remember, the Chiang Mai nights are brisk. An hour in the sun is nothing, for a pool this big that's been refrigerated all night.

I warm up, stretch, then dip my toes in the water again. I can't do it. I tell myself it's ridiculous, it's just water, but it terrifies me. Even the slightest feeling of cold sends shivers not only through my spine, but through my soul. I'm reminded of the nights I spent huddled by the heater, sleepless, convulsing as if it were snowing inside, desperate for my skin to hold in some heat, any heat. Like a mini PTSD, I realise that winter, *that night*, it's traumatised me. Any feeling of cold against my skin freezes me – both my body, and my mind.

I sit in the stands, stare at the water. Pep talk myself, two times, three times. Nearly an hour goes by. The fat guy is still doing laps. A machine. I savour the sun on my back, how divine it feels. If I hadn't driven so far to get here, I'd have given up by now. Gone back home to some scrambled eggs and a duvet. But I'm here.

I have to do it.

The deal is simple, I tell myself. Forget about swimming. Just conquer this fear today. Jump in, and you can get right back out. As long as you get in. As long as you conquer yourself for that five seconds.

Deal.

I stand by the edge of the pool. Brace myself. It's just a swimming pool, but it feels as if I'm skydiving, as if I should have an instructor behind me screaming, you sure you wanna do this?

Yeah. I'm sure.

Then go.

I jump. I feel the cold hit my blood like an electric shock. It lasts half a second. Maybe less. But it jolts me. And then it calms me. I stay under the water and enjoy the calm, let it flow through me, let it take over. Then I come to the surface and laugh.

So scary in my mind. And not scary at all. Like so many things in life.

I have memorised the training plan for the day:

4 x 200 metres relaxed.

4 x 150 metres vigorous.

4 x 100 metres relaxed.

4 x 50 metres vigorous.

30 seconds rest between sets.

Can't lie, sounds like a stroll.

I fit my goggles, then take off for my first set. Four laps.

I manage one. Then stop.

Yeah.

No way I'm finishing this workout.

Huffing as if I've just run a half marathon, I look over at the fat guy. He's still going. Lap after lap after lap.

What's his secret?

After catching my breath, I swim another lap. Now I'm really demolished. I don't remember swimming ever being this exhausting. I forget about doing the sets, and the speed. I forget about resting for thirty seconds like in the training plan. I do one lap, fifty metres at a time, and I rest as long as I want. Sometimes two minutes. Sometimes five. What matters is the plan asks for forty laps total and I tell myself I can go as slow as I want, as long as I finish every one of them.

Deal.

I figure out many things as I swim these laps. First, I figure out I really can only do one lap at a time. But if I swim really slowly – like a beginner – I can do two at a time.

I also figure out it's not my arms that get tired, or my legs. It's my lungs. My Mum can't even swim, I've probably swum ten thousand more laps in

150

my life than she has, and somehow she still understands more about swimming than I do. Even here, lounging against the wall while I recover, watching the fat guy sail through the water like a canoe, I can hear her voice from all those years ago. *Swim more laps. Get strong lungs.*

I'm in the pool over an hour. I get to forty laps, and my head is spinning. I climb out of the pool, proud, and smiling. The fat guy is still swimming. I wonder if he's training for some kind of swimming marathon, because he's obviously superhuman.

I wash off with the firehose by the side of the pool, then sit in the stands and watch him a while. His body is covered in dark brown hair. He's obviously not Thai. Maybe Italian, or Lebanese, something like that. Somewhere people swim a lot, because watching him now, it's as if he's on automatic pilot with an engine attached to his feet. His strokes are so effortless, his round body not only moves through the water, it glides, like a sailboat. I study him – at first watching only his legs, then only his arms, then only his breathing – trying to figure out how he's doing it. But his arms seem to move in slow motion, and he barely kicks, his breaths barely last half a second, and somehow, he just glides and glides. This guy must have the strongest damn lungs in the world.

The next morning, I can't wait to get back to the stadium. I call a cab and we take the same drive – out onto the highway, into the middle of nowhere, under the 700 Year Stadium arch. But we don't go to the pool. We go to the main arena. Today, I want the running track.

The driver pulls into the carpark, asks if this is the right spot.

I say yes. Even though I have no idea.

I walk up the stadium steps, expecting to see another *Foreigner – 50 baht, Local – 25 baht* sign, but I see nothing. Not even an open door. Everything is closed, boarded up, locked. So I walk around the outside of the arena, down some stairs, up some stairs.

Nobody.

Eventually, I come to a side entrance. The gate is slightly ajar. I slip inside, walk through the tunnel into the stadium, and see the running track sitting abandoned in the sun.

There's no way this entire track, this entire stadium, is just here, forgotten. Is there?

I step onto the track and walk a few metres. It is well worn, peeling in places, but clean. Even though the stadium stands are empty, it feels epic. Like some kind of abandoned Colosseum.

In the distance, on the opposite end, I see a groundskeeper peacefully cutting grass. I wonder if I'm allowed to be here, if I'm trespassing, if this is a UNESCO site, but he takes a quick look at me and looks away.

Either he thinks it's fine, or he doesn't care.

Both are cool with me.

It's my first run since Singapore. It's also my first time training on a track. I love it instantly. It's invigorating – reinvigorating. I'm not sure if it's from the week off or the rubber track, but my legs have so much bounce I feel as if I'm running faster than I ever have, like I'm being carried, like I can run forever.

The training plan for the day says run one kilometre, then sprint two hundred metres, and repeat it six times.

I'll raise you, I say. I'll go seven.

As soon as my watch hits one kilometre, I hit that hundred-metre line and go. Gritted teeth, knees high, everything I have. For that two hundred metres, I scream and curse and sputter and run to the edge until I hit the line again. Then I relax, jog in slow motion, get ready for the next one.

The stands of the stadium go up so high, they block the sun off the left side of the track, while the right side cooks. But Chiang Mai's midday sun is so strong that even half a lap in the sun is tough. I've forgotten my hat, and feel my face on the brink of burning. So, running on the right side I speed up, and then, as soon as I hit the shade I slow down. Each change breaks the run into mini goals, like aid stations – sunny half, shaded half, sunny half, shaded half, two hundred metres, go!

Before I know it, I've churned through my six reps. As promised, I do a seventh. For the first time in my life, I think to myself, maybe I don't hate running?

Feeling worn later that night, I indulge in one of my old Thailand traditions: Noodles and a massage. It was my nightly luxury when I lived in Bangkok, but after the last two days, it's looking more like a nightly requirement.

There is a massage shop ten seconds from my apartment, right next door. I push the door open. The bell goes *ding-a-ling-a-ling*. A trio of old ladies greets me inside.

Nervous about my skin, nervous that Dr Sato would be scolding me about allowing my body to be touched by massage oil, I opt for a leg massage only. Luckily, it's all I need. My body is fine, neck and shoulders fine. Legs in pieces.

A Thai woman, probably my mother's age, sits me down on one of the mattresses in reception. Cleans my legs and feet, then goes to work. On my long list of things I would do if I ever healed, a massage was at the very top. It feels as magical as I'd imagined.

After the massage, I walk. If walking Thai streets looking for noodles were an Olympic sport, I'd win. At the very least, I'd come second only to Mark Wiens.

I wander the main strip by my apartment, not wanting to go too far, but willing to walk until I find what I'm looking for. Chiang Mai nights are cold – much colder than I expected – and even in a hoodie and jeans, I need to sink my hands into my pockets to feel any kind of warmth. I pass a few food carts, but none grip my senses the way I'd like. They are sparser here too, the streets resembling quiet suburban roads rather than those of a big metropolis where noodle stands occupy every corner.

A few blocks down I find one which smells worthy, and the lady running it looks like she's been doing this a long time. I order the chicken drumstick noodles, then sit on my lonesome at one of her little plastic tables on the sidewalk. My order arrives in a few minutes. Just the sight of the little pink plastic bowl and the stainless steel soup spoon warms me up inside, more than a hoodie ever could. I sprinkle a little chilli, a little fish sauce. Eat my first spoonful. They're tasty, certainly not life-changing, but they give the stomach that familiar happiness. More than the flavour, it's the setting. Sitting here at a noodle stand, slurping my favourite food. My old life.

Remember to feel blessed this time, I tell myself. Remember to cherish it. Remember how fast it can be taken away.

The following day is bike day. I'm excited for bike day, except for one problem. Similar to the problem from swim day.

I don't have a bike.

I ask Google: Can you train for a triathlon on a gym bike?

The answer is yes. But you need a spin bike. Not an exercise bike.

I didn't know there was a difference.

I Google nearby gyms. There's one a ten-minute walk away. I go downstairs, say good morning to Kiet, then follow the map. The gym is across the road, which is a good thing, because it's been three days and I still haven't crossed this road. It's the main road that runs by my apartment, three lanes one way, three lanes the other. It's intimidating. Any time I find a road like this on my travels, my mind floods with worst-case scenarios – what if a cop sees me and decides to shake me down for jaywalking? What if it's super bad etiquette to cross here and everyone stares? What if a Vespa comes swerving out of nowhere and hits me? Then I'm that idiot tourist who lies dying in the street, all because he tried to cheat the highway instead of walking five minutes to cross at the lights like a good citizen.

So for the last few days, I've resisted crossing. I stick to the mall on my side of the street. I buy water from the 7-Eleven on my side of the street. I look for noodles on my side. Now that the gym is on the other side, I don't have a choice.

So I cross.

Like jumping in the swimming pool two days earlier, it's nothing. Just like crossing any other road, and it's over in five seconds. Stupid.

The gym is a boutique gym, popular with wealthy Thais and foreigners. It's on the ground floor of a small, glitzy hotel. It's one hundred baht for a day pass, and I don't even need to ask if they have what I want. As soon as I get there, I see two spin bikes right behind reception, and that's all I need.

The schedule today: Four minutes easy riding, followed by eight minutes standing, repeated four times.

Forty-eight minutes.

It sounds twice as easy as yesterday's run, and fifty times easier than Monday's swim. And it is. I'm on the bike and off the bike with my legs still feeling fresh.

Monday, Tuesday, Wednesday.

Swim, bike, run.

Welcome to tri-life.

After it's done, I sit in the yoga area and stretch. I stare at myself in the mirror as I work on my hamstrings. I look different. I've let the top of my hair grow out, but I've kept shaving the sides and back because those are the spots that tend to flare and flake. What's left is a mini mohawk, a furry grass patch running along the top of my head. I've been walking around in public like this? I hadn't noticed how ridiculous it looked until now. Maybe I just didn't care.

The best part? I still don't.

The next day I visit the pool again. I do the same number of laps as last time. My lungs still suffer. But slightly less. After training, I indulge in another round of massage-and-noodles. I head to the same massage place, for the same massage. Push the door open. Hear the bell go *ding-a-ling-a-ling*. My massage therapist is younger this time, maybe twenty-five, and speaks some English. Her name is Mi.

Your legs strong, she says. You play sports?

I run, sometimes.

You run today?

I swam.

Ooh, she sighs. Me no. Swimming cannot.

You should learn.

Yes, should.

Want me to teach you?

Really?

Sure.

She grins, then asks, what about running?

Running?

Yes. You teach me.

You don't know how to run?

Can, but not good.

Me neither.

She slaps my leg.

You good! Strong leg!

I think back to my day in the pool, laugh inside.

Strong legs? Who needs 'em.

Strong lungs – now *that* would be something.

After my massage, Mi says she will take me up on my offer. I will teach her to swim. We swap phone numbers. She is now my one friend in Chiang Mai.

The next day, I do the usual schedule – gym, lunch, shower, rest. Then send Mi a text in the afternoon. Ask how her day's going.

Do you like Japanese food? She asks.

One of my favourites.

I feel like eating it later. Want to go with me?

She gives me an address, says to meet her there in the evening after work.

Evening arrives. The cab is late to pick me up. He drives me through several backstreets, narrow like alleyways, filled with open-air restaurants, scooters swerving around us.

The look of this part of town, the aura, even the smell – especially after sundown – it's all very Chinatown.

We pull up fifteen minutes late. The driver looks around. Asks if this is the place.

Was hoping you could tell me.

There's no English on the buildings, but on the sign beside me I notice the Japanese writing. Must be it. I get out and look around, see Mi waving at me. Sitting on the patio alone, halfway through a beer.

It's a cute place. The tables are like park benches, and they're all full, smoke from the grills shooting up from the centre of each one. She holds up her glass.

Beer?

I shake my head.

I don't drink.

So healthy!

She opens the menu. I expect her to ask what I want to eat. Instead, she tells me what she's already ordered. Beef and pork, oysters, vegetables. In front of us, there's a smoking hot grill ready to be put to work. Not exactly what you think of when you hear Japanese food. I don't mind. This looks ten times better.

When the food arrives, I don't even have time to move. She grabs the plates and tongs and starts grilling away. Just sitting and watching, sweat starts collecting underneath my baseball cap. I start to worry about my skin. It's going to get red. Is it red yet? What about the flakes under my eyes? Can she see them? But she's not looking at me. She's looking at the grill, and soon she starts moving pieces from the grill to my plate. We eat everything slowly, piece by picce, dipped in garlic sauce and chased with fresh ginger. Spectacular.

When it's time to go, she asks how I'm getting home.

I'll walk.

She frowns.

It's okay. I like walking.

Okay, then I walk with you. Or you get lost.

Sure.

157

We head outside onto the pavement. Then, just as we're about to move, she hesitates.

You sure you don't want me drive you?

You have a car?

Of course not.

She points to the row of scooters parked behind the restaurant.

Oh, right. Well in that case ...

I watch as she pulls her scooter out to the main road, revs the engine and gestures me on. I hop on behind her. Just as she's about to take off, I tap her twice on the head.

Helmet?

She laughs.

Don't need!

There's a long list of dead guys who would disagree, but okay.

I tell her I live beside the Maya Mall. She nods and starts zipping through backstreets until we finally get to the main road. Then at a red light, she turns to look at me.

Your first time Chiang Mai?

Yeah.

She smiles.

You want tour?

Seeing a new city by scooter is marvellous. Literally. You marvel at the city, breathe it in, hear it, smell it. As we coast through Chiang Mai's streets, Mi manoeuvring through cars like a video game, me holding on to her for dear life, I quickly forget about the freezing wind and my helmetless head and my flaking skin. Instead, I start to marvel at this version of Chiang Mai I haven't seen before. Dirty streets, but tidy. Noisy but peaceful. Busy but relaxed. Modern but underdeveloped. A city of opposites, making it a city that has everything.

We drive past my apartment. Past the mall. Past the gym. The streets are free-flowing, save for the odd traffic light. Once we've crossed the city and my cheeks are chilled to ice, she pulls over onto the sidewalk.

Tha Phae Gate, she says, pointing.

It's like the entrance to a castle – a huge brick wall that runs the entire street, a moat surrounding it.

Come, look.

She leaves her scooter in the middle of the sidewalk and we go wander around the wall.

All around it, people are selling desserts and souvenirs. Locals lounge on benches and talk. Across the road is a Starbucks and a McDonald's. On the other side, a Burger King.

Like I said – city of opposites.

We head through the gate. She points down the main street.

You come here Sunday. There is famous market. Good for tourist.

We walk until we've circled back to her scooter. She clunks it off the sidewalk and I hop back on behind her. This time, we turn off the main road, zip down a street with open-air bars and neon lights.

Loi Kroh Road, she says.

A few girls in skimpy shorts loiter outside. Music. Bars filled with foreigners. All men. And Thai women.

Many bar, she says. But bar for man.

She waves her hand dismissively.

I pretend it's not interesting.

A few streets down, she parks the scooter again. We walk a few blocks, this time to another market.

Ploen Ruedee, she says.

It's not a usual Thai market. It's set up like a fairground, and vendors sell food from every continent – steaks, hot dogs, pasta, donuts – and of course, plenty of Thai food. In the centre, a band plays live on stage. Mi ignores it all and beelines straight for the ice cream.

She orders one for herself, then looks at me.

No, thanks.

Sure?

I don't eat ice cream.

So healthy!

But if he's so healthy, why is his skin so bad? That's what I'd be thinking.

She gets me a spoon anyway, and we sit at the trendy tables and eat. I steal a spoonful, then another. One more.

Man, I miss ice cream.

Once we've walked the whole market, we go exploring the streets outside. The sidewalks are filled with souvenir stands selling Chang beer singlets, jewellery, phone covers and crafts.

Everywhere sells elephant, she says, pointing at every second shop. Tourists really love elephant!

It's true. Every second shop has elephant carvings, elephant keyrings, elephant tee shirts, elephant jewellery.

We find another night bazaar. It's an enormous warehouse, packed with more shops.

See? More elephant. Everywhere elephant. You want elephant? I buy for you.

No, thanks. I don't eat elephant.

But only I laugh. She doesn't get it.

It is Day 207.

Saturday. The big day of training for the week, and it's bike day. One hundred kilometres.

Two things jog my brain during the walk to the gym. One – spin bikes don't have distance counters. I'll have no way of knowing when I've ridden a hundred kilometres. And two – it doesn't matter, because I'm not riding a hundred kilometres. It's impossible, at least without losing a leg. And I need my legs. I'm committed to this week of training, I really am, but riding a hundred kilometres will take around five hours, and I'm not a psychopath.

Still, it's the final day of the week. I've survived it all up to now, and I want to finish strong. So I cut myself a break: Ride for three hours. Then you can go home.

Deal.

I get to the gym, and as I pay my entrance fee, I also ask for three chocolate bars and three bottles of water. Then I head to my bike – the same spin bike from earlier in the week. It's only our second date, but I'm attached now. It wouldn't feel right riding any other bike.

I put my headphones in, line my refreshments up on the reception desk beside me, and pedal.

The sweat comes quickly. I'm always surprised when I sweat on a bike. Maybe because I'm sitting down, my brain is saying, this is easy, you're sitting. My brain has a lot to learn. And we do learn, fast. We learn that sitting on a spin bike makes things even harder because it scrunches up your hips and curves your back and kinks your neck. That's already wildly uncomfortable, but then you need to pump your legs in that position, which is just misery all around.

Twenty minutes pass. I look like I'm in a sauna. Even though there's an air conditioner working at full blast, sweat rains off my face. I feel blobs of satisfaction as I see the droplets hit the floor under me in rapid-fire – drip, drip, drip, drip.

I'm almost through my first bottle of water. I should have bought five. Then I eat the first chocolate bar. I should have bought twenty. It takes legendary self-control to resist opening up the other two and eating them straight away.

There's a cleaning lady who roams the gym, wiping down machines and continually mopping the floor. She's walked by me a few times. She glances at me now and I can tell by her two-second look that she doesn't want to stare, but she's thinking – *that's* going to need a good cleaning.

One hour down.

A guy gets on the bike next to me. White guy, chunky like a rugby player. Eighty percent chance he's Australian. You can always pick Australians, miles away, just from the way they walk, the fluoro shorts they wear. He fires up a Gary Vee video on his phone and gets to pedalling.

A Thai guy arrives soon after. Older man, maybe fifty. There are only two spin bikes. He walks straight past us, but I can tell from the way he flicks his eyes at us both, he wanted one of them. This must be his bike day too. He must be saying, who are these two *farangs* on my damn bike?

He walks by us again minutes later, lost, looking for something else to do. I see him looking at my bike, the pool of sweat on the floor.

Gross, he's thinking. That's my bike!

Then he looks up at me and we catch each other's eyes for a second.

I bounce an eyebrow, he gives a half-smile.

Sorry, mate. My bike now.

The second hour is longer than the first. Sweatier. More painful. Already on my third bottle of water. Chocolate bars long gone. Sitting is the true enemy now. My back aches, hunched like a rainbow. Anything but sitting, please. I stand on the pedals as long as I can, until my thighs cry, then sit upright until my hips cry, then go back to hunching over the handlebars until my shoulders cry. Then repeat.

Two hours down.

Now in the final hour, the finish line in sight, my legs still hurt, my back still hurts, but my mind is recovering. I've got half a bottle of water left.

That's the challenge. Get through this last hour. Make that half bottle last. Every ten minutes you get a sip. Six sips of water and you can go home.

It's only me now. The Aussie guy has done his workout, gone home. The old Thai guy got on the bike, did his workout, went home. Another Thai girl with a nicely shaped bottom in maroon yoga pants warmed up on the bike, did her workout, went home. And in half an hour, I can go home too. Just another half hour. Three sips of water. Home.

As I watch the second hand on the clock tick through the last minute, the last thirty seconds, the last five, I don't realise until I've gotten off the bike, until I've emptied the last few drops from my water bottle, until the receptionist girl smiles back at me, that I have a goofy smile plastered across my face.

As I collect my things, scrunch up the chocolate bar wrappers, I look at the splatters of sweat under the bike, already drying up. The receipts from a three-hour pedal I didn't know I could finish, and now I do.

And if I can do three hours, surely I can do four?

What about five?

What about an Ironman?

Yes, Brendan. Good question. What about an Ironman?

It is Day 208.

I wake up feeling invincible. It is Sunday. The best day of the week.

Rest day.

There's a big UFC fight on. I head to a small sports bar in the Old Town, find a seat in the corner next to two American guys. From the way they talk, the way they look, I guess they're kickboxers, probably in Thailand for training. I order a platter of tropical fruits and a hot tea, then spend the morning chatting with them about fights, sucking on cubes of fresh mango and pineapple.

When the fights are over, I go for a walk around Chiang Mai's Old Town. My legs are soft from yesterday's ride, from a week of punishment, but it doesn't matter. I walk all afternoon, unhurried, and it feels like time has slowed down with me. The hours pass lazily. The sun stays high and bright. Chiang Mai is rustic. Many shops are here just for the tourists, and filled with tourists – western-style coffee shops, smoothie bars, souvenir stands – but everything still has old wooden construction, bamboo adlibs. The smell of hot woks is inescapable and rows of scooters line the sidewalks on every street. It is everything Thailand.

On a quiet shopping street, I am drawn to a second-hand bookshop. I have walked past two already, but I can't resist entering this one. It's set up like a souvenir store – bargain bins, open-air, a cashier counter with brochures and pamphlets all over it. The shelf at the entrance is filled with famous books: *Eat Pray Love, 1984, The Lord Of The Rings.*

Down at the bottom, one with a bright pink title stands out.

The World Of Suzy Wong.

I haven't heard of it, but I feel like I have. I grab it, read the blurb, study the front cover. Flick the front page open.

150 baht.

Deal.

The store owner is a retired European man with a scraggly beard and unkempt hair. As soon as he opens his mouth, I know he's Scottish. Or Irish. I mix them up sometimes.

Do you need a bag?

No thanks.

Do you need a receipt?

No thanks.

Then enjoy, sir.

He hands me my new book and I wander the streets with it, looking for a cafe that looks inviting. Something roomy and quiet.

Across the road, not far from the Tha Pae Gate – where Mi brought me for the first stop on our city tour – I see a place that's almost empty, with outdoor seating amongst hanging flowers and palms.

It's perfect.

I nestle myself in the corner and order noodles – *khao soi* – and sesame chicken, and a matcha latte. I can hear my legs singing underneath the table, loving this day of sitting down and reading and eating cheat meals even more than I am.

The food arrives. The noodles are just okay, the sesame chicken is just okay, but I could be eating cardboard and would be no less happy than I am right now. I don't need to remind myself to be grateful. I am.

When night starts to fall, I look across to the Tha Phae Gate and see things livening. Now I remember, Mi had told me about this – the Sunday market. I ask for my bill and, for once in my life, I don't care what the price is. I would pay a thousand dollars for this afternoon. I leave the biggest tip of my life, grab my book and stroll across the street.

The Sunday market is a walking street, filled with the usual goodies – plates of noodles, Nutella crepes, fruit bags, massages, knock-off wallets and purses, and of course, elephants. The air is perfect, the afternoon heat is gone, but it's not yet late enough to be cold. I walk the street twice, then stop at a patio halfway along, where carts are serving ice slushies and fried noodles, and a talented pair of musicians are performing covers of classics in a small courtyard. I find an empty table, order a pad thai, a tonic water, and sit for an hour, listening to covers of Stevie Wonder and Maroon 5 and The Script.

When they finish, it's suddenly gotten late. My day had started so slowly, now feels gone in a flash. I start heading for home but as I walk back towards the gate, a crowd draws me to a stop one last time. They're watching four guys sitting on the pavement, singing Thai songs. Two have drums, the others have a keyboard and a guitar. They are all so into the music that their eyes are closed, lost in the harmony. The crowd loves them. I love them.

I see the box at the front, getting hammered by tips. I go to drop some coins in, and that's when I notice the sign.

Their eyes aren't closed from the music. All four of them are blind. This is how they make a living.

Fighting through your pain. Making something of it. Pushing yourself to keep on living when life deals you the rough hand. I've learned a little about that recently. I stand and enjoy their music for another half hour, leave them what's left in my pockets and head home inspired.

Now I know for sure, without a sliver of doubt – I'm going to do this Ironman.

Lying in bed at night, I feel a peace I haven't felt in a long time. I have never enjoyed a day of travelling so deeply. It wasn't just cheat day, or rest day, or Sunday. It was everything I've missed, everything I prayed to be returned to me. Five years ago this was an ordinary Sunday. Now it's extraordinary again, and always will be.

It is Day 215.
My final weekend in Chiang Mai.
My alarm clock goes. Three a.m.

Since leaving the corporate world, there's only been one thing I'll let an alarm clock wake me for – a flight. But now there's a second thing.

A race.

My clothes are prepped. I tape my feet. Lace up. Pin my race number to my shirt. There are no nerves this time. This is nothing new to me now, except for one thing.

My race number doesn't have my name on it.

Instead, today I am running as Kriangsak Boonnopamorn.

Earlier in the week, I'd noticed the training plan had a twenty-one-kilometre run for Saturday. A half marathon. And it seemed almost like fate, finding out the Chiang Mai Marathon was being held the same weekend.

How much cooler would it be to run in that, instead of running around the track fifty times?

But of course, things weren't so simple. The half marathon event had sold out weeks ago.

I start thinking – surely there's a way. Surely. At least one person has to be injured. At least one person has flunked on their training and isn't showing up. At least one.

Surfing through some Chiang Mai running groups on Facebook, I eventually find hundreds of people exactly like that. Kriangsak replies first.

Yes, he says. I'm stuck in Bangkok this weekend. Please buy my race number.

Would be my pleasure.

The following day, after going to the athlete check-in and picking up his race number, I tell him I don't have a Thai bank account. If I could send him some money some other way.

Don't worry about it, he says. Donate the money to a charity you like.

What a guy.

As usual, my charity is Stand Tall International – founded by my friend Masha, who arranges spinal surgeries for kids in East Africa. Then, all over my socials, I share Kriangsak's donation, asking if people would repeat his small act of kindness. Let's pay it forward. Many do. We raise over two thousand dollars.

I've barely slept. Two hours, maybe. But I feel good. Fresh. I slug as much water as I can. Then, with Kriangsak's name and number pinned proudly on my chest, knowing I'm running for him, and for me, and for Stand Tall, I head downstairs in the morning dark to catch my cab.

Kiet is there, asleep in his booth. I tiptoe past, not wanting to wake him, but there's no need. He's in another dimension. Snoring away. Gate unlocked. Wide open.

Airtight security. Nothing to worry about.

My cab is waiting in the driveway. As I hop into the backseat, the driver looks at me in the rearview.

Tha Phae Gate?

Yes sir.

Mayaton?

Excuse me?

Ma-ra-ton?

Oh. Yes. Marathon.

Okay!

The city is asleep. Only a few cars are on the road, but we're all going in the same direction. Not only do I see them, I feel them. That familiar buzz of race mornings – I don't know if it's in the air or just in my mind, but you feel it, like everybody's energy funnelling together, ready to create a massive collection of magic moments. For some people, this will be their first marathon. This will be the race where they cross that line and nothing is ever the same again. There may even be a TSW warrior on that course, running through the same battle I fought two months ago. I know it better than anyone – lives change forever on race day.

We pull up to the Tha Pae Gate, and it's unrecognisable. It looks nothing like it did on Sunday market day. It looks nothing like the day Mi first brought me here. All of Chiang Mai is silent except here, where thousands of us are being herded in blue and pink Chiang Mai marathon singlets. A huge festival tent and stage are plastered with sponsors. Mini stalls are everywhere. Ushers are waving people down the street. I've arrived just in time. The full marathon has already started, the half marathon has about ten minutes until the gun. No time to stretch, no time to even check I'm in the right place. I just follow the crowd, to the start line.

It's messy. No seedings, no pacers. No one even checking race numbers. Anyone could walk in here and run. Not only is it messy, the crowd is scrappier too. Less fancy running gear, more everyday socks and sneakers. I like it. This is the kind of race I belong in. I push myself as far forward in the crowd as I can go.

What's my time going to be?

I don't know, I've never run in a half marathon before. But let's try and go. Fast.

The gun bangs. Cheers whimper out of the crowd. Slowly, we inch forward to the start line, faster, faster, until I'm jogging – and then we cross.

I weave in and out of bodies for a while, as the crowd starts slow, like the Singapore race. I'm restless. I want to clock a good time, and I'm not going to do it starting like this. To the side, I see a pair of guys, technically off course, but running free of the crowd, zooming down the sidewalk.

Great idea.

I join them for at least half a kilometre, and we pass hundreds of people before the sidewalk ends and we merge back into the crowd.

Up here, we're moving smoother, at a pace I like.

Perfect.

I have no idea what roads we're pounding, but I know we're around Tha Pae Gate, because of the big stone wall beside us, and the moat. I knock the first few kilometres down comfortably and as I see the markers pass by me on the roadside – Kilometre 1, Kilometre 2 – I can't believe how good it feels to know I'll only be running twenty-one kilometres today and not forty-two. It's as if you sat down for an algebra exam and the teacher said; don't worry about doing the second half, we'll give you that for free.

That's what this feels like.

The first aid station arrives. I zap two cups of Gatorade. I feel fresh, strong. One thing about racing this early in the morning – the weather is perfect. Literally. No wind. Cool, but not nippy. Air clean. If God gave me an app and asked me to design the weather for race day, it would be exactly like this.

As my pace wavers, a little too slow at times, I remind myself it's a short race, to keep working. I tell myself at each kilometre marker to pound out thirty big powerful strides, like it's the last kilometre of the race. I count them out – one, two, three – all the way up to thirty, every single time, to make sure each kilometre starts strong and finishes strong.

The first ten kilometres go down like a milkshake. Easy and delicious.

The race is not a big deal here in Chiang Mai. Or at least it seems that way. The roads aren't even closed. They're just cut in half by orange cones, and we're sharing them with morning traffic. The aid stations are manned by only one or two people pouring Gatorade. Somehow, though, everything is operating flawlessly, like clockwork. The course is uncrowded. There are no lines at the aid stations. The cups are arranged perfectly on the tables. And it's a joy to run. Completely flat. Perfect weather. And takes you right across the city.

Things toughen as the second half starts. My legs are softer now, my knees are softer. I'm hanging out for Gatorade more and more. I see a guy in front of me and instantly I know that's the guy I need – calm, and running steady. I slot in behind him and stick to his heels, match his rhythm, so I don't need to think. I just run.

I hang with him until fifteen kilometres. We enter a more industrial area. Wider roads. Very quiet. Every race seems to have this point – on the back half, where things start to feel a little lonely, a little more painful. The sun still hasn't risen. The street lights beam strongly, but above them the sky is still pitch black. And the roads are still silent, except for us.

A girl passes me. White girl. Twenty-five maybe, or a little younger. Sandy blonde. Very pale. I get a quick glimpse of her face – freckles, quite pretty.

I don't know her, of course, but I recognise her from fifteen minutes ago. We passed each other several times a few kilometres back. Looking at her now – her nice New Balance singlet, her running belt, her purple shoes – I can tell she's super serious about this running stuff.

Alright Purple Shoes. Me and you. All the way to the end.

I look at my watch. I have time. If I put on a little gas right here, I'll beat two hours. I'm conscious that I need to refrain from destroying myself today, that I'm straight back into Ironman training tomorrow, but I feel good. I pick my legs up and get moving, leaving Purple Shoes behind me. But I know I'll see her again.

It's the last quarter now. Five kilometres left. We run through another park, a few side streets. I have no idea where we are, just that we're shrouded in trees and it looks like some kind of cycleway. Then we emerge onto the highway for the final three kilometres.

There are barely any cars. Still no hint of a sunrise. And Purple Shoes is back. Beside me.

My legs are heavy. She passes. I know I can stick with her but I'm hurting, and I'll hurt a lot more if I try to tail her. I let her go. Three kilometres doesn't sound like a lot, but it is. Especially when you're so close to the end and you wish it were just one kilometre, and it isn't. So all you can do is say *fuck me* and keep on running.

We hit the Kilometre 19 marker.

Two to go.

On this final stretch, the road is perfectly straight, down the side of the highway. Nothing but wide open pavement ahead of us. Beside me, on the other side of these cones, the highway is slowly coming to life. And I guess – I know – all these people in their cars and trucks are staring at us through their windows saying – did you know there was a marathon today? Or, look at all these runners! Or, what I would be saying – who would want to wake up early on a Sunday to do something like this?

One kilometre left. Now I can let it all go. I look at my watch. I'll break two hours easily. If I really go, I'll break 1:55.

I flick the switch in my legs and we move. By the last kilometre of a race I am usually half dead, but today I'm not nearly dead at all. Just tired, just hurting, but easy-mode hurting. Holiday hurting. Half marathon hurting. It would be an insult to even think about *that night* right now.

Up ahead I see Purple Shoes. I gain on her. Pull up beside her. Pass her. I think she's surprised to see me. I've named her Purple Shoes. She's probably nicknamed me Pink Shoes.

This Pink Shoes guy is back? Really?

As I pass her, I can hear the finish line in the distance. It's minutes away. We turn off the main road, up a little ramp into the final park. As I'm running up, Purple Shoes pulls beside me again. I get a glimpse of her flickering eyes, the grimace on her face as she edges ahead. She wants to beat me, she must beat me, she's giving it all, every last step. I can almost feel the weights in her thighs as she goes past.

In David Goggins' book, *Can't Hurt Me,* he talks about *taking souls.* When there's something, someone, trying to beat you, when they think they've done everything possible to defeat you, when they've given every last drop and they know there's no way you could possibly give more, that's when you do it. You stand up and roar with the strength of a thousand men – and take their soul.

It's exactly what I think about as I see Purple Shoes' face flash beside me. Like the Chinese girl at the lake took my soul that night, I'm going to take her soul right now. In front of us is a two-hundred-metre stretch right to the finish line. I can see the Thai dancers waiting at the end. I give Purple Shoes three seconds in front of me, then I sprint. Right past her, so close our shoulders brush.

I know she has nothing left. I know she can only watch the pink soles of my feet as I tear away at full speed, all the way to the line. Wondering how I had the legs. Thinking, damn, Pink Shoes. Too good for me today.

I sprint across the finish line with a smile on my face and my arms outstretched. Thai dancers welcome us to the finishers' area filled with free food and bottomless Gatorade and a cute little medal. As I sit there in silence, eating and drinking with hundreds of other runners, the sun finally breaks the horizon.

We've all run twenty-one kilometres, and Chiang Mai is just waking up.

When I get back to the apartment, limping up the driveway, Kiet sees the medal around my neck and beams, clapping. He speaks no English, so doesn't know how to say what he wants to say, but his eyes say it all. He's very impressed.

I want to tell him, don't be. Everybody gets a medal. He's smiling at me as if I won the whole thing.

Normally, after a race, I spend the day basking in the post-race glow, but not today. Not only is today race day, it's also my last day in Chiang Mai. I know the Maya Mall inside out. The 700 Year Stadium has become my personal playground. I've half-marathoned the city streets. In three short weeks, it's become home. And now it's time to leave.

Sadness pinches me like it does every time I leave a new city, but I'm okay this time. I've spent most of my time alone, training. I don't have anyone to say bye to – except maybe Mi. I haven't seen her since that one night we met, my first week. The Japanese feast and the scooter tour. I text her.

Hey. I'm flying tomorrow.

Already!?

Going home for Christmas.

So sad!

Let's meet after you finish work?

Okay. Want to go here?

She sends me a poster for the Nimman Sunday Market.

Yes!

Ok. Meet you there ten o'clock.

I lie on the couch, still half dead. Groaning at the thought of hurrying to cross the road on race day legs.

I grab my phone again.

Can you pick me up? I can't walk.

She sends the frown emoji. I send the smiley one back.

Evening arrives and Mi picks me up at ten o'clock sharp. I get on the bike and tap her head again.

Still no helmet?

Don't need!

This time, I might even agree with her. The Nimman Market is less than a minute away, opposite the Maya Mall. It's a big market – half outdoor and half indoor – lively and chic and not what I'm used to from a Thai market. There's spaghetti and donuts and lattes and a giant wok of hot coals where people roast their own marshmallows.

I buy us a couple, oversized and fluffy and white, perched on sticks and ready to toast. As we stand there waiting for them to melt, we talk about the race, how I never taught her to swim, what I've been doing this last two weeks.

So you just 700 Year Stadium every day?

I shrug.

Why so much?

I think of how to explain it.

Well ... a long time ago in Hawaii, some swimmers and runners started this race ...

I can't. It will sound too ridiculous. To both of us.

After we've scoured the market and eaten the oiliest, unhealthiest, heart-attack-inducing foods in Thailand, she points to the rooftop of Maya Mall across the road.

You been to top?

Again, I wonder if I can explain.

Yes, once, I was looking for swimming goggles and the lady told me there weren't any but I didn't believe her, so I spent the whole morning looking through every store, and ended up at the roof ...

But I just say yes.

Yes I have. Once.

She nods.

It have nice view at night. I show you.

We take her scooter down into the basement carpark, ride the elevator up. The whole mall is closed, but the roof is open for the one bar up there that opens late. The balcony is large – the size of a tennis court – and charming in the evening moonlight. A few people are milling around, taking selfies, a few couples are having a romantic moment over the view of the city.

Chiang Mai – people rave about the place, but it's not much to look at from above. Ordinary. Unimpressive. But you soon learn it's the little things, between the streets, the second-hand bookshops, the roasted marshmallows, the marathons that give you free McDonald's at the finish line. I think that's where people fall in love with the place. At least, that's what I'll remember.

Mi pulls up a photo on her phone.

My daughter.

You have a kid?!

Yes.

Are you married?

No.

Where is she?

My home. Chiang Rai.

But you live in Chiang Mai?

For job.

You must miss her.

Of course. What about you? You have kid? You marry?

I laugh.

Why it's funny?

I point at my face.

Do I look like I'm married?

No. You look like just gym every day.

We laugh.

Exactly.

It's late when we finally leave. She pulls out of the carpark to drop me home, and as we wait at a traffic light she turns and asks:

Do you know temple?

Temple?

In Chiang Mai. Famous temple on mountain.

I shake my head.

I take you? Tomorrow, before you go airport.

I bite my lip.

I can't. I gotta go to the gym.

You can miss the gym for ONE DAY!!

She slams the handlebars with her palms as she yells it. I almost brace myself for a crash.

It is famous! You need to see.

I'm in shock from being scolded. I don't say anything.

We pull up at my driveway a few minutes later. Miraculously, Kiet is awake. I wave at him, then climb off the bike and smile at Mi.

Okay. Temple.

She nods.

But have to go early. I pick you here, seven o'clock.

Where is it?

Far. Driving forty-five minute.

On your scooter?

She looks at me as if I'm stupid. I am stupid. It's Chiang Mai. Of course we go by scooter.

Okay, I'll meet you here?

I point to the ground.

She nods again, happy.

Seven o'clock.

Then, just as she's about to drive away, I stop her.

Mi, wait.

She looks back at me and I tap her on the head.

Can you bring me a helmet?

The morning air is crisp. I didn't have a chance to appreciate it when I woke up the day before, preoccupied with getting to the race on time. But today I notice it the minute I step out the door. The kind of morning freshness that makes you think, why don't I wake up this early more often?

I say good morning to Kiet. He's surprised to see me up so early again. Second day in a row.

Then, as he opens the gate for me, I see Mi waiting at the bottom of the driveway. Or I assume it's her, because it's her scooter, I just can't see her face.

She's wearing a helmet.

She pulls the visor up and gives me a dry smile. Then gets off the bike, lifts up her seat. Pulls out a second helmet and hands it to me.

Okay!?

Yes, I smile. Okay. Very okay. Thank you.

The helmet feels brand new. It's not, I can tell by the fade, but I can also tell it's been worn three times and been on a bookshelf ever since. I pull it on. Fits like a glove.

We head out of town on a road I've never been on before – the opposite direction from the gym and Tha Phae Gate and Maya Mall. Of course, to Mi, this is a bore, she's driven this road a thousand times, but to me, everything on this road is new – every restaurant, every 7-Eleven. I smile under my helmet. Maybe I should've spent a few more days away from the stadium. I'd forgotten about this – this feeling of being fascinated with the everyday. This is why I fell in love with travelling.

Mi points up, into the distance.

Mountain. You see? We go there.

I've never noticed it before. It's huge, half hidden in the fog. She wasn't lying, it is far. And tall.

As Mi drives, I doze into a slight daydream. My legs ache. It's too early for me to be awake. I don't even realise we've reached the mountain until we're very obviously driving up the mountain. Mi senses me starting to look around and shakes her head.

Only halfway, she says.

The road up is steep and winding, but wide and well paved. Luckily it's early, so the cars are few. In fact, there seem to be more cyclists than cars. And not just cyclists going for fun Sunday rides. Hardcore cyclists with expensive bikes, multiple bottles strapped to their frames and spandex suits. They're all foreigners. Is there some international cycling club in Chiang Mai? Or is it just a secretly great city for cycling?

Then I realise – if I do this Ironman thing, this is going to be me for the next few months. Cycling up hills, early in the morning. Judging by the looks on their faces, it doesn't look fun at all.

Finally, we arrive at the summit. It's nothing but a carpark. Several groups of tourists and tour buses. Some souvenir shops lining the sidewalk. Not much else.

As she locks up the helmets, brushes all the hair out of her face, Mi grins at me.

Buy water. We walk many stairs!

I have a handful of coins in my pocket that need spending before my flight. We buy three bottles.

Two minutes later, I see what she means. We get to the staircase to the temple, and it's big – but not three bottles of water big. Maybe a couple of sips big. You can see the top. It will take us ten minutes, tops. Then I'm reminded, it only looks that way because I've been living in running shoes this month. Correction: This year. Not for Mi. It seems like this will be the most exercise she's done since high school.

We climb for five minutes, then stop and rest. I hand her the water. A few more stairs. Stop and rest again. She looks at me and laughs hopelessly.

This is why I go to the gym, I tease.

She scowls.

Very funny.

Once at the top, we take off our shoes and she leads me through the temple. It's actually a collection of temples, or at least looks that way. Lots of gold. Lots of statues. Lots of locals lining up to pray. In a sacred place like this, after the year I've had, you'd think I'd be compelled to say a prayer as well. But I don't. I'm compelled to behave like every other tourist, taking selfies, asking stupid questions, standing at the viewing deck looking out over Chiang Mai. But she was right, I did need to come here. Not even for the temple. Just for the morning scooter ride, the mountain air, so I could go home and tell everyone I climbed the staircase.

Thanks, Mi.

When we finally get back to the city, it's barely ten o'clock. Still three hours until I need to hit the airport.

Breakfast?

She drives us back to the Old Town, to a quiet street with a couple of restaurants. As usual, she pulls into a tiny alley and parks her scooter. I'm amused at how unworried she is about it being stolen, or her helmet being snatched from her handlebars. There's also no parking warden to be afraid of, no machine to fill with loose change so your scooter doesn't get towed.

Just think – my own stadium, tropical fruits, massages, no parking fees. I think I'd quite like living in Chiang Mai.

The restaurant is nothing more than an abandoned garage with a wok at the front, street food style, slabs of roasted pork hanging in the display cabinet. Out the back, a pair of grandmas laugh while making salads. There are five or six tables with the usual four-sauce combo on each, and a tray of spoons and chopsticks.

Mi orders rice, I order noodles. They come out steaming and fragrant. It's the type of smell that makes even your nostrils salivate, but they're so spicy I choke on the first slurp and can't stop coughing. Luckily we still have two bottles of water from the mountain. Over the course of one plate of noodles, I drink every drop.

After we're done, we sit and talk, picking at a plate of peanuts until Mi has to go to work. I tell her I'll get a cab home. We say goodbye with a hug. She smiles sadly. I tell her I'll be back to teach her to swim, someday.

It's astounding, how fast you become connected to someone, especially on the road. This is only the third day Mi and I have seen each other. I've spent maybe seven or eight hours with her, if that. I don't even know her last name. But she's my only friend in this city, and it's a thousand times more a home because of her.

I get back to the apartment with just over an hour to pack and hit the airport. I start gathering my clothes, and as I'm rolling up my gym gear, I think about it.

Could I?

I could ...

But will I miss my flight?

No – if I really try, if I go right now, I can do it. Unless I want my first black mark on the calendar today, it has to be done now.

I throw my gym clothes to the side, then start packing at rapid speed. I've packed this backpack so many times, I should have a degree in packing backpacks by now. I can do it in three minutes. Less, if my life depends on it.

Laptop, toiletries, clothes – I whiz around the apartment and snatch it all up, manoeuvre it into my backpack the usual way, like a game of Tetris.

Done. Record time.

I fill up my water bottle, throw my gym gear on. Run down the stairs to the second floor, to the apartment gym. It's not the best gym – quite a shitty one in fact – but doing this here instead of at the nice gym down the road will save at least fifteen minutes in walking time.

There's also a spin bike in here. It's shitty too. But it's all I need.

On the training plan today is a one-hour bike ride, but I figure if I go extra hard for forty-five minutes, it's the same thing. I was wrong. It's harder. Luckily the gym is empty, because I'm whimpering and groaning and blaaa'ing until the agonisingly slow clock hits forty-five. Then I'm out. Drenched in sweat, I run back up to my room, shower, change, call the cab.

It arrives in a few minutes.

Not only will I make the flight, I'll be early.

Too easy.

There is one final person to say bye to. I come down with my bags, and Kiet gives me the same smile he's given me every morning and afternoon since I arrived. I wonder if it's just a mask, or if he really is always this happy.

While the driver loads my bags, I walk over to Kiet, shake his hand, say thank you. I pull out the last two hundred baht I have in my pocket. He looks surprised, and suddenly the smile on his face is gone and he's serious. He puts his hands together, makes a praying motion.

Kop kun krap, he says, bowing.

No man. Don't bow, you're making me feel weird.

He timidly accepts the cash, and his smile comes back.

That's more like it.

I shake his hand one more time.

Thanks, Kiet.

And goodbye, Chiang Mai.

14

It is Day 225.

January first.

After Chiang Mai, it was a short week in Sydney for Christmas and I'm back in New Zealand.

New Year's Eve comes and goes. I spend it sober, eating sausages with friends. They laugh at my new haircut. Laughter with love, of course. I wear long sleeves to cover the scars on my arms, but the ones on my face, I wear proudly.

Just like that, 2019 is gone.

The worst year of my life is officially over.

I've made something else official, too.

Ironman.

In nine weeks, I'll be lining up for the toughest race in all of sports.

New Year's Day is traditionally a day to reflect, be grateful, rest, but as soon as my eyes open I can only think about one thing. I check the training plan. Thirty-kilometre ride.

I pull my old bike out from the garage. It's an old hybrid mountain bike, barely used. I kick the tires and give them a nod.

Yeah, they can handle thirty.

Since I'm not a cyclist and never have been, I mix and match a cycling outfit with what I have in my wardrobe. An old jiu-jitsu rash guard, aviator sunnies, some yellow compression leggings I bought at the outlets. As I head out the door, I do a once over in the mirror.

Glorious.

I start down the driveway. Past Laura's house. Past James' house. Up the hill. The same route I've run over a hundred times. Now I ride it. And the first surprise comes quickly. On my first run, all those months ago, I gassed out after two kilometres. On my first ride, I'm gassing out after one. This is nothing like riding a spin bike. There's no uphill on a spin bike. And this bike is heavy as a truck. Even on the lowest gear, I barely make it to the top.

Then the downhill starts. Sweating heavy, breathing heavy, I rest my legs and let the bike roll. One cool thing about the bike: If you stop working on a downhill, you still keep moving.

I wish running was like that.

I ride past the shopping centre, all the way to the park with the skateboarding ramp. Over these few kilometres, I realise that first hill wasn't so terrible after all. Just a shock to the system. They get easier, and after an hour around the neighbourhood, my thighs have been worn in. But it's still only one hour. Can they handle seven?

For the week that follows, I spend every evening reading about bikes. Spokes. Tire tubes. Gears. The difference between a road bike and a triathlon bike. Alloy versus carbon. Women's frames versus men's frames. Aero bars versus no aero bars.

Seriously – what the hell are aero bars?

That's before I find out there's practically aero everything. Aero helmets, aero frames, aero bloody drink bottles.

If I can't even figure out which drink bottle to buy, I'll definitely never figure out which bike to buy. But one thing will certainly save me. The same thing that saved me with TSW.

Facebook.

I join the biggest triathlon group and introduce myself. I tell them my grand plan to race at Ironman New Zealand on twelve weeks training and I'm already a few weeks in. I share the free training plan I got online from some random website. And then I ask: Please tell me which bike to buy.

I expect ridicule. They're going to laugh at me. They're going to tell me I'm delusional and to stop wasting their time. But one by one the comments come in, and I couldn't have been more wrong.

You're mad, but good luck.

Cheering for you!

Will be tough. But anything is possible!

That's when I know I'm in the right place. Still, I don't suspect for a second that this group could be anything more than a bunch of internet strangers. But they will be. They'll never meet me, never even see my face, but they'll end up teaching me everything I know about triathlon. And they'll be watching it all from afar on race day.

Right away I get good tips. Great tips.

Buy a road bike, someone says. A tri bike is a special monster you don't want to deal with yet.

Roger that.

Get aero bars, says another. You need them.

Sure, once I find out what they are.

Get the right size bike. Too big or too small and you'll be miserable. And most importantly, get your bike right now! Yesterday! Last month! Ironman is fifty percent bike! You need to ride, ride, ride, ride, ride!

I don't like shopping in general, but bike shopping is the worst shopping of all. Especially second-hand bike shopping. Sometimes the bike is good, but the size is wrong. Sometimes the size is good, but it doesn't come with wheels. Sometimes there are great wheels, but it's twenty years old. Sometimes it's almost new, but the colour is terrible.

You can't ride a lime green bike, can you? You'll look like a cartoon character.

By the time Saturday rolls around, I'm still bikeless. Nothing but my trusty old mountain bike sitting in the garage. And it's a 100-kilometre ride today.

I go and kick the tires.

Yeah, they can handle a hundred.

Except this time I'm not sure if I believe it.

Then I give my thighs a punch.

Can they handle a hundred? That's the real question.

I've got the perfect place where I can find out. Out in west Auckland, a forty-minute drive from my house, is a public park. There's a playground, a walking track, lots of grassy fields, and hidden away to one side is a treasure I've never heard of.

A velodrome.

I make the long drive out, and it takes me a little while to find it. When I do, my heart sinks. It's an outdoor track, littered with leaves and fallen twigs, the odd broken bottle, but worst of all – it's built funny. It slopes up steeply on either end, so that I'll be riding on a lean as I ride around the bends, like in the Olympics. Doesn't that mean I'll fall off? Unless I'm riding really fast, which I won't be.

Of course, I don't know this yet, but this is exactly what every velodrome is supposed to look like.

Already convinced that I can't ride here, I almost get back in the car and drive home. Then I think – since I'm here, might as well try.

I walk around the track, kick off the twigs and beer cans. It's shrouded by two huge overhanging trees on either end. In the middle is a grass field made into a running track with lanes painted on. That might be the oddest part of all, because if not for that, the place feels totally abandoned. Like me before today, I'm sure most people in Auckland don't even know this thing exists.

I haul the bike out of the car, wheel it onto the track. At first – when riding around those up-turned bends on either end – I ride up the slopes, then turn around and come down, like I would on a skateboard ramp. But as I get warm and move a little faster, I learn to turn the bends cleanly, pedal into them, lean with them, and the slopes actually help.

So that's why they build them like that.

Excited, I stuff my earphones in and put on an audiobook. *Can't Hurt Me* – David Goggins. Yes, again. I've already read the book, but I can't think of anything I'd rather listen to on this ride. It's different too, reading it through my ears instead of my eyes. Listening to it with my thighs burning and the wind on my cheeks.

It starts with the story of his childhood – Goggins' maniacal father making him work all day and night, tormenting his mother, beating him from the neck down with a belt buckle. I'm so absorbed, I almost forget I'm riding a bike.

The chapter ends. I look at my watch.

Four kilometres.

REALLY. FOUR KILOMETRES.

Feels like thirty already.

I measure the next few laps with my watch, and realise I've got around two hundred laps to go. Since a lap goes by reasonably quickly, two hundred doesn't sound like too long. But I'm wrong. It's going to be very long. Longer than a marathon. Longer than I've ever exercised in my life.

My watch beeps every five kilometres. The first five take sixteen minutes. The second five take sixteen minutes. The third five take sixteen minutes.

An hour passes.

Two.

Man, this is a lonely sport.

And this velodrome is a lonely place.

This audiobook is a lonely story.

Only fitting, since TSW was the loneliest journey of them all. Maybe that's why this lonely velodrome will soon become my third home, after the lonely stadium in Chiang Mai, and the lonely loop around the lake. Maybe it's not a coincidence I keep finding these places. All those nights spent suffering on my lonesome, I became good at being alone, and in pain. Now it seems that's all I know how to do.

I hit fifty kilometres. Halfway. Three hours.

Time for dinner.

I ride off the track, through the carpark and up the road to the gas station. There's a little bakery cabinet in there and I load up on junk food – the best kinds of junk food – chicken nuggets, mini pies, beef jerky, a couple more bottles of Powerade. With brown bakery bags scrunched in one hand, I ride back down to the track, sit and eat. A bag of soggy chicken nuggets never tasted so good.

In my absence, an Indian guy has arrived. As I nibble on chicken nuggets, I watch him stretch on the grass. It's around six p.m., and the sun is starting to set. My guess: He's some corporate guy, working Saturdays for his big company, but knows he needs to get some running in if he wants to live long and not go crazy.

A few minutes later, a guy arrives with his kid and a soccer ball. My guess: Judging by the hypo kid, he's been bugging his Dad all day to take him to the park to kick the ball. Now that the temperature's cooled a bit, they're here.

In the background, a few couples are out for their evening walks, strolling down the walking path along the far side. In the playground by the carpark, a guy shoots hoops with his son. Place doesn't feel so abandoned anymore. But luckily nobody else with a bike arrives. The velodrome stays empty, still all mine. All mine with fifty kilometres left to go.

I knock off another thirty. Now the sun is long gone. The kid and his soccer ball, the Indian runner, the romantic strolling couples – also long gone. Luckily, I at least have the moon, because there are no lights on this track. If not for the moonlight and a few lights in the carpark, I wouldn't be able to see five metres ahead of me.

Suddenly David Goggins' voice cuts off, and I get a beeping in my earphones. It takes me a few seconds to realise it's a phone call.

Hello? Bren? Are you okay?

Yeah.

Where are you?

Riding my bike.

Still?

Yes, Mum. Still.

Are you nearly finished?

Yes, I lie.

Okay, please don't be riding in the dark. It's dangerous.

She's right, it is dangerous. But not the kind of dangerous she's thinking. She's thinking I might crash into a car because it's dark and people won't see me. She doesn't know that's impossible because I'm at the velodrome, and there's literally nothing on the velodrome, not even light. The kind of dangerous I'm thinking of is; some lurker might be watching me, hiding in one of these tall trees. He'll throw a bottle at me and steal my bike and car, then leave me bleeding on the track and nobody will know I'm there. Because why would anyone be riding a bike at the velodrome at eleven o'clock at night?

Luckily, I'm at ninety-five kilometres, which means only ten more laps. Maybe twelve. Unless this lurker makes his move in the next twenty minutes, I'll be home drinking protein shakes before midnight. I think about the first time I saw a hundred kilometres on the training schedule, that first week in Chiang Mai, and I knew it was impossible. Didn't even try. Just sat on the spin bike for three hours. Today, I've been on the track more than six.

Ninety-eight kilometres.

My legs don't even feel anything anymore. I'm a robot. Round the track. Pedals go round. Wheels go round. Round and round and round. Batteries still charged with Powerade and chicken nuggets.

One hundred.

The watch beeps. I smile at the screen. I'm not just smiling. I'm laughing. They say it's a special feeling, one of the most special, to finish your first hundred-kilometre ride. I finish the lap, ride to the carpark, dismount. Load the bike in the car. I have two chicken nuggets left, drowning in their grease stains at the bottom of the brown paper bag. I savour them one by one, while sitting in the driver's seat and staring at the track.

They're right. Pretty damn special.

It is Day 230.

I can't remember – is this lap seven? Or eight?

You wouldn't think keeping count would be difficult, since there's literally nothing to distract you. You can't listen to music, can't look at anything around you. Just the big black line at the bottom of the pool. But I've already lost count once, now it's happening again. I'm sure it's lap eight. Isn't it?

I have a two-thousand-metre swim today. The outdoor pool at the gym is finally open for the summer – a fifty-metre Olympic, like the one in Chiang Mai. Only it's nowhere near as big, or peaceful. There are kids playing on one half, three swimming lanes on the other. A lifeguard too.

Two thousand metres is forty laps. This lap must be number nine, I think. I need to check somehow. I try to figure out a way I can look at my watch while swimming, without interrupting my stroke.

Maybe when I turn?

I try it. Impossible. Too many bubbles.

Maybe, when my hand enters the water, I can turn my wrist and pause for juuust a split second and look?

I try it.

LOL. Nice try.

And are we on lap ten or eleven now? Now I've really lost it.

Let's say it's lap eleven, and it's probably more like lap thirteen but you're going to over-swim today because you got distracted trying to look at your watch. So now just swim and concentrate. And count.

So that's all I do. Every stroke I say lap eleven, lap eleven, lap eleven … until I hit the wall and it becomes lap twelve, lap twelve, lap twelve.

My shoulder starts to hurt. I think back to the swimming lesson I watched on YouTube last night. My elbow needs to be higher. I try to prop it up on the next stroke.

Like this, right?

But that doesn't feel so good.

Let's try something else. Maybe it's like ... that?

I dunno. I need to watch the video again tonight.

Anyway, what am I going to eat after this swim? Chicken? Nah, steak. Definitely steak. Oooh – and eggs. Maybe some tomatoes. That sounds good. I wonder what happened to that pretty Pocahontas girl who was running at the lake last year. Haven't seen her in months.

Oh shit. Is this lap thirteen or fourteen?

Thirty minutes pass. Lap thirty-nine now. I think. Only one more left. But I feel good.

Keep going?

Let's keep going.

I do a few more. Make it to lap forty-five.

Keep going?

I hit lap fifty. How odd. Not feeling more tired. Nor less. Just the same.

Let's do sixty?

Lap sixty. If my counting is right, I only need to do sixteen more laps – just sixteen – and I'll have done the Ironman distance. Seventy-six laps. 3,800 metres.

Deal.

I'm reinvigorated. These lungs have come a long way since Chiang Mai. Literally. The final sixteen laps are easier than the first.

I hit the wall.

Stop my watch.

Rip my goggles off, check the screen.

3,800 metres.

A miracle.

Not the distance. The counting.

I was right all along.

After a few deep breaths, I sink into the water, look back at the lane. One hour, thirty-three minutes. Even I'm surprised. Other than a sore shoulder, fresh as a bunny. I did it, Mum. Stronger lungs than ever.

Once I've had a moment to recollect myself, I head straight to the sauna. There are three types of guys you meet in the sauna. There's the guy who just smiles at you when you walk in, then never looks at you again. There's the guy who might say, hey, how's it going, and that's it. And there's the guy who says, hey, how's it going, and then won't shut up the entire time. When I step inside, there's one guy in there alone. I've never seen him before. Tall, wiry, looks like a science teacher. And before he even opens his mouth, I already know he's the third type.

Do anything interesting for New Year?

I shake my head.

You been working hard today? In the gym?

In the pool.

Oh yeah, training for something?

Yeah, actually. Triathlon.

Oh wow! That's fantastic. I did a triathlon, once. Never really much of a runner or swimmer, but spent a lot of time on my bike. It's the hills that hurt you, easy to underestimate them. The hills. You find that?

I nod.

Me too, he says. Every time. I usually need to stand up. And go down a gear. If there's a gear to go down to!

He hoots with laughter. Must be a teacher. Teachers are masters at laughing at their own jokes. Plus his voice – it's a lecturer's voice. Doughy and poshy. Like a history professor.

Do you practise your transitions a lot? You pretty fast at 'em?

I can see it, looking at him now – he's lanky, but there's some muscle in his legs, his calves. Old cycling legs.

I shake my head.

It's actually my first tri.

Oh! Great! When's the race?

Taupo. In March.

Is it a sprint? How long's the bike?

Hundred and eighty.

Kilometres?

I nod.

Sheezus, what kind of triathlon is this?

I squirm a little in my seat. It feels weird to say it.

It's Ironman.

Wow, and your first one! That's something.

He laughs again as he stands up. He's reached his sauna limit.

Well, you're brave. Good on ya. Good for you. Good luck. Best of luck.

It is Day 237.

I'm back in the pool. I'm excited to swim these days. Every night, I watch a YouTube video from my favourite channel, *Effortless Swimming*. I write notes on each one. After a few nights, these notes have become an endless list of things to try – moving my head less, keeping my elbow higher, keeping my stroke straighter when I pull. Swimming used to be my nemesis. Now it's one big physics experiment.

After each swim, I post my stats on the Facebook group. I tell everyone what I changed, how much faster it made me. I even record a few clips on a GoPro and share them, asking for tips. Like my personal coaching team, they pick my form apart and point out all my uglies.

Rotate less.

Kick less.

Glide more.

I like the sound of that. *Glide more.*

The sky is spotless today. Splendid day for an outdoor swim. I'll have the sun on my back, my skin will love it. The water will be warm. A perfect day to learn how to glide more.

As soon as I start my laps, I slow everything down – my kick, my arms – and put all my effort into gliding. Each time I pull, I pull with everything my shoulder has, *whoosh*, and let myself glide.

Two laps, rest. Two laps, rest.

Am I doing it wrong?

I must be doing it wrong.

I'm half a second more glidey, but ten times more tired. Everything looks great when you watch it on YouTube. Then you try it in the pool and it's like you've never swam before.

After a handful of laps, I notice a kid beside me. At first, I thought it was just a coincidence – this person constantly swimming at the same speed as me in the next lane. For one lap, maybe, but every lap?

Now as I'm about to start my next lap, I see why. This kid is ready to go, goggles on, staring at me, waiting for me to start.

He's racing me.

I take off. Once again, he takes off with me. My eyes stay on the black line on the floor, but I still see him alongside me, a good glimpse of him every time I breathe. All I want to do is practise my stroke, work on gliding more, but this kid is churning his arms at full speed, and he's going to beat me.

C'mon. Let him go. He's a kid.

I ignore him, and he flies off ahead. As I finish my lap, I see him already lounging against the wall, waiting for me again. Looking smug. He can't be older than ten. Twelve tops. He watches me pull up my goggles, grins. A grin that says, I beat you.

Yeah, kid, you beat me. But did you glide like me?

Sixty seconds pass. I pull my goggles back on. He does the same.

Here we go again.

We take off together. I stay relaxed, stay thinking about my elbow, stay thinking about gliding more. He starts pulling away again. I can't resist. I put on a little speed, stay with him. I can see him kicking furiously, giving everything he has, but I give just enough to stay an inch ahead, nothing more. We hit the far wall and turn at the same time. I feel him tiring, but he's still giving everything. He knows. He knows I'm racing him this time. His arms are frantic. I see his face as I turn to breathe, and can tell he's using the last bit of oxygen his lungs will give. Then, about twenty seconds from the wall, I can't resist.

Let's do it.

Let's take his soul.

I peel away from him at full speed, like there's prize money waiting at the end. Instantly I see him disappear behind me. I can feel his eyes follow me as I surge ahead, watching my feet propel away from him in a cloud of white water. Then, as I'm about to hit the wall, I know he's expecting me to stop. He's expecting he will hit the wall just a couple of seconds after me, and we'll both stand and huff and puff, exhausted.

But I don't stop.

I dive into a turn, bounce off the wall and burst into another lap.

As I take off, I glance behind me underwater and see him stand and watch as I leave him behind. He's not coming with me. I try to picture what his face looks like. Watching me swim away for another lap like I'm just warming up, while he heaves in buckets of oxygen.

Of course I'm not just warming up, my lungs are busted as hell, just like his. But I don't let him see that. All he can see is the glide.

I knock off two more laps. As I'm about to finish, I look ahead to see if he's still at the wall waiting for me. But his lane's empty.

Where'd he go?

I hit the wall, pull up my goggles and look around.

There he is. Sitting on the benches. Given up swimming for the day.

Sorry, kid. Just killing some demons.

It is Day 240.

Here to pick up a bike, I tell the guy as I walk in.

Which one?

It's a red Giant. Extra small.

Oh yep, saw it this morning. I'll bring it out for ya.

After second-hand bike shopping for weeks, I've given up. Today I'll be getting a brand new bike.

The guy disappears into the back of the store, comes wheeling it out seconds later.

I love it instantly. Slick. Fast. Shiny brand new. GIANT in big red letters along the frame.

You sorted all the parts for it? Pedals, bottle cages?

I pause, look up at him.

Did he just say pedals? Two thousand dollars for a bike and it has no pedals?

I shrug.

Actually, I have no idea. This is my first road bike.

Oh yep! Yep.

He pulls two boxes off the shelf behind him, drops them onto the counter.

You should probably start with these. Pretty standard Shimano pedals. Most roadies have 'em.

As I'm checking the price tag, he walks over to the middle of the store. Pulls a few things off the shelf.

These are bottle cages. Got a favourite colour?

Yeah, red.

Cool, red it is. How about bottles. Red as well?

I nod.

Yes. Everything red.

By the time I leave, I've got a new bike, and a whole two boxes of shopping. Pedals, shoes, bike pump, chain lube, bottle cages, bottles, toolkit, glasses. I thought training a million hours for Ironman was bad enough. Looks like you need a million dollars as well.

The weekend arrives. I'm back at the velodrome. I pull my new bike out of the trunk, roll it onto the track. Lean it up against the railing.

I decide, if we're going into battle together, I better give this thing a name.

Tokuko.

She started me on this journey. Now she'll finish it with me too.

My first ride with Tokuko isn't what I expected. I'd imagined myself effortlessly zooming around the track, holding fifty kilometres an hour like a speed demon. Instead, it's awkward. She's definitely fast, but my back aches quickly, and she's hard to balance, and for some reason, I'm barely coordinated enough to click my shoes in and out of the pedals without falling over.

I do a short ride, then go home and share the news with my Facebook group.

They all have the same answer.

You need a bike fit!

It is Day 246.

It takes me a while to find it. Out by some car yards, down a back alley, hidden away from everything. It's the kind of alley where you'd expect to find a bunch of old warehouses, a fleet of delivery trucks, maybe a few car mechanics. But this is where my new bike guy is supposed to be.

I know nothing about him, except that he fixes bikes, and he's the first result on Google for bike fits. Now, driving through this scruffy back alley, I start to doubt whether I've chosen the right bike guy.

I don't see it at first. Then right in the corner, down the back, I spot the little sign.

Performance Bicycle Tuning.

It's an old garage. Big roller doors. Small row of bikes outside.

I pull Tokuko out of the car and wheel her across the alley.

How's it goin' man?

He appears almost out of nowhere.

Hey. I'm here for a bike fit?

Awesome! I'm Ben.

He stretches his hand out.

I shake it.

Ben looks like a cyclist. He is tall – borderline freakishly tall – like he could play in the NBA. He has a shark-toothed grin, sharp blue eyes, and spiky blonde hair caked with gel. At a guess, he's forty-something, but could pass for late thirties – maybe from all the cycling. His arms are a little doughy, but his calves are the size of cannons.

Cool Giant, man!

He runs his fingers along Tokuko's frame, checking her out. Then his eyes stop on my front tire. He frowns.

What have you done here?

Ran over some glass.

Hmm. We'll have to fix that up first.

He grabs her and wheels her over to the far wall. Clamps her into his little machine. Raises her up. Pulls the wheel off. Peels the tire off. Cleans it out. Grabs a new tire tube, slides it in. Pumps it up. Lines up the chain, clinks the wheel back in.

I watch him in silence, amazed. I already know getting the wheel in and out like that, would have taken me three YouTube videos and an hour to figure out. He cruises through it in less than a minute – like making a bowl of cereal.

Maybe he is the right bike guy?

Once he's cleaned up Tokuko's tires, I follow him upstairs to his office, or second workshop. A blend of both, maybe. He fits Tokuko into a stationary trainer, then tells me to hop on, lean down on my aero bars and pedal. While I do, he asks questions, like a job interview.

Your first Ironman?

My first tri, actually.

It sounds ridiculous saying it out loud. Even more so, saying it to a guy like him. So I add – I've run a couple of marathons though.

Awesome, he says. Awesome. And how's your training going?

Good. Kinda crazy.

196

Yeah, it is crazy, right? You done any long bike rides yet?

I've been riding at this velodrome, actually.

Oh yeah, out west?

He knows it. Of course he knows it.

I can't ride anywhere else, I shrug. I get spooked by cars on the road.

Yep, he nods. Takes a while to get used to.

It's only been three or four minutes, but I start breaking a sweat. I didn't realise a bike fit was going to involve a workout. He asks me a few more questions, fiddles with some tools at his desk.

More minutes pass.

Now I'm sweating for real.

How much longer is he going to make me pedal? He's been talking, looking at his phone, looking around the room – everything except watching me ride.

Then, almost as if he's reading my mind, he grabs his pen. Kneels down beside me.

See that?

He points his pen at my knee, as my legs go round and round. We both look at me in the mirror on his wall.

Too much bend, he says. We want your leg almost straight when you reach the bottom of the cycle. Not totally straight, just almost. If there's too much bend, you're giving up power. If it's too straight, you'll hurt your knees. So we need to lift you up. Half an inch.

Now look back here, at your bum. Your seat. It's too far back. See your shoulder?

He taps it with his pen, then taps my elbow.

We want you to be ninety degrees here, and ninety degrees here. So we need to move you forward. Just a bit.

As he talks, he circles me, like a mechanic fine-tuning a car, explaining each adjustment methodically, like a math teacher.

He pulls up my sleeve next. Taps the back of my arm with his pen.

Your triceps. See how they're flexing? They're too tense. You shouldn't be tense. Nothing should be tense up here. We want relaxed. You're going to be in this saddle a long time. We want comfortable, relaxed. But powerful too. And *aero*. Some fellas have a big gut hanging down here, they can't lean forward too much.

He grabs his pen, pokes my stomach.

You don't have that problem though. So we can get you more aero. We'll drop your handlebars a tad, slide this seat forward. We'll get a bit more weight to the front of the bike, and we're gonna get you way more aero.

Alright, hop off.

I get off and take a seat on the couch. Try to hold back my smile.

He's definitely the right bike guy.

First thing he does is pull my seat off. Rips it apart. Starts clinking all the pieces around.

What were your marathon times like?

About four and a half.

Woooo. He reaches over and gives me a fist bump, catching me off guard. Wasn't expecting that to impress him.

At Taupo though, I'll probably be running around six?

He stops playing with my bike seat for a second. Takes a quick look at me.

I'm gonna guess you'll run around five.

Really?

It's not too hard, the run course. You've been training. It's easy to tell who's been training and who hasn't.

Ben keeps talking about the race. He talks about it as if he's been there before, many times. Then he starts telling me stories – one year this happened, another year that happened. I start thinking – Performance Bicycle Tuning – it sounds familiar now, I've seen it before, heard it before. And then it clicks – it was in the Ironman rulebook. Hidden somewhere in all those pages.

The crew from Performance Bicycle Tuning will be on the course to give mechanical support.

It's his team, his company – the official bike crew for Ironman New Zealand. It's Ben who will be out there on race day, driving around fixing everyone's punctures and broken chains. Ben won't just be my bike guy. He's *the* bike guy. Everyone's bike guy. The entire country's bike guy.

After this clicks, I spend the next hour bombarding him with questions. How to navigate the mass start in the swim? How hard is the bike course? What are the aid stations like? What happens if I break a chain? Have you ever had someone crash super bad? Like they couldn't continue? How many people quit on the run?

Everything I've wanted to know, everything I thought was too stupid to post in that Facebook group, I ask Ben – and he knows. He almost knows too much. He talks about the bike course in terrifying detail.

All depends on the weather, he says. I was down there last weekend and the headwind was so strong, it cut our speed in half on the way back.

He grins, as if it's funny. Doesn't sound funny to me.

Then as the course zig zags, he continues, the wind blows across you at an angle. So you have to lean into it one way. Then the course bends and you lean into it the other way. The people down the back, the really slow guys – it gives them some trouble.

I wasn't nervous about the bike before, but I am now.

Don't worry, he says, like he's reading my mind again, or maybe just my face. That's not going to be you. You're going to be fine. You're a little guy, covered in muscles. Lots of power. You're going to be just fine.

After about an hour of tweaking, Tokuko is a different bike. He's tilted her aero bars up slightly. Moved them closer together.

More aero, he says.

He's also lifted the seat up. Lowered the handlebars.

More aero, he says again.

And he's shifted the saddle forward – a lot. And tilted it down.

So it doesn't crush your balls, he says. And – more aero.

15

It is Day 249.

If a fortune teller had told me six months ago I'd be going to Japan in the middle of winter, I'd have laughed and said, you couldn't even pay me to do it. And if she insisted I'd be there, I'd already know the reason. I'd be there to check into Dr Sato's clinic, because TSW has me on suicide watch.

Yet I've just landed in Tokyo. It's the middle of winter. I'm not on suicide watch. And I'm not here to see Dr Sato.

I'm here for a better reason. Maybe the best reason.

Love.

I've been friends with Shinji for twenty years, and in two days he's getting married. I hate winter, my skin hates winter even more, and when my skin hates something, I know I'm going to hate it too. But I love Shinji, and Shinji's in love, all my best friends are here for love, more than anything I love noodles, and Japan makes very lovable noodles.

Strength got me through an entire New Zealand winter. Surely love can get me through one week more.

Shinji has booked us rooms at the Prince Hotel – the nicest hotel in Yokohama. I land in Tokyo and it takes me an hour to get there from the airport, jumping trains and asking strangers to translate maps and signs. In my old life, I used to live for this, craved it – talking to strangers, adventures in strange places, ready to check into my hostel dorm and paint the town with my new roommates. Right now though, all I want to do is get to the hotel and put the heater on. All I think about is my skin, how long I have before it flares, how much my skin hates the cold. Because there is only one word to describe Japan in winter: Cold.

I get to the hotel. The rest of the boys – Peter, Tam, Andrew – flew in earlier in the day. They're waiting for me in the lobby.

Heeey, yooo, Japan, eeeh.

Dinner?

Of all the things we could eat in Yokohama, it's burgers for dinner. Not even Japanese style burgers. Good old-fashioned American hamburgers. We walk one block, two blocks, see the burger joint. Next minute, we're inside.

Since there's nothing much else to do except eat, after we down the burgers, we walk another one block, two blocks, end up in a noodle joint.

Shinji joins us a few minutes later. I'm surprised to see him.

Aren't you getting married tomorrow?

He shrugs it off. Then looks at me.

Thanks for coming, Bren.

Wouldn't miss it brother.

He pauses for a second. Then reaches over and hugs me.

That's when I realise, he gets it. Travelling to the other side of the world – it was the last thing on my wish list these days, and he knows. Maybe that's why he's out here, late at night on his wedding eve, eating noodles with us.

I wake around seven o'clock the next morning. My first look in the mirror tells me what I already knew. My skin hates this place. My face is starting to peel already, the troubled spots around my body have been itching all night. But even on vacation, even if the skin sucks, one rule still applies, every day until race day.

Gotta get one in.

I lace up. Sweatpants. Hoodie. Beanie. Take the elevator down. As the doors at the hotel entrance slide open, an icy gust smashes me in the face like opening a freezer door. It doesn't just feel miserable, it looks miserable, sounds miserable. It's six degrees. Feels more like minus sixty.

I've got ten kilometres on the schedule today. I run out of the hotel entrance, hood up and tied tight, breathing fog as I drift through the city streets. Yokohama is a grey city, at least in February. Clean, free-flowing, lots of tall buildings, some colourful signs, but the buildings themselves – all grey, everything generic. Every street lines up straight, in a perfect grid, all indistinguishable from one another, except for the odd familiar logo I see on every second one – McDonald's, 7-Eleven, Starbucks, Lawson.

I know there's a river a few blocks over. It runs right through the city. I could see it from the hotel. I go looking for it, find it. It's wide with well-paved banks and stretches further than I can see, with a pleasant surprise: Runners. One or two. Then as I run a few more minutes, three or four more. Five, six, seven, eight. Plus some walkers. Some bikers.

In Auckland, you'll hardly find anyone running on winter mornings. But here, we're quite a few. Maybe around here, we're a little less crazy.

Or more.

I'm still figuring that one out.

I don't know where this river goes, or when it ends. All I know is my face feels like an ice pack and I'm going to run until my watch beeps ten times – that's ten kilometres – then I'm going home. To be warm, and eat. That's the only thing on my mind. Food. Hot food. Our hotel rooms include a breakfast buffet. I wonder if they have salmon. It's Japan, they must have salmon. Right? And udon noodles. Am I allowed to eat udon noodles?

Dude, you're running in the freezing cold on holiday at seven o'clock in the morning. Eat as many udon noodles as you want.

I come to a bridge. Not wanting to go too far and get lost, I cross to the other side of the river, then start heading back towards the hotel. It stands in the distance, towering over the rest of Yokohama.

I look at my watch.

Two kilometres.

Eye roll.

The body slowly warms. The cold weakens. It starts to feel good, the iciness on my face. Eventually, the riverbank intersects with one of the highways of the city. As I'm waiting at the lights to cross, I notice a park under the highway. Tennis courts, fields, a big running track around the outside. And people. Not just a few people. Lots of people. Hundreds, maybe. Running, jumping, playing soccer, tennis, doing aerobics.

What's up with these Japanese people? It's not even eight o'clock. Cold enough that my fingers are feeling like ice cubes.

More crazy. Definitely more crazy.

The crossing light turns green and I get moving again. But now I veer away from the river, down towards the park.

I have no idea how to get down there, but I'll run until I do.

Hunting for a way into the park leads me across one bridge, two bridges, through a few more lights. I finally see a narrow path off the highway leading down below. It takes me exactly where I want to go.

I get there, and I'm dazzled. Ten years on the road, hundreds of cities, and Yokohama might be the fittest city I've been to. This is the last thing I expected to see when I left the hotel this morning. Old people, young people, kids, couples. Jogging. Training. Playing sports in the morning fog. I've never seen this so early on a winter morning, anywhere. Then I realise – of course I haven't. I'm never awake this early in the morning.

The running track is cool. It's not a perfect circle, or oval. It winds and swerves, past different sports fields and tennis courts and ponds and trees. From the back end of the loop, I can just see the Prince Hotel, standing tall in the distance.

How far away is that? Two kilometres? Two and a half, tops?

That's my guess.

I decide I'll run the loop until my watch hits eight kilometres, then two kilometres back to the hotel will make it ten.

As soon as my watch hits eight, I take the first exit I see. It leads me past the big Yokohama sports stadium, through some tunnels, up some stairs and back onto the main road.

Yokohama is coming to life now. Sun in the sky, morning traffic, morning faces. That unmistakable hum and smell of a waking Asian metropolis. I have no idea where I am, but luckily, it's impossible to get lost. I just look up at the sky. For the Prince Hotel. It towers over everything.

A few blocks pass. I recognise the subway station. The big coffee shop. I'm getting close now. I look at my watch.

9.6 kilometres.

I remember this street, we walked here for dinner last night. Two more blocks. Maybe three.

9.7 kilometres.

I've judged it perfectly. I know I have. I can see the hotel building. I take the back entrance. My watch reads 9.9 kilometres when I go through the doors.

The back entrance takes me through a shopping mall, then a long stretch where it connects to the hotel lobby. I see reception in front of me, across the wide-open space where the escalators are.

I'm still running. People turn and stare as they hear the *tack-tack-tack* of my sneakers on the tile floors. Then, just a few metres shy of the lobby, my watch beeps.

Ten kilometres. On the dot.

The boys are at breakfast. If I were hot and sweaty, I'd shower first, but because I'm cold and sweaty, I feel kind of fresh. I head straight to the restaurant.

Yes, there's salmon. And udon noodles. And steak and bacon and eggs and cookies and cakes and fruits and sausages and potatoes.

Ironman diet? What Ironman diet?

I eat it all.

Two hours later, we arrive at the church suited and booted. It's been a while since I dressed up, since I saw Shinji's family, since I hung out with my friends. Thinking of it now, it's been a while since I did anything normal. Normal as in, drinking with the guys, going out for burgers – the stuff I did in my old life. I don't look like my old self either, with my half-shaved head and new skinny face. And my old self certainly never ran ten kilometres on holiday before breakfast.

As I walk in, I wonder if people will recognise me. Shinji's sister, mother, old friends. If they do, will they say anything? Will their eyes linger on the skin peeling on the side of my face? But they recognise me just fine. They look at me just the same. They either don't notice I look different, or don't care.

Maybe it's about time I started doing the same.

After the ceremony, as we sit at our tables in the wedding hall, the hostess starts calling names for speeches. She walks by our table and stops. Looks at her sheet. Calls my name.

Me?

Yes. You.

I stand up and take the mic. I know what people must be saying to each other. Or thinking. What kind of haircut is that? His skin looks kind of red. Is that the new fashion in New Zealand?

I don't mind. I'm doing it already – not caring.

Then I find out, it's not an impromptu speech. Thankfully. She just wants to ask some questions, hear a few stories.

How did you meet Shinji? What are some things that make him a good friend?

I can do that, no problem.

I say a few things. Even get a few laughs. Only when it's over, when I'm sitting there with a full belly eating all the foods I shouldn't be eating, and taking the honourable shot of sake – the first taste of alcohol I've had in a year – do I see how special this is.

Laughing, eating. Pain-free. On holiday. Surrounded by my best friends. How I'm already forgetting to be grateful.

If Shinji had gotten married six months ago, I wouldn't be here. No way I could have shown my face then. No way I'd have had the strength to get on a plane. I barely had the courage to leave my house, let alone fly across the world. In forty years, when we'd reminisce about Shinji's wedding, looking at the old photos, I would have been missing. Another moment TSW would have taken from me.

But I'm here.

16

It is Day 269.

I'm back at the velodrome. Now armed with Tokuko 2.0 – fitted by the bike wizard Ben – I'm ready for my final training challenge. I've done a 3.8-kilometre swim. I've done a marathon.

All that's left – the 180-kilometre ride.

I arrive mid-afternoon, armed with half a dozen bottles of electrolytes and half a dozen Clif Bars. If it takes me six hours, I'll be beaming. If it takes me seven hours, I'll be happy. Eight hours and I'll be satisfied. Nine hours will be disappointing, but still a win. Truthfully, as long as I survive it, that's all I need to know.

In my headphones, Goggins. Again. I listen to his book, his podcast interviews, and with his words in my ears, it's impossible to quit. I don't have a team, I don't have a coach, so I've had to invent them. My swim coach is Brenton, the *Effortless Swimming* guy on YouTube. My bike coach is Ben. I won't talk to him again until race day, but he's turned this bike into a rocket, and answered a hundred questions. My teammates are the triathlon Facebook group, even though I've never met any of them except through words on a screen. And my personal trainer, my motivational coach, the guy who tells me to stop being a bitch when things get really hard – Goggins.

This is my Dream Team, and they don't even know it.

I start easy, down a gear.

Get to twenty kilometres without a problem.

Up to full gear.

Thirty kilometres ticks by. Forty.

It's long and slow, but my legs are used to long and slow now. They don't mind it at all.

Two hours gone. Fifty kilometres.

Sore back. Sore balls. Time for a break, but I don't need one. Just a Clif Bar, a few sucks of my water bottle.

On to sixty kilometres.

Seventy.

My watch beeps every five kilometres, and each beep is like a jingle of joy. One more down. One less to go.

I stop for a minute, change out my bottles, get straight back on.

Three hours gone.

It's five p.m. now. Early evening. Kids are arriving in the carpark, bunches of them, carrying soccer balls and wearing long yellow socks. Two guys drag soccer goals onto the grass in the middle of the track.

Shit. It's game day.

I don't know what kind of mini-field soccer this is, but apparently, it's super popular. There are five, six, seven teams. Eventually they're standing all over the track, kicking balls against the railing, jumping out of my way at the last minute.

Are they serious? Don't they know what this race is?! That I'm training for *Ironman*?! The most important race ever invented? In the history of the universe?

I look at my watch.

Seventy-five kilometres left. Three hours, give or take.

There's no way I can finish this here.

This is the third week in a row my ride has been stopped short – by a track team, a soccer team, the rain. I'm boiling inside. Wishing I could just tell everyone to fuck off so I can suffer in peace.

I drive home angry. It's almost six p.m. The sun is setting, darkness is an hour away. I grab my old headlamp from my backpacking days, affix it to my helmet. Put on my Dad's safety orange vest. Tie one of my fluoro headbands to my arm. I'm not sure if it's enough to stop me from getting killed, but it's all I have, and right now, I don't care.

Tokuko and I hit the roads. Seventy-five kilometres left. I know if I ride the same loop that I used to run, past Laura's house, past James' house, all the way to the skateboarding park and back, that's seven and a half kilometres.

Ten loops of that and we're done.

Darkness falls. I know I need to ride fast-ish, to keep my pace, but it spooks me, riding too fast in the dark. All it takes is a guy to whip out of his driveway, a guy to turn up a side road without seeing me, and Tokuko's in pieces. I'm in pieces. I'm already in pieces, but I'll be in more pieces. Unfixable pieces. My skin already doesn't work. I don't need legs that don't work either.

But I can't resist. When the downhills come, I soar. Not only because I want this ride to end, and I need to milk every bit of speed out of every downhill, but because I'm still seething, still cursing at those stupid soccer players, and the rush is too much. Riding in the dark, alone on the road, no cars in sight, bike wobbling at fifty kilometres an hour.

Sheesh.

Then as we hit the uphills, I need inspiration. I can't have my headphones in while riding on the street, so I can't listen to Goggins. Instead, I listen to myself.

Hey Brendan, how's it going?

Yeah, fine. Just riding my bike for seven hours.

Why you doin' that?

Good question. Not really sure. To heal my skin.

Really? Riding a bike heals your skin?

No. Not really.

Then?

Your mind – it heals your mind.

And your mind heals your skin?

Something like that.

How?

Because the evil that broke my skin is the same evil that's going to break my mind. And I won't let it. I'm going to finish this bike ride. This evil is trying so hard to stand in my way – sending me shit skin and shit weather and stupid soccer players – and at the end of this bike ride I'm going to laugh at it and say, you tried so hard. You tried so hard to break me, and I'm still here. And then my watch is going to say 180 kilometres and I'll smile and say, you failed. All this time you've been trying to break me, and you failed. Look at what the fuck I just did.

I pass my driveway again. It's been four hours at the velodrome, three hours on these streets, and now there's just one more lap. Seven and a half kilometres. I ride the first quarter easy – past Laura's house, past James' house, up the hill. Then I hit the downhill and thrash it. I should keep my eyes on the road, but I can't. I keep glancing at my watch going up – fifty, fifty-three, fifty-four kilometres an hour.

Can I hit fifty-five?

I hit fifty-five.

In the back of my mind I'm thinking, you're going to crash. It's the last lap, middle of the night. In the movies, this is exactly when the guy would crash.

But I don't crash.

I get to the skate park. This is halfway. As I turn to go back, I put the gas on. It's completely dark now, the air is crispy cold. I don't even know if my head torch is still on. I don't care. I'm riding uphill, and it usually smokes my thighs, but the end is so close, I don't feel anything anymore. All I can think about is getting home, having a hot steak and a hot shower and an icy cold protein shake.

I top the hill. Cruise the easy downhill past James' house. Past Laura's house. And just as Laura's driveway runs past me – a minute before home – my watch beeps.

180 kilometres.

I laugh loudly into the night.

One eighty!

I scream it again and again.

One eighty!!!!

If anyone were walking past me, if anyone were watching me from their window, they'd think I was a lunatic. I don't care. Just the sound of it is absurd. Is this watch right? Did I really ... ride one eighty?

Then I think back to when I started at the velodrome, back in the afternoon. So many hours have passed, it feels like that was a different day.

I pull into my driveway. Ride Tokuko into the garage. Dismount slowly on wobbly legs. And as the garage door closes, I take one more look at the night sky.

Yeah. Look at what the fuck I just did.

It is Day 278.

My last big training day before the race.

140-kilometre ride. Twenty-kilometre run.

I arrive at the velodrome early for once. Sun is high and bright. Little wind. Couldn't have asked for better.

Seeing the empty track, bathing in sunshine, the thought of spending the day here is almost peaceful. The lake felt like a second home, 700 Year Stadium felt like a second home, but this velodrome really is a second home. Some days, I spend more hours here than I do in my own house.

I think back to the first time I came here, when I almost didn't get on and ride because the slopes looked funny. Now I know everything about this place. The hall beside the velodrome is a running club. That's their track on the grass in the middle. They train on Tuesdays. There are soccer goals out the back, which they bring out for the mini-league on weekends. There's an Indian guy who comes on weekday evenings, runs around ten laps and goes home. Two guys sometimes come down and do a circuit in the afternoons. One guy – I think he's a sprinter – comes to practise his starts every now and then. On Saturdays, a church group uses the clubhouse for rehearsals. In fact, everything here seems to get used a lot – the hall, the running track, the playground by the carpark. Everything except the velodrome. Sometimes the odd kid arrives on his bike, rides around twice, gets bored and leaves. Other than that, nobody seems to ride here except me.

Since I've arrived early, there's no rush. I start slower than usual, eating my breakfast cookies as I knock off the first laps. I've done so many laps of this thing, it doesn't even feel like work anymore. Just round and round, automatic pilot. 140 kilometres doesn't even sound hard in my head. Just long. I've got a podcast on, some girl named Courtney Dauwalter. She's just won the famous MOAB 240-mile ultra-marathon. Blitzed the guy who came in second by over ten hours.

As I listen to her talk, it strikes me how normal she sounds. Like a girl you might meet waitressing at Denny's. She giggles at her own jokes. Says she likes nachos and beer. You would think someone like her would be famous for being superhuman, but she isn't. Like the rest of planet Earth, I've never heard of her.

There's no prize money in ultra-running, she says. No fame up for grabs. We do it just for us.

I nod my head as I pound the pedals.

I get it, Courtney. Spending my Saturday riding around this track three hundred times. Maybe it's stupid. But there's nowhere else I'd rather be.

I guess the ride will take me five and a half hours. By the second half, it looks like I'll clock in just under, but the last ten kilometres is a killer. Somehow on these rides, the first ninety percent ticks over in normal time. Then the final ten kilometres count down in slow motion. A special kind of torture. All I want to do is get off the bike and run, set my back free, set my hips free, set my aching ass and balls free. But this final ten kilometres feels like it's hanging on by its fingertips, like some jaded politician, dragging out a few more years to secure a pension.

Finally the watch beeps. 140 kilometres. I load the bike back in the car, walk onto the track.

Twenty kilometres to run. Then home. Play some Nintendo. Eat some steak and watermelon.

Strangely, after a ride like that, a twenty-kilometre run is almost an afterthought. A warm down. It's not, obviously. It's going to be long and painful, but in my mind, it just feels like the last little bit of training for the day. As if, now that the bike is done, this is the easy part.

I've been riding in circles for nearly six hours. Now I run in circles. I run barefoot this time. The grass soothes the feet. Raw. Wholesome. There are triathlon motivational clips on YouTube and I have my favourite one on repeat, banging in my headphones.

Why pay the price?

Why work this hard?

It's the back half of the afternoon now. The sun is starting to dip, but still shining hot and bright. It hits me in the face as I run the far end of the track. Some people hate running in the sun, but I love it, I crave it. The cold gives me PTSD, the sun heals me. My bottles are stashed on that side of the track, and every few kilometres, I reach down and grab one as I run past, do a lap while sucking on it, then throw it back in the pile.

Twelve kilometres down.

Now it hurts. Everything hurts. My lungs, my feet, my hips. I shake my head. No way I'll walk. No way I'll stop.

Fourteen kilometres.

The same clip continues in my headphones, over and over.

Why try to do everything?

Why try to be everything?

Because nobody knows what I went through. Because nobody else is out here running as far as I am.

Why try to become all that you can possibly become?

Because I can run forever, and nothing can break me. Ever again.

Sixteen kilometres.

My legs are starting to give up. I've been moving for nearly eight hours non-stop, and they're begging for me to stop. But I can't stop. I don't know how to stop. The more it hurts, the higher I lift my knees, the higher I push my chest out. *Run to the edge.* I move faster and faster until the pain has withered away, I feel nothing but strength. I'm screaming now. I don't know what I'm saying, but I'm screaming to the world, to the track. To TSW.

You don't know me! You never knew me! You chose the wrong guy. You never dreamed I would fight you like this, did you? Have I taken your soul yet, TSW? Are you even still here?

But I don't need to ask. I already know. TSW saw me on the bike earlier and didn't even bother to look twice. It wants nothing to do with me anymore. I don't even have time for those three letters anymore. I've got something bigger in front of me, something greater.

Nineteen kilometres.

Pain rumbles through my body, from the creases in my toes to the tips of my earlobes.

If your goals aren't powerful!

The words blast in my headphones.

If your vision isn't clear!

You sure you want this? Every step counts. All or nothing. You can't stop one kilometre short on race day, and you can't stop one kilometre short today. Every piece makes up the whole. Push. Push! You didn't ride for five hours and run around this track fifty times so you could stop one kilometre short.

The old prophet said, without a vision we die!

Final laps.

Without a vision we perish!

I can see the end.

Without a dream, we are nothing!

A hundred metres left.

I sprint it.

My watch beeps.

Twenty kilometres.

One hour, fifty-six minutes.

I walk over to my bottles. Sit cross-legged on the grass. The sun is sitting just above the horizon – low enough to be only lukewarm, but still high enough to shine on my face. I sit there for a while, let my mind unwind. My legs are destroyed, but my lungs feel brand new. I'm ready. I know I am. I've never dreamed of doing anything this big, never even dared to think about it. Yet I've never been more ready for anything in my life.

That's when the words bang in my headphones one last time.

Without a dream, we are nothing.

17

Almost 27,000 years ago, the Oranui eruption occurred. The earth's largest volcanic eruption in 70,000 years.

Although it happened in the very heart of New Zealand, nobody was there to hear or see it. It wouldn't be until 25,000 years later when the Maori finally settled these lands, that human eyes would set sight on the marvel that happened here all those years ago – a hollow in the earth so enormous that, even when standing right on the edge, you weren't able to see the other side.

This hollow filled with water – fresh water – courtesy of the Waikato River that flowed healthily from the north. Over the centuries, it became a source of life, sustaining those who lived around it for miles in every direction. Even today, if you look at a map of New Zealand, you won't have to search for this crater of water. It will be staring you in the face – a big splotch of blue, right in the centre.

Today, we know it as Lake Taupo.

These days, Taupo is a lot more than just an old volcano. It's one of New Zealand's most visited places – modern, peaceful, boasting a modest population of 25,000. Outsiders consider it a town, locals insist it's a city, but nobody denies the charm it holds from top to bottom. It's known for many things – its gorgeous lake of course – but also its single set of traffic lights, its collection of hot springs, its prawn fishing farms where nobody ever catches anything. But this week I would learn, it's also famous for something else.

Hosting the number one Ironman race in the world.

Taupo is an easy four-hour drive from Auckland. I arrive late in the night, check into a motel two blocks from the water. I spend the evening practising my tire changes, over and over. Have a big dinner. Sleep like a baby. Then, first thing in the morning, I ride Tokuko down to the athletes' village.

As I ride along the lakefront, a girl walking towards me looks at my bike, my shoes. Then up at my face. Then down at my wheels again. I start to wonder if there's something wrong.

As she walks past, she looks me in the eye. Smiles.

Good luck for the race!

I say nothing, just stare at her, semi in shock.

That's when I start to notice the red Ironman logos on every lamp post, the athletes training – running, riding – up and down every street, the good luck signs in the shop windows.

They say all of Taupo shuts down for race week. Now I see, they really mean it.

It's slightly odd, then, when I arrive at the athletes' village and it's almost empty. I'm a week early, but I expected everyone else would be too. Yet there are only a few athletes around, getting wetsuits checked, lingering in the merch store. And only one busy tent, which is the one I'm going to.

Even from a distance, I can see Ben's entire crew in there, six, seven of them, tinkering away on expensive bikes. There's a short queue outside, but I see Ben in the back and wander right in. Hopefully he remembers me.

I wheel my bike over. A friendly frown comes across his face. Wondering why I've been allowed into his work area.

Now I feel like an idiot. He has no idea who I am.

I quickly take off my sunglasses and say hi.

Oh, hey brother!

Phew.

We shake hands. He's got a silky black bike up on his stand. Thick frame, sharp angles. Looks like it was made at NASA.

You just get in?

Last night. You guys look busy.

Oh mate, this is nothing. Wait until Friday.

I ask him a few questions about my wheels, my chain. While I'm there, I decide maybe he can help me with some shopping.

I need some tire tubes, I say. And a mini pump.

Easy as.

One of his guys rounds it all up and brings it over.

These tire tubes are your size, he says, handing over a couple of boxes. And, this is the inflator we use.

He hands me a couple of CO_2 canisters, and a little gadget for attaching them to your tires.

I take the inflator, flick it between my fingers.

Umm. Can you show me how to use it?

I'm down there every day. As soon as I wake up each morning, I stretch, do a little training session, then walk through the centre of Taupo to the athletes' village. I love it. There's always something on – Q&A with the pros, athlete registration, buying last-minute supplies, checking out the swim course.

Each day, Taupo gets a little more crowded. Soon, it's athletes everywhere – motel carparks filled with triathlon teams, sidewalks packed with perfectly sculpted calf muscles. Even the roads have been taken over. Bikes zoom past you on every street. The pitter-patter of sneakers echoes on every footpath. Everywhere you look, any time of day, people are pumping out kilometres, grooming the legs for race day.

On the Thursday morning, two days before the race, I'm leaving for my walk to the village, just after breakfast. A woman follows two seconds behind me. One glimpse and I know, just from the legs, the clothes. She's a triathlete.

Heading to the village?

Yes I am.

She's from Canada. Her name is Deb.

Deb has spiky bleached blonde hair, and soft eyes, and walks slightly pigeon-toed, like Andre Agassi. She's a great person to take this morning walk with. It's not her first Ironman, and I still have so many questions. What does she eat the day before? What does she eat the day after? Does she wash her bike? What made her come all the way down here, from Canada?

If you race Ironman, she says, you have to do Taupo. It's the best one in the world.

We get to the village just in time for the first timers' tips session. Before it starts, I quickly visit the bike tent and say hi to Ben. He wasn't lying; he is twice as busy every day. Twice as many bikes outside, twice as many people in the queue. I'm not surprised. Bikes are our cavalry, our lives will depend on them on Saturday. And Ben is the bike whisperer.

Later that evening, we're all invited to the welcome dinner. The hall is enormous, packed with thousands of athletes from across the world. I sit next to a guy called Dom. Mid-forties, maybe. Long shaggy hair. Looks like a drummer from a punk rock band.

We don't say much – dinner is mostly quiet, as we eat while listening to speech after speech. But once dessert comes out and the room starts to clear, we start to talk.

Your first one? Dom asks, grabbing at a donut.

Yeah. That obvious?

Mine too, he shrugs. How'd your training go?

Could've gone better.

It's a lie. It couldn't have been more perfect.

He tells me about the charity he's racing for, how this race isn't just for him.

I was at the finish line today, he continues. I stood there for a while, just visualising. Watching myself cross, over and over.

I don't say anything, just think back to the other day, when I'd been doing the exact same thing.

Besides, he says. I'm not here to set the world on fire. I'm just here to finish what I started.

But he doesn't know, and neither do I, that's exactly what we're about to do. We're about to set our worlds completely on fire. More than either of us could have imagined.

Journal entry

March 6, 2020.

When I was a teenager, she gave me one of those little desk plaques from a gift shop. It read:

TO ACHIEVE ALL THAT IS POSSIBLE
WE MUST ATTEMPT THE IMPOSSIBLE
TO BE ALL THAT WE CAN BE
WE MUST DREAM OF BEING MORE~

I guess she knew me well, because time always stopped when I read it. It took me into a daydream. I even travelled around the world with it in my backpack for a couple of years, long after we broke up. You might think, maybe it was because of the girl. It wasn't. It was because of the words.

Every time I read it I would think, what is going to be my impossible? What is the more I'm going to dream of? Money was always on my mind back then, so I would always guess, maybe I'm going to become a billionaire, start some huge company, something like that. But life changed, and so did my dreams. But I never thought they would lead me here.

Tomorrow I will line up with 1,000 other athletes to take on one of the hardest races in the world. The first time I ever heard about Ironman, it sounded so absurd, I looked at the photo of the guy crossing the finish line and my first thought was, "Impossible." And I knew I wasn't like him, would never be like him. Some people were just born to be special, to do impossible things.

And now here I am.

This journey of mine was born out of anger. Back on that winter morning in August last year, running in the rain with half my face falling off, rage burning in my stomach. But I'm not angry anymore. No matter what happens tomorrow, I finally understand, all that pain had a purpose. It was to bring me here. It was life's way of telling me, "You're capable of so much more, I'm going to beat you down, in the suffering, you'll see who you really are." Now it feels like everything in my life, everything I ever learned and studied and experienced – it was all preparing me for this moment.

I have that plaque sitting in front of me right now. It's a little busted around the edges, faded, a few chips in it from clanking around in my backpack. But now I see why I had to hold onto it for all these years.

Tomorrow, I finally get the chance to attempt my impossible.

18

It is Day 291.

Race day.

Six a.m.

I walk down the athletes' chute, toward the bike racks, gear bags over both my shoulders.

It's dark, other than the spotlights. Sun still yet to rise. People are everywhere – athletes, volunteers, supporters, but it's silent. Maybe I'm just not hearing. Too alone in my thoughts.

Ready for action brother?

It takes me a second to realise he's talking to me. I turn and see a face, grinning, tinkering on a bike, but my eyes need a moment in the morning darkness to make out who it is.

Ben.

I respond with a nod, a half-smile, but I can't manage to put any words together. I keep on walking.

I get to my spot on the bike racks. Tokuko is hanging there, right where I left her.

How about you? Are *you* ready for action?

I smile at her, and almost see her smile back.

I pull out my checklist. Salt pills into my tube bag. My secret cookies. Bottles in their cages. Double-check my gears.

Slowly, I tell myself. Relax. Don't forget anything.

I check my tires. Ben said the pressure should be seventy, but I pump them to eighty. Eighty sounds better. Feels better. I check them two times, three times. One more time.

As soon as I'm done, a girl walks up to me sheepishly. Japanese, I think.

Could I borrow your pump?

Yeah, of course.

Now the chain. I run the bottle of lube across it, give the pedals a few spins. Then I wipe it clean. Just like I've done on countless mornings in my garage, before those long rides at the velodrome. But this time I wipe it a little cleaner, a little more carefully. Until I can see it shine.

The girl brings my pump back.

Two seconds later, another tap on the shoulder.

Excuse me …

I turn around. Skinny guy. Big smile. Maybe Korean.

May I borrow your pump?

Yeah. Course.

I give the chain one more spin, just to be sure. It purrs.

Tokuko is ready.

Which means I'm ready, to head down to the lake. The start line. But I don't want to leave. Not yet. In all the race videos on YouTube, they always linger at the bike transition on race morning, and just seeing it on screen gives you chills. Now standing here on my own two feet, I can see why. Even the air shivers with anticipation. The athletes fine-tuning their wheels, their outfits, their tires. Still dark. Silent, yet somehow screaming with the sounds of nervousness and anxiety and belief. I think back to that first Ironman video, watching them shine their bike helmets in the pre-dawn darkness. Now three months later, here I am. I stare at my name tag on the rack – BRENDAN: 592 – and feel proud, prouder than I've ever felt in my life. Like the whole world is watching.

It's still early when I finally get to the lake. I find my parents waiting, watching the half Ironman event about to start. I stand at the barrier, my wetsuit hanging over my shoulder, watch the athletes entering the water. Every single one looks nervous. The blind stare in the eyes. I've never looked into a mirror minutes before a race, but I already know that's what I look like. That's what we all look like.

They have a rolling start, just a few athletes entering the water at a time. It's a lot less dramatic than the mass start we're about to have, which is good. Not only does it bring their nerves down, it brings mine down too.

The final athletes enter the water. An hour zooms by.

They call us to the start line.

Main event.

Words boom from the commentary box. I pull my wetsuit on. Slowly. Breathing. Keeping my heart rate low. My swim cap. I pull it a little forward, push it a little back. Just right. Goggles. I have two pairs. The pink ones, which I've used for all my ocean swims, and my blue ones, which I've been using in the pool lately. The pink ones leak sometimes, but are battle-tested in the ocean. The blue ones never leak, but I've never used them in open water before.

Golden rule: Nothing new on race day. But I choose the blue pair anyway. My gut chooses them. They might only be pool tested, but looking out over the lake, I tell myself this won't be too different from a morning in the pool.

Before I head to the start line, my pre-race tradition: I hug my Mum. I hug my Dad.

Good luck, sweetie.

Good luck, boy.

I say nothing. But they know.

We head through the race entrance. The crowd cheers. Commentators are hooting on the microphones. Photos – everywhere photos. But as I walk to the start line, all the noise fades. Everything blurs, except the water right in front of me.

I've heard about this happening, the world blurring around you. I've read about it in books, seen it in films. Now I know why it happens in real life. Because there is something you've been preparing for, lying awake at night agonising over, and it's finally here. Standing right in front of you. Nothing else in the world matters now except this one thing. No room in your mind for the guy in the commentary box, the people taking photos, whoever is screaming your name, how cold the water looks. The only thing your eyes and ears and spirit have room for is dominating this one thing, with every piece of yourself, to be more relentless than you ever believed you could be, and to not stop until it's over. Because you know if you can do that, your life will never be the same again.

When I finally see the water at my toes, electricity bolts through my body. They say your life flashes before your eyes, just before you die. No one tells you it also happens when you're most alive. I see it all now, Polaroids flashing in my mind of the mornings in the mirror, suffering on that first flight home, every winter morning run where I whimpered in pain, the patches of tears soaking into the bloodstains on my pillow. I fight to hold in my tears. I have to, or I won't stop. Then I look around, and see the tears are not just mine. They're all of ours. The hours of training for weeks, months, years to get here. For some, maybe even a lifetime. Now our feet are finally in the water, on an Ironman start line. Only two things matter now. The demons that drove you to start. The redemption you'll feel when you finish.

I wade into the lake, neck high, middle of the pack. This is what Ironman New Zealand is famous for – the mass, deep-water start, one of the only ones left in the world. Up ahead, the confident swimmers crowd together on the green buoy line, treading water. The rest of us linger a few metres behind. Then, at the back, the less certain swimmers, maybe only knee-deep, steering clear of the crowd.

I dunk my head under. I can't tell if the water's cold. I feel nothing. Just. Electricity. At my first marathon, and even my second, I'd felt like a poser at the start line. That morning in Auckland, looking at everyone's special shoes and running belts thinking; this is going to be a long day, I'm not even a runner, I'm not even supposed to be here. But this crowd of athletes is the most special I've been in, and among all these bobbing swim caps, I know this is who I am now. This is exactly where I'm supposed to be.

BOOM!

What the ...?

The cannon?

It's frantic. Furious. White water everywhere. No time to think. Just. Swim.

Not even two minutes pass and I realise I've already made two mistakes. I should have started further forward. This crowd is swimming slower than I want and I'm boxed in, eating feet.

The second mistake – wrong goggles. The sun is just starting its rise, and every time I look ahead to sight, I can't see the buoys. There's no tint on my lenses and all I see is glare. During a typical breath, you have half a second to sight, or even less. Now, even if I slow down and keep my eyes up for two whole seconds, I see nothing but white. Like God is shining a torch right into my eyes.

I shrug it off. I'm boxed in the crowd. If I'm going the wrong way, we're all going the wrong way.

Ten minutes pass. I find some space and hit a rhythm. Swimming, like running, is all about rhythm. Three strokes, breathe. Swim easy. *Glide more.* I hold the pace for the next kilometre.

I still try to sight every six breaths, but see nothing. Nothing until the buoy is right in front of me, and I make out a blob of yellow. YES, I think. I'm swimming straight! And then between buoys, I'm back to swimming blind. Eventually, I start breaking my second golden rule – never follow the person in front of you. But it's either that or stopping to tread water and sight every six breaths. All that sighting practise, and now all I can do is trust that the guy in front of me has practised as much as I have.

The swim course is straightforward – around one and a half kilometres out, then one and a half kilometres back, then just over half a kilometre down a river to the Taupo Yacht Club.

We get to the turnaround buoy. I feel fresh. The crowd has thinned, and I make the turnaround as tightly as a pro, swimming inches from the buoy. Confidence starts to soar – even with these dud goggles, I've finished the first leg of the swim unscathed and feeling brand new. About two kilometres to go, then we're back on dry land.

On the return leg, I drift out to the side to find some room. I've got gas in the tank, and want to swim freely now, without weaving through bodies. I get to the outside and finally it's open blue ahead of me. I swim smoother, and faster. *Gliding more.* But now the buoys have changed from yellow to red. If sighting was ninety percent impossible before, it's ninety-nine percent impossible now.

I go several breaths without seeing a buoy.

The next breath, I hold my head up a second longer, but still see nothing. Just glare.

Finally I stop, tread water, lift my goggles to see the course properly.

Oh, shit. They're over *there.*

Sighting doesn't get easier. The next time I stop, I'm even more off course. I adjust again, swim a little faster to make up time.

The third time I stop, there's a safety kayak about two metres away from me. The guy doesn't even look at me, but I figure he's paddled out here just to make sure I don't swim to Australia.

Mild panic. I lift my goggles, find the buoy line again. I've been swimming almost a full ninety degrees off course. I swim back to the crowd as fast as I can, feel a wave of relief as I rejoin them. I've only been off course for five minutes, but I don't know that. It feels more like thirty.

Now, I don't mind eating feet. In fact, I tell myself to keep eating feet for the rest of the swim. The more feet the better. Beautiful, delicious feet. Not only that, I need to turn the engine on. The plan had been to swim easy the whole way, like a warm-up. But one more screw-up, I wonder if I'll even make the time limit.

Swimming fast, feasting on feet, I finish the return leg. I'm breathing heavy, but feel good. We've passed a bunch of people. I'm nowhere near first, but I'm also definitely not last. The sun is higher now, the glare less intense. Sighting still isn't easy, but if I really focus for that split second, I can catch a tiny glimpse of a blurry red buoy, and that's all I need.

We enter the river swim. Final stretch. For a moment, the buoys change back to yellow and it throws me, because I'm looking for red and can't find it. Then the course hits the wharf of the yacht club and I'm good. Not only can I see it right beside me, I can hear it. The people along the wharf, cheering and clapping, waving us along.

When I finally see the boat ramp leading up to the finish line, I let my arms fly. I don't even bother breathing, five strokes, six, eight, nine, twelve – maybe fifteen. I sense the shallow water and stand. My ears are still blocked, hearing only muted sounds, my head is floating, dizzy, like I've been spun in circles underwater.

But I can see.

The huge crowds gathered behind the barriers, plastered with sponsors, hundreds of people screaming, waving, snapping photos. My eyelids peel open, wider than they ever have in my life. I can't blink, I can't look away. I can't believe this is me running up this boat ramp. The commentator is yelling our names. I don't hear him, only the echoes. But my eyes are crystal. Everything is slow motion, times one hundred. Like they won't dare let me miss a single second of this.

This is really me, I think. I'm really doing this.

As I pass under the arch, I glance up at the clock.

1:24.

I check my watch.

1:23 and change.

Running up the boat ramp, trying to shake the dizziness, I hear my Mum. She's behind the barriers, screaming.

I see her, but am too zoned out to wave or even smile.

1:24? Are my eyes working properly?

After the race, I'll learn I've actually swum four kilometres – over two hundred metres more than I needed (or four extra laps of the pool). And still clocked a personal best by five minutes.

On to the transition tent. It's a four-hundred-metre run, up the boat ramp to the bike racks. I feel lost. My head is still spinning, nobody is in front of me. This is my first triathlon, I've never done a transition before. I look behind me, make sure everyone else is running the same way. The path is filled with spectators on both sides, waiting for family and friends to run past, but all of them are clapping and hollering. Many of them look me in the face, as if I'm their own son.

Good job! They scream. Awesome stuff!

I reach the top of the hill. An usher waves me towards the tents, and as I arrive, I see about thirty volunteers lined up on the grass with all our gear bags.

592! The lady at the front shouts, eyeing the race tattoo on my arm.

A man near the back shoots his arm up.

592!

He screams at me, waves me over. I run past and he hands me my bike bag.

Doing awesome mate! He says with a smile.

I've never had so many people tell me how great I am in such a short time. And if there was ever a day I needed it, this is it.

I step inside the transition tent. The moment I do, it's like I've entered another dimension. It's packed with laughter from front to back. Boisterous, like a bar during happy hour. All the nerves and silence and anxiety from the starting line has vanished. Now, all I hear is joy. Smiles, back slapping, fist bumping. Everyone feeling like superstars.

I sit down to pull off my wetsuit. As soon as I hit the grass, a volunteer rushes over and kneels in front of me. She doesn't need to say anything, just looks me in the eye and wiggles her fingers.

Hurry up, she's saying.

I carefully pull my arm sleeve over my watch, my leg sleeve over the timing chip on my ankle, then she yanks the suit off me with a few vicious tugs. Before I can move, she's emptying my bike bag on the grass, stuffing my wetsuit inside it, wishing me luck and moving on to the next person. She's the angel we all need today. I can see in her eyes, she knows exactly what this race means to all of us.

Time for my race kit. I pull my race top on. Helmet. Glasses. Shoes.

When shopping for this race kit, the brands didn't matter. The design didn't matter. Even the price didn't matter. There was only one rule.

Red.

The colour of the flares that had covered every corner of my body. The colour of the bloodstains that covered my sheets every morning. The colour of my eyes after crying through countless sleepless nights. The colour I never wanted to see in the mirror each morning, but it was always there. I bought a red bike, red bike bottles, red bottle cages, red tube bag, red armband, red race top, red hat, red gloves, red sunglasses. Red – the colour that had tried to conquer me, and failed. Now, there was no reason to run from it anymore. Red was the colour of TSW, and today I would wear it into battle, like spoils ripped from a conquered enemy.

I run out to the bike racks to meet Tokuko. She's glistening, right where I left her.

Hey, kid. Time to make magic happen.

There's a bunch of us – five or six – hitting the road at the same time. The mounting spot is right on Taupo's main boulevard. It is not new to me, but I've never seen it like this. Barriers stand on both sides, crammed with the crowds of Taupo. I don't know who they're screaming for, but it's loud and festive and fantastic. Now the first challenge of this bike leg – don't look like a fool.

I've imagined this moment already, many times, while lying in bed. I'm a bike rookie. What if I can't clip my shoes in properly? What if I fall over? The same way I've fallen over in my driveway countless times. What if I fall into someone else, and they fall over, and they hurt their leg or break a spoke, and now I've just ended someone's race because I'm an idiot?

I take Tokuko by the handles and run. Sprint. My cycling shoes clacking on the pavement.

I mount, clip one shoe in.

Perfect.

Then the second.

Perfect.

Couldn't have been smoother.

I jack the gears up, *click-click-click.*

180 kilometres. Time to work.

The bike leg is two laps of a ninety-kilometre course. Ride to the logging town of Reporoa and back. Then do it again.

I have a game plan for this ride. Everyone starts too fast, Ben said. People will pass you. But it's a long race. You'll see them later.

No reason to doubt him, my game plan is to start slow. A gear down, and ride easy, for at least twenty kilometres. Then, up to top gear, but still ride easy for another twenty kilometres. After that, just do whatever feels good.

I soon learn, Ben's right. At least about the first part. I ride easy, like I'm riding down to the supermarket to buy milk and bread, and people are passing me. Not just one or two. Ten, twenty. All these people I beat on the swim, now riding by me like it didn't even count.

I'm not even sweating. I can ride faster. I want to ride faster. Should I ride faster?

Don't ride faster, I hear Ben say. My coach who doesn't even know he's my coach.

Okay Ben. We won't ride faster.

The road to Reporoa switches between tar seal, which is great, and sealed gravel, which isn't. But it's wide and straight, and is closed to traffic for the day. By the roadside, all you see are open fields and paddocks and the odd rural home. But that also means there's nothing to shield us from the wind.

In these early kilometres, when it's still early morning and the sun is still weak, I'm exposed in my sleeveless race top (sleeved ones didn't come in red). Not only am I not sweating, I'm cold. The wind hits my arms and I feel it cutting. Almost painful. But somehow it doesn't faze me today. On a training ride, this would be miserable. On race day, it only adds to the occasion.

Besides, there are bigger things to worry about than my arms. Each time the road shifts angles, even slightly, the wind hits the bike differently. It hits me now, and I'm unprepared. I swerve off the road, onto the gravel. My eyes bolt open, the gravel crunches under my tires and the judder in my handlebars quickly jerks me back to reality.

Slowly I recompose myself, get Tokuko under control again.

Sheesh.

Keeping these legs riding for seven hours will be tough. But keeping this mind sharp might be even tougher.

This is when I'm reminded why I hate riding. Ever since Day One. Bike day is always the longest and loneliest training day. And now, I like the bike even less. Nothing can go terribly wrong on the swim, or the run. At worst you get a cramp. Maybe you fall over. No problem. Just sit there for a minute, get yourself right. But now I'm seeing *everything* can go wrong on the bike.

What if next time I lose control, there's no gravel bank on the side? What if it's a ditch?

Nice knowing you.

What if, as you're riding fifty kilometres an hour, you nick a stone on the road and flip? Maybe the wind decides to U-turn and blows your wheels out from under you?

Any of those could end your day. One bad crash and you kiss everything you've worked for goodbye.

I'm mindful of this now. Hyper-mindful. Because I'm here. We're so close, and now, after months of suffering on this bike, today's ride is the only one that's going to matter. As we hit the downhills, I don't dare go over forty kilometres an hour. Above that I might wobble, and nothing good can happen when you start wobbling. Even during this downhill right now – which is long and straight and could put so many watts in the bank for me – I don't pedal it. I just grip my aero bars tight, hold my body still as a rock, hunch over and keep my eyes glued to the road – *more aero!* – and coast this downhill, and every downhill. I don't need to go fast to finish. I just need to not crash.

One hour gone. Twenty-three kilometres. People are still passing me. Some are polite, saying things like: Coming to pass! Passing on your right! Others just fly by. I've passed maybe six people, been passed by about fifty. Still, I don't break my pace.

I'll be seeing you later, I whisper as they go past. Ben told me so.

Reporoa is a long time coming. By the time I get near, the crowd has thinned so much that sometimes several kilometres pass before I see another athlete. Even the volunteers look bored, lounging at their posts, ready to go home, waving us along like we're the last few customers on their shift. When I finally see the turnaround point, it feels like I'm the last to arrive.

A few supporters are crowded around, waiting for family members, but they cheer for me anyway. I don't think they know how special it is. To have someone scream for you, someone who has no idea who you are, and will probably never see you again. But they stand there all day, and scream for you to keep going.

I make the turn carefully, around the cones, disoriented after riding fast and straight for so long. As I clear it, I notice the bikes lying by the toilet stalls at the roadside.

Looking good! A voice screams to me from nowhere.

I look quickly. See Deb, standing by the toilets.

I wave back.

Hey!

That's all I have time for. Just hey. Then I'm already too far, too many more kilometres to think about.

As I start the ride back towards Taupo, I see I'm not back of the pack. A stream of riders is still coming toward Reporoa. In fact, I'm not doing badly at all. The watch says I'm exactly where I should be – an hour and forty-five minutes on the dot. If I can hold that pace for the rest of the course, I'll break seven hours.

A few kilometres later, I hear that familiar voice again.

Looking strong!

I look behind, see Deb pulling up beside me.

As she passes, I notice she's dressed smarter than I am. She's in a windbreaker jacket, which my arms would love right now. It's bright yellow, like the yellow highlights in her hair. Her bike is bright yellow too (yellow demons, maybe?). Her legs are not especially muscular, but still look strong as they hammer the pedals.

I pedal hard enough to stay with her, keeping her in my sights, just a few bikes ahead. I need something, someone, to keep my mind switched on, and she's it.

Deb is going to be my pacer now.

There's a hill on the return leg, just before you reach Taupo. They call it Heartbreak Hill. I've never ridden or seen it, just heard the stories. Long and gruelling, the last thing you want to see at the end of a ninety-kilometre lap. Earlier in the week, at the tips session with the pros, they told us to pedal a little easier in that last twenty kilometres of each lap. Just in case. Because Heartbreak Hill really does break hearts if your legs have nothing left.

Translation: Heartbreak Hill takes people's souls.

I'm waiting for it. Bright yellow Deb is right there, keeping me on pace just a few bikes ahead, and each time I see a slope in the distance I'm wondering, is that it? Is that Heartbreak? But each time we ride a hill I'm also realising, they always look scarier than they are. Sometimes there's a monster looking slope and I think, oh man. This one will be interesting. I stand on the pedals, hammer it hard, expecting a battle. But in thirty seconds it's already over.

However, now there's a hill ahead, and I think this might be the one. It's not too steep, but it's long and stretches into the distance, far enough that you can't see the top. I notice people slowing down, but my legs feel good so I carry on. I pass one or two riders. Then I pass Deb.

The incline steepens. I stand on the pedals and go to work. After riding easy for three hours, my thighs finally start to burn and sweat beads on my forehead.

This is it. This is what we've been saving our legs for.

I pass another rider. And another. Is this the hill? It has to be. We're almost back at Taupo.

I push harder still. Minutes pass. I don't know how many, but I know this is not the time to ride easy. This is the time to push.

I pass more people. Three, four.

I can see the top now.

Already? Can't be. This is not a hill that would earn the name Heartbreak. But as I reach the top, there's a surprise.

False peak. Still lots more hill to go.

I get it now. The heartbreak isn't impossibly steep or long. Just plays with your mind. Says to you – almost there, almost there, and then right at the end – surprise! But I don't mind. My legs have plenty left. The second half is even easier than the first.

Minutes after I reach the top, I see the big highway bridge from the start of the course. It brings a wide smile to my face, because I know what that means. We're almost home. It also means I was right – that was Heartbreak Hill. And now I know I can do it.

Ten kilometres still remain before the first lap is over. After passing under the big highway bridge, we turn into Taupo's suburban streets. As a ten-year-old, I used to ride my bike on streets like these around my neighbourhood, but I would only ride the footpaths, pumping the brakes down the hills, not going too fast in case a car pulled out, or kids were out playing. All those years I would wish that for one day – just one day – I could close all the roads and zoom down those hills as fast as I wanted. No cars or pedestrians, only me, the wind blowing madly in my face.

Twenty-five years later, I'm about to get my wish. Orange cones line every road. The streets are all closed, just for me. I fly through a collection of downhills, a beaming smile plastered across my face. I'm fast, too fast, I'm a Formula One driver, swerving from one street to the next, racing through intersections on my personal race track. Ten kilometres of empty suburban roads wind all the way into town. My childhood dream come true.

We finally hit the lakefront. It is alive. Spectators line the barriers from start to finish, howling. The half Ironman is already in the middle of their run.

I see my parents on the sidewalk. My Mum screams and waves as I ride past. My Dad smiles silently, his phone out in front of him, snapping photos. I wave, then within seconds, I am gone.

In that moment, I know one thing is for certain. Seeing them here in this crowd, in Taupo, watching me chase this ridiculous dream, standing in the sun all day for hours, just to see me ride past for five seconds – I know. Even if I crash and my bike is smashed to pieces, I will carry it a hundred kilometres to the finish line. If both my ankles break, I will crawl across the line on my knees. I don't care if it takes seventeen hours or seventeen days. They are going to see me cross.

I hit the turnaround point. It's the same place we started the bike leg hours ago. The commentary booth screams my name.

This is Brendan Lee, from Auckland!

I'm already nervous making the turn, but hearing this makes me doubly nervous. The turnaround is sharp, and unlike Reporoa, this one is crammed full of spectators.

I wobble slightly as I take it.

Please don't fall. Not in front of all these people.

I make the turn. I don't fall.

Ninety kilometres to go.

I see my parents again minutes later on the way back up. They're in the same place, same pose. Mum waiting. Dad with his phone out. I ride strong and wave, give a smile. I don't want them to be doubting I have the legs to make it back.

Just around the corner is the halfway pit stop.

592! A girl screams as I ride in.

I get to the tent and my bag is on the table waiting for me. I lay Tokuko on the grass, quickly swap out my bottles, then head for the toilets.

As I get in line, a guy walks past. It's Dom. The guy from the athletes' dinner.

Hey, man!

He laughs as he stuffs something into his mouth.

How's your ride? I ask, giving him a fist bump.

He sits on the grass to tend to his feet.

Yeah, going great. Until some hills got in the way!

We both chuckle. Often, Ironman is described as a day of torture. But I'm not seeing it. All I'm seeing in everyone's faces today is strength. All I'm feeling in my heart, is joy. I've already done my suffering. I'm not going to suffer today. Today is going to be the best day of my life.

I get back on the bike, ready to turn up the volume. I start eating. This was always the plan, to ride on an empty stomach until halfway, nice and light, then pack in some calories and go to work. For the first few minutes of eating, I can't stop. I just laugh, listening to my stomach sing while shovelling food into my mouth.

The mysteries of the bike are over now. I know the course, and I know I can do it. I zone out and ride. One hour passes. Two. We're spread thin now. The course is twice as empty, and ten times as lonely. Not a problem. Empty roads are my favourite, and loneliness is my specialty. I arrive again at Reporoa. Check my watch.

Five and a half hours.

It's a good feeling at first. Then I do the math, and frown.

I'm way behind pace.

I can't understand why. My pace has been steady and rising the whole way. Watch broken? Missed a turn?

Then I figure it out. I spent too long at the pit stop.

I feel urgency again. Like the swim. Not only am I behind pace, if I meet any nasty headwinds on the way back, if I have to stop to change a tire, not only will I miss seven hours by a landslide, I may end up riding closer to eight.

But I have gas in the tank. Plenty of it. I start putting weight on the pedals, doubling down on the calories. I ride by the next aid station in full race mode, scream out like one of the pros – Clif Bars!

A volunteer holds one out and runs alongside me as I grab it. I've been chewing on white chocolate Clif Bars, but this one is different. The zing of it dances on my tongue.

Oh yeah! Raspberry!

I hear them laughing behind me.

A few kilometres on, I see Deb again. Her yellow bike stands out from miles away. I pull up behind her.

Found ya.

Yes you did!

She is so Canadian.

I ride with her for the next few kilometres, using her to keep pace. Then, at the final aid station, she slows to grab a banana and I power past her.

You're doing great! She yells as I go past.

It's the last time I'll see her.

Heartbrcak Hill approaches. I feel even stronger than the first time. I know it's only a six or seven minute climb – no reason to hold back now. I attack it at full speed. In the distance, I can see several people who passed me earlier, some many hours ago, and I think back to Ben's sage advice. I really am seeing them all again. I stand on the pedals once more, knock the hill off as fast as possible, passing many of them on the way up.

As I hit the peak, I check my watch. Give myself a nod of relief. I won't be clocking seven hours. But I also won't be riding eight.

Just as I'm finishing the final kilometres before Taupo, there's a sign by the road.

That was the easy part. Just a marathon to go!

Marathon. That word used to be so enormous. Mythical. Another word for impossible. Now, it doesn't sound scary at all. I know it's going to be forty-two kilometres of agony, five hours of mangled feet and busted knees, but I'm not even dreading it. I'm up for it. My legs are waiting. Ready to smash it to pieces.

I coast cautiously through the final suburban streets this time. Even the huge downhill near the end, which would have been a dream flying down as a kid, I pump my brakes and ride it slowly.

We've made it this far, I say to Tokuko. Let's not crash and break our legs now.

As I turn back onto the lakefront, everything has changed. The mood. It's different. Half the runners are walking, exasperation on their faces. It's the face of having nothing left, wondering how the hell you will make it through ten, twenty, thirty more kilometres. It's what bonking looks like.

Singapore flashes in my mind.

Yes, I know exactly what that feels like.

This time, however, it's a welcome sight. I wish every athlete every blessing in crossing the finish line, but many of these walkers are people who had zoomed past me on the bike, and I want to get that back.

I roll into transition and dismount, handing my bike off to one of the volunteers. She accepts it keenly, like it's the most important job in the world. I love her for it. Santa – please give her whatever she wants for Christmas. I bolt down the transition carpet to the tents. I had expected wobbly legs, but they feel free and fast.

Biked too easy? Adrenaline? Both?

Another volunteer is waiting with my transition bag. I take the first seat in the tent, empty my bag on the grass. Shoes, socks, tape, running belt, hat. Lots to do, but I run through it slowly. There's no reason to rush now, nothing left to be nervous about. I know I've ridden 7:15 on the bike, maybe 7:20, meaning I have over eight hours to run the marathon. All my doubts had been about the bike. Now that it's over, the doubt is gone. I'm going to be an Ironman today.

Transition 2 is not like Transition 1. It's calm, far fewer people. The tent is almost empty. The guy sitting next to me is having a long, slow conversation with the volunteer. Talking about family, work.

You got plenty of time for your run, he says. Over eight hours, bro.

Guess I'll try do it in six, the guy replies.

I look over at him, as he calmly bites into a sandwich. It calms me down even more.

A minute later my feet are taped. Shoes on. Race belt filled with salt pills. I slather Vaseline between my thighs. Visit the toilet. Then just before I set my watch, I look down at my shoes.

Hey. Got a tough few hours ahead. How about we go make this marathon our bitch?

The marathon course is three laps of a fourteen-kilometre loop. As soon as I come out of the transition tent and hit the pavement, I feel at home. I've been here before, more than once. I know what kind of pain it's going to be. I don't even bother checking my watch for pace. The only rule is no walking, no stopping. Fifty thousand steps and I'll be home.

Immediately I recognise two people who whizzed past me near the end of the bike. I pass them within minutes. As the second kilometre starts I pass my parents standing lakeside. Mum screams. Dad takes photos. I manage to smile at them while I scale the first hill.

As my legs start finding their rhythm, I find more familiar faces. Although "faces" isn't quite the right word. It's a funny thing about races – you see the same people over and over again, but you only know them from their backs, their bums, their shoes, their calf muscles, their running style. When you see them you recognise them instantly, even though you have no idea what their faces look like, and almost never find out.

That's what's happening right now. I recognise a bright orange tri-suit, from many hours ago on the bike. I pass him. The green tri-suit with all the advertising on the back is familiar too. I pass her moments later. Each pass pumps me up a little more, like I'm Pacman, eating monsters and getting stronger every time.

But even this early in the run, my legs are soft. I know what's coming. Already, I need to play games with my mind, to trick myself into believing how short this run is going to be. The same way I do during every training run – those three-kilometre laps around the lake. Thinking in laps is my favourite trick, it makes the numbers smaller, less tormenting. And of course the first lap never counts, because it's just a warm-up, and the last lap never counts, because by then you can taste the finish, soon it will be all over. It's the laps in between that hurt. Those are the ones you need to fight for.

So I don't call it a marathon. I don't call it a long and unbearable forty-two kilometres. I call it three laps around Taupo. Just three. And if the first and last laps don't count, there's only one that's going to hurt – the middle one.

The goal reverts back to the same goal as always: Get to the aid station. They come every two and a half kilometres. As I hit the first one, I almost start laughing. This isn't an aid station. It's a buffet from a five-year-old's birthday party. Potato chips, chocolate chip cookies, Coke, oranges, bananas, pretzels, candy.

With miraculous willpower, I resist the potato chips. I know it's too early, if I start now I won't stop. I take two cups of electrolytes and keep on moving.

The course winds through Taupo's suburbs, up and down hills, each street looking the same as the next. Not knowing the course beforehand taxes me. I want to visualise how far I have left, where the hills are, whether I'm on the easy part or the hard part, but I have no idea. All I can do is follow the cones.

Finally, I hit the wristband checkpoint, at the halfway point of the first lap. I pass through the arch and a volunteer holds the band out for me to collect. It's yellow – the colour for lap one (Deb will be happy). On lap two

I will collect pink, and on lap three I'll get green. Once you have all three wristbands, you're ready to run home, to the finish line.

It feels so far away, I don't even think about it.

Still, it's a different race now with a yellow band on my wrist. As the course converges and athletes are running alongside each other in opposite directions, that's all we seem to be doing – looking at each other's wrists. I see some guys with green bands, and I'm impressed. Wow, I think. He's fast. I see some guys with nothing and think, cool, I'm ahead of that guy. And now that I've got one wristband, I can only think about one thing. Getting another.

The second half of the loop is easier than the first. It's filled with downhills, and the crowd starts to pick up. As we emerge from the suburbs, the people of Taupo are out in full force. They have picnic tables set up on their lawns, drinking and cheering each of us on as we run past.

At the bottom of one hill, a local triathlon club has set up its own aid station filled with chocolates and beers. I pass on both, but gladly accept the high fives and cheers. Then, as I hit the lakefront again, it is non-stop. My name is printed on my race bib, so all I hear is GO BRENDAN! C'mon Brendan! Keep it up Brendan!

Only then do I start to understand, this isn't just our race. It's all of Taupo's race. The whole town has been out here on these streets since sunrise, cheering. Most people only need one person to believe in them to achieve something great, so how can you possibly fail, when an entire town is ready to believe in you?

I run along the lakefront, buoyed by the crowd. Familiar territory now. The loop ends at the athletes' village and I know it's there, it's just there. As I get closer, the crowd thickens until finally I hit the village, greeted by cheers as I turn around to start my second lap.

As I do, I know things are about to get real.

The blisters on both my big toes are pulsing. I taped them carefully, but they swell up anyway. Always. My knees have gotten so soft, even making this U-turn makes me wince. My feet are starting to get the miserable sharp jolts with each step, common on long training runs. And I've been here enough times to know it doesn't get better from here. It gets worse.

But I'm a different athlete now. A better one. I've trained better, and I run better. I breathe better. Everything hurts, but I even hurt better. I know if any lap is going to give me suffering, it's going to be this one. But I'm ready.

The sun starts to set. Darkness is an hour away. I get to the first aid station atop the hill, and there's no holding back now. Time for a sugar high.

I see the oranges and that's suddenly all I want. Three, four slices, I suck them down as fast as possible. Then I grab two cups of energy drink and knock them down, like tequila shots.

One, two.

Grab two more.

Three, four.

Go time.

After two aid stations, I feel the sugars surge through my blood. My legs find a second life. I feel the extra muscle on the hills, and as I climb, my pace doesn't slow a beat. It's oranges and electrolytes, every aid station, as much as possible, as fast as possible.

Halfway through the lap, I start looking for a pacer. I find one. He's Japanese, I think, and older than me. I'm guessing fifty. Maybe even older. His tri-suit is navy and white, and looks expensive. But his calf muscles tell the story. Dense and chiselled like stone. The kind of legs that can only be carved through decades of numbing battles, just like this one.

I sit on his tail, and spectators start to cheer for us as if we're one team, always in the same breath:

Let's go Hiroshi! Let's go Brendan!

Keep it up Hiroshi! Keep it up Brendan!

But there's a glaring difference between us. It's the first thing I notice about him. The pink band on his wrist.

He's on his third lap. I'm only on my second.

It doesn't matter. All that matters is I keep moving forward. And Hiroshi is going to get me there.

We hit another aid station. I slow to a walk and down two cups of electrolytes, take some oranges for the road. Hiroshi does too, but I only allow myself a few seconds, and he allows himself several more. I speed off well before him and try to put some distance between us.

It lasts about as long as a TV commercial. He runs me down and passes me not even a minute later. I pull in behind him again and sit on his tail, matching his cadence. If he's running six-minute kilometres, so am I. If he's speeding up to five and a half, I am too.

Staying in Hiroshi's rhythm does wonders. It takes my mind off the screaming blisters on my toes, the razors in the soles of my feet.

Almost an hour passes. Hiroshi and I are still going back and forth. Of course, we haven't said anything to each other. Still haven't looked at each other. But I'm marking him, and I know he's doing the same with me. Any time I pass him, he pumps his legs and edges back in front.

We hit another aid station, and he stops to a standstill while I take my two cups on the run. This time, I'm sure I've left him behind for good, but minutes later, there he is again, right by my side.

This is the game we play. Not fighting for the podium, but fighting simply to fight, because fighting is how we got here. I have no idea who this guy is. I will never see him again after today. But I have to beat him. I have to. Nobody will care who actually won or lost in the morning, but if we're fighting for something it means we can't give up. And if we can't give up, we'll make it to the finish line.

We hit the wristband checkpoint again. I run through the pink arch this time, and as soon as it hits my skin, it's a different race. We've been out here since six o'clock in the morning, eleven hours in, and now I have just one wristband left. *Just one.*

All the people I've watched enviously running with their pink wristbands – I am now one of them. As I run the return leg to the lake, I can see people looking enviously at mine. These wristbands, they're more than just lap markers. They're status symbols, like stripes or medals on an officer's chest. If you want one, you have to work for it, and when you get one, it makes you want to work even harder. It might just be a scrappy piece of cloth but when dusk is falling and you have half a marathon left to run, there's nothing more important in the world than collecting one more wristband.

Coming up the final hill out of the suburbs I pass aid station number four. It's the noisy and crowded one. In the backyards of houses around it, people have tents set up, with tables of wine and snacks and couches set out on the sidewalk. Music is playing. I run through and slam my two cups, then hit the hill strong.

Brendan!!!

A tall lanky figure is screaming at me, his hand outstretched.

Ben.

After spending a whole day out fixing bikes, he's winding down here at aid station four with some wine and a boogie.

I high five him. I'm glad he's seeing me now, running strong. Even though he doesn't know he's my bike coach, that he's part of my team, I still want him to be proud of me. He was part of this journey too.

After losing Hiroshi for a few kilometres, I catch him again. It's the second last aid station, just before we get back onto the lakefront. He stops as usual to drink, and I zip past him. Moments later, I'm not surprised to see him edge past me again. We're in the heart of the lakefront now, on the final stretch towards the village.

And then he stops. Right in the middle of the course. Hands on his hips. Sighs.

There's a Japanese lady among the spectators. She says a few things to him.

He's stopped to talk to his wife.

I see this and I take off. Baring my teeth, I push my pace as hard as my legs will let me. Seeing the way he was standing there, the grimace on his face, there's no way he's coming back. He's stopped to tell his wife his legs are messed up. His knees are finished. Needs a few loving words, perhaps.

Either way, I've seen the last of him. He's on his final lap anyway, but in my book, I've won this one. I start to look for a new rival to bring me home.

It's dark now. Nighttime dark. I relax into my run, working on breathing easy through these flat lakeside kilometres. My eyes wander and as they hit the shimmer of the lake, I'm spellbound for a moment. The water shines like I've never seen, purple in the moonlight, but an immaculate purple, more perfect than any sunrise or sunset I can remember. Even days, months later, I will see this image so vividly, like a postcard plastered in my mind. I let my pace slow as I stare, for five seconds, ten, maybe even a minute.

This is why people come here, I think. This is why they come from all across the world to race in Taupo.

Then, snapping me out of my daze, someone blows past me. I barely see him, but I look ahead and can't help but laugh.

Fucking Hiroshi.

I don't bother chasing. He is flying, with the sudden superhuman strength only a nearing finish line can bring. Even with a brand new pair of legs, I'd never catch him. In ten minutes, Hiroshi will be an Ironman.

Congratulations, mate. Couldn't be happier for you.

Me? Still one lap to go.

I hit the turnaround point and start my third lap. I know the first aid station isn't far away, it's waiting at the top of the first hill. I get there. Electrolytes again. Oranges again. I know I should only eat two – I don't want to bloat, or need to take a crap. But I don't care. I eat five. They taste like fairy dust. I grab two cups of drink for the road. Slam them down. I look at my watch.

Eleven kilometres left.

On the brink now – of the marathon's final ten. As I've learned well, this is when the good stuff begins. Passing out, vomiting, broken dreams, limping to the finish line with ankles swollen like grapefruits – it all happens here in the final ten kilometres. But the goal hasn't changed. Wherever you are, no matter how close you are to collapsing – just get to the aid station.

Only five aid stations remain.

Five more aid stations, you'll be an Ironman.

Five more aid stations for the rest of your life.

I pass the second aid station, and find my next rival. She's moving at about my pace, just far enough ahead that I'll need to push to catch her. She's in a sleeveless green tri-suit, short ponytail bobbing down her neck, solidly built, but lean, with strong tapered legs, like an Olympic sprinter. Although I can't see her face, I imagine it to be incredibly beautiful. But even that's not what is drawing me to her. Instead, it's her perfectly toned, perfectly tanned shoulders.

Another quirk of these races. Everyone is half naked on the course, or at least in skin-tight clothes. Dripping with sweat. You're bound to see nice-looking members of the opposite sex. But the kinds of thoughts you might expect to have, they're nowhere. Any other day you'd think, wow, I wish I could take this nice-shoulders girl on a date. But not today. Instead, all I can think is, how does she get shoulders like that? My shoulders don't look like that. She must swim a lot. Probably swims three or four times a week. Because biking doesn't do that to your shoulders, does it? Maybe I should bike less, and swim more. You think she uses a pull buoy? Yeah, maybe that's the secret. Alright, I'll start swimming more. And get a pull buoy.

I catch nice-shoulders girl by the next aid station, but she barely stops to drink, while I come to a standstill at the table. It's the potato chips that capture my eyes this time. I have never eaten potato chips in training, ever, meaning I shouldn't try them now. But I can't resist. I let myself take one, then two more, then five or six. Then a whole handful. *So good.* I finish off with oranges. Two more cups of electrolytes. I'm barely there thirty seconds, but it's a long time compared to the five seconds nice-shoulders girl spends. She's left me in the dust. It's worth it. All these carbs have me bouncing. Still battered, but bouncing. Like a busted-up car with flat tires and rusted panels, but a brand new engine inside.

I finally see her again on a high, straight stretch of suburban road, just after a short but meaty hill. I remember this road. It's an odd point in the course, far enough in that you feel comfort, since you've made it "this far", but still far enough from the end that you groan, knowing there's still a long way to go. Most others are dawdling along it. Walking. This is perfect. I step just outside the cones and run unimpeded, as perfectly as my legs allow – chest out, knees high, arms rocking, eyes forward. *Run like Lange*. I pass four, five, maybe more. Then, just before the road ends and we turn down the hill, it's nice-shoulders girl.

I pass her. I can tell from her stride, she's struggling. I don't think I'll see her again soon.

It's a hard slog to the next aid station. The sun is well and truly down. It's pitch black, nearing ten o'clock, only streetlights light the course, and sometimes not even that. As we enter the smaller streets, race volunteers are directing us through with flashlights.

Another aid station. I take a toilet stop. I've been holding it for a while, not wanting to stop, but soon it's coming out whether I want it to or not. I shut the door behind me, and everything falls eerily silent. More eerie is the feeling of standing still. It takes a while for my stream to start. Normal bodily functions aren't working, because there's nothing bodily normal about what I've been doing for the last thirteen hours. Eventually it comes. It's weak and abnormally hot. I can't see, there's no light, save for a thin stream of moonlight coming in the top, but I already know it's orange and cloudy. Even now, standing still in the darkness, I can feel sweat rolling freely off my forehead. I'm losing too much fluid. I need to drink more. I'm hitting two cups and oranges at every station, but I need more.

I'm in the toilet box less than a minute, but as I step out, it feels like I've been gone an hour. It's darker and colder suddenly. There are fewer athletes. Is this the same course? I barely recognise it. I start to move, but even that short break has been enough for my muscles to cool. My feet are clamped up, like glue that's been left to dry for a few seconds too long. I almost hear them gristle as I start to run again. And just a few metres in front of me, I see a familiar backside.

Nice-shoulders girl.

I tail in behind her.

Getting my final wristband is joyous. I see the three arches atop the hill, and run triumphantly to the green one. The volunteers can see the beam in my eyes.

Congratulations!

This is it now. The final leg. Seven kilometres.

Seven more kilometres, you'll be an Ironman.

Seven more kilometres for the rest of your life.

On any other day of the week, that's an appetiser. Seven kilometres is garlic bread and chicken wings. But not today. Today, at this hour, even seven metres is misery. Nobody is running now. Perhaps one in four, maybe less. Now and then someone breaks into a run for ten metres. Then gives up. Back to plodding.

But I run. I have to. I don't look at my pace, but I know I'm running strong. Stronger than I have in the past hour or maybe two. There's nothing to hold back now. My knees are shredded, feet are shredded, but I remind myself the pain is good. It's supposed to hurt. It's supposed to break people. This is the reason you worked so hard. This is the moment you trained for.

By now spectators are on their tenth or eleventh hour of wine, and are chirping mad. I run past a crowd sitting in their backyard, and they lift me.

Here we go, look at this fella! This is strong running! STRONG running!!! All the way home mate!

I catch nice-shoulders girl again. I can tell she's surprised to see me. Surprised, dismayed. I don't see her face, but I just know. I feel it. We hit the second to last aid station together. Like all the others, it's filled with chips and fruit and candy, but this time I barely stop. There are only three kilometres left, maybe four. I don't need anything but spirit now. I gulp one cup and keep moving. So does she.

Running on each other's tails, we climb the final slope onto the lakefront. She powers past me again. I can see she's giving her absolute last legs to the road, running with concrete shoes. She wants to sprint but her legs have nothing left.

I have plenty left.

Watching her grinding away in front of me, I know this is where I'll be doing it one last time. The same way I'd done with that girl in Chiang Mai. The same way I'd done with that kid at the pool. The same way Hiroshi had done with me fourteen kilometres earlier.

I'm taking her soul.

I lift my legs and boost. I run calmly and strongly, like it's the first kilometre of the race, litres of bounce in my stride. As I pass her, I can picture her face in my rearview mirror.

Damn, she's saying. He's gone.

It's the last time I see her.

I hold that same energy all the way into town. The lakefront is packed. With the green band on my wrist, the cheers change to victory chants.

All the way home Brendan!

LET'S GO!

Congratulations!

You're going to be an Ironman!

Seeing the finish line in my mind, tears start to pool in my eyes. I shake my head. Lock them away. Not now. Not tonight. No more crying. Tonight you will smile. You will laugh and celebrate. I run faster. More tears well. I curse them away and run faster still. When your legs hurt enough, you can run as fast as you want. They can't hurt any more than they do now.

I get to the turnaround point, and the volunteer sees my wrist and smiles. I'm not turning around this time. I veer left, into the finishers' chute. The people behind the barriers roar as I go through.

Then all of a sudden, it's strangely quiet. And dark. For a second I turn around to check I'm in the right place. The chute gets narrower and narrower, darker and darker. I can see the lights in the distance, hear the music, but it feels like I'm running the chute forever.

Then, red. It's all I see. The red carpet laid out in front of me, red lights, red flashes. It's almost eleven o'clock, and everything glows in the night. At the end I can see the big red arch, the red Ironman logo, towering over the finish line, waiting. The Serengeti sunrise, the Great Wall of China, Machu

Picchu in the clouds, even the night sky of the Sahara. I've stood before all of them. None were a more beautiful sight than this. The announcer is on the mic, he's yelling at me, screaming my name, but my ears aren't working. As my feet step onto the red carpet, I hear, I *feel*, the bellow of cheers, the crowd packed full on either side, screaming, clapping, banging the barriers.

Tears flow. I let them. I won't be able to stop them, even if I try.

He's emotional! The announcer screams into the mic.

I know my Mum is here, my Dad is here, in the stands somewhere. But I don't look around. I can't. My eyes are flooded, my mind is numb, even more so than my feet, the lights and noise fade into one big blur around me. All I see is the finish line arch, towering in front of me, and all I know how to do is keep on running, so I do.

Ten more steps.

Five more.

Two.

One.

And then, after fourteen hours and thirteen minutes, after 291 days, after five hundred hours and five thousand kilometres across pools and oceans and roads and running tracks, I step across the finish line.

I raise my arms, point my fingers to the sky. He screams his famous words into the mic.

Congratulations, Brendan. You are an Ironman!

But I barely hear him. All I feel are tears streaming down my face, free flow, like a broken dam set free.

Journal entry

March 7, 2020.

When TSW first started,
It felt like I was crawling through the deepest valley.
That there was no finish line.
That this demon would keep me buried forever.
But every day,
I fought.
A little bit more.
And took one step forward.
Today, I finally stood on the highest of mountains.

19

It is Day 292.

The day after race day.

They call this day the "learning to walk again" day. Knees that no longer bend, back muscles moulded stiff like concrete poles. But somehow I wake with limber legs and only mild aches down my body. I feel normal.

I have lunch with Mum at one of Taupo's cafes. A few other Ironman athletes are in there. I don't know them, I can just tell by the athlete ID bands around their wrists. Still wearing them proudly. Not yet ready to rip them off.

I know the feeling. I'm still wearing mine too.

I'm finally allowed to eat junk food, so I have a raspberry slice for dessert. Mum and I sit there and talk for a while. It's odd, not having to hurry off to train, or stretch, or watch swim videos. Normal life doesn't feel so normal anymore.

The athletes' village is just across the road, so after lunch, we visit the merchandise tent to buy a few things. I grab a couple of singlets and take them to the girl at the counter.

Did you have a good race?

Perfect, I say, and I mean it. And then I add — it's kind of sad though, now it's all over.

Isn't it! She lets out a sigh. It was so quiet out there this morning. Almost feels like a dream, doesn't it?

Later that evening, I stand out on the balcony of our motel room. I can see the lake in the distance. After darkness falls, it shimmers under the moonlight, the same purple glow that had captured me during the race.

I grab my shoes and head for the door.

Going for a walk, I tell my parents.

It's three blocks to the water. The winds are out strong. I tuck my hands into my hoodie, shivering as I shuffle down the footpath.

As I get to the lakefront, it's a ghostly shell of what it was the night before. Not a person in sight. Just a few kids standing around a parked car, drinking, listening to music.

I start walking towards the finish line. It's two kilometres away. I know, because I still remember the distance markers from yesterday, their exact places on the footpath. But tonight, the silence is bizarre. In my mind I can still see the cones and the ropes, still hear the cheers. The cashier was right. Feels like a dream. The cameras, motorbikes, aid stations, all gone. How could something that changed our lives so deeply disappear so quickly? Like it was never here?

Then I see the chalk on the pavement.

Keep going Chris!

GO SAM

My Dad is an Ironman!

Go Cam, Go Janna, Go Dougal!!

I'd noticed these during the race, but only now do I see the extent of it. Messages in chalk literally cover the entire sidewalk, non-stop, every kilometre into town.

I get to the athletes' village. I smile at the finish line arch, still standing tall, but silent, and empty. It had shone last night, but now in the shadows, I barely see it. I imagine myself, again, running down the chute, and a roll of memories flashes in my head. The pro triathlete who put the medal around my neck as I crossed. *That's a tough run, ain't it?* He'd grinned as he said it, holding my shoulder, as I choked on my tears, unable to reply. Then the volunteer, an old lady, who held me as she walked me to medical check. *It's okay to be emotional*, she'd smiled, holding me proudly as if I were her own grandson.

When I finally turn to walk back to the motel, I notice the coffee shop across the road has its lights on. A few patrons linger outside. It's the only place open. The rest of town is completely empty and silent, not a car on the streets.

It's with this glimpse of a sleepy Taupo that it finally sinks in, what I've been a part of. Everything is gone now, but the people of Taupo put together something spectacular here, if only for a week. To them, it may have been just a few days of fun, another race week, an excuse to scream at strangers and drink wine on the lawn, but thousands of athletes from around the world travelled to this small town by the lake, and thousands of dreams came true on this one street. For us, it wasn't just a race. It was a calling – a chance to chase something deep in our souls – *deeper than most people ever go*. They'll probably never know it, but this week, Taupo saved lives, wrote books, was the scene of a thousand defining moments. This week, Taupo set all our worlds on fire, forever.

Epilogue

It is Day 600.

Early afternoon. I'm running. Same streets – past Laura's house, past James' house. A quick six-kilometre loop around my neighbourhood. I rarely run more than that now. Six kilometres is enough to get the sweat glands pumping, to give me that little jolt of life. Most importantly, to remind me of where I came from. Of who I am now.

My world has come full circle. I can finally smile at the irony. The medications that were supposed to heal me are what almost ended me. The sport I've always hated is what saved my life.

Life has a funny way of teaching you these things. Almost mockingly.

But that's what life is, isn't it?

Lessons. A collection of lessons. It's how we learn things, how we grow into different people than we were five or ten or fifty years ago. And if the quality of our lives depends on the quality of our lessons, the most trying lessons are the ones that will change us the most.

Pain is a great teacher. Maybe the greatest. Broken hearts, empty wallets, the deaths of loved ones, suffering in health. But as humans, we never seek those lessons. It is our nature to avoid them. We look for pain in the gym, lifting weights until our legs turn to jelly, or by working so hard we fall asleep from exhaustion. But the pain that reduces you to tears, the pain that makes you question if you even want to be in this world anymore – we never seek that pain. We run from it at any cost. To experience that pain, we have to be forced into it.

I cursed TSW. I cursed it with swear words, with tears, I cursed it with darker thoughts than I knew I was capable of. I try not to allow hate in my life – I don't like to hate things, or people – but I hated TSW with every ounce of me. I hated it because my life had so much joy, and TSW took it all away.

It's only now I can look back and see TSW wasn't trying to take anything. It was giving. Giving me a second chance, to stop being dormant. Giving me the opportunity to achieve something great. I wrote in my journal that this was God's way of showing me I was capable of so much more, of giving me the opportunity to fight, to find out "who I really am."

And there were many moments I found out who I was. In the moments I gave up, I found out who I was. In the moments I triumphed, I found out who I was. I found out I was too weak to save myself. I found out I didn't know how to be strong. And then I found out I was more powerful than I ever thought possible.

When TSW strips you of your skin, when it takes away everything about who you thought you were, remember there is something good waiting on the other side. Maybe nobody is trying to take anything from you. Maybe it's the opposite. Maybe it's forcing you to become everything you were supposed to be. They say you never know how strong you are until being strong is the only choice you have. And it is a deep, dark place in hell that brings you to that point. But I say this from experience: If you survive that place – and you will – life will never be the same again. Nothing will ever be impossible again. Life will never be more beautiful. People will ask how you got so strong, and you will try to explain. But they'll never know. Only we will. It's a fact of life – the biggest trials are given to the strongest warriors. And you and I already know, the strongest warriors are us.

My battle with TSW is still ongoing. Healing from this is a process. It's up and down, still exhausting, still unpredictable, and we know it will likely take several years. I still go through flares, my skin flakes, reddens. There are days when I wake up and look in the mirror, wondering when it will finally be over. But I also know that each day my skin is getting stronger, each day I give it love and time, and it heals a little more. And on every bad skin day I am able to smile into the mirror, because I know this skin that covers me is no longer normal skin, this is Iron Skin, and it's already achieved the impossible.

You will too.

Have faith.

Strong always.

Love and healing to you all.

B.

The Author

Brendan was born in Sydney, Australia and grew up in Auckland, New Zealand. He has been writing and living nomadically since 2011.

He is passionate about providing support and guidance for fellow TSW survivors and hopes this book will raise awareness.

He continues to run, bike and swim regularly and compete in races.

This is his first published book.

Printed in Great Britain
by Amazon

17013711R00157